The Making of
the Modern
Philippines

The Making of the Modern Philippines

Pieces of a Jigsaw State

Philip Bowring

BLOOMSBURY ACADEMIC
LONDON • NEW YORK • OXFORD • NEW DELHI • SYDNEY

BLOOMSBURY ACADEMIC
Bloomsbury Publishing Plc
50 Bedford Square, London, WC1B 3DP, UK
1385 Broadway, New York, NY 10018, USA
29 Earlsfort Terrace, Dublin 2, Ireland

BLOOMSBURY, BLOOMSBURY ACADEMIC and the Diana logo are trademarks of
Bloomsbury Publishing Plc

First published in Great Britain 2022
Reprinted in 2022

Cover design by Graham Robert Ward
Cover images: hiroyuki nakai/Getty and freevectormaps.com

A catalogue record for this book is available from the British Library.
A catalog record for this book is available from the Library of Congress.

ISBN: HB: 978-1-3502-9681-7
        ePDF: 978-1-3502-9683-1
        eBook: 978-1-3502-9682-4

Typeset by RefineCatch Limited, Bungay, Suffolk
Printed and bound in Great Britain

To find out more about our authors and books visit www.bloomsbury.com
and sign up for our newsletters.

CONTENTS

FIGURES

MAPS

PREFACE

This book went to press four months before the 2022 presidential and congressional elections. At one level they represented an encounter between different views of the roles of individuals and institutions in delivering good government. At the same time the result was likely to be significantly influenced by factors having little to do with policies – name recognition, money, regional loyalties, even gender bias. Policy specifics were in short supply from almost all the candidates.

The election would – barring a last-minute shock – mark the end of six years of the presidency of Rodrigo Duterte, an unusually powerful personality as well as ruthless and autocratic leader. His successor will be very different and possibly less divisive. Whatever the election result it may have less impact than some hoped and some feared. Ferdinand (Bongbong) Marcos Jr, front runner early in the campaign, bore the name of his father, ruler for twenty one years, fourteen of them as kleptocratic dictator. But despite some success in using social media to re-write the history of the Marcos era, he had not been noted for the same set of political skills nor the personality of President Duterte. Early front runners have a poor track record in presidential elections. If Bongbong's running mate, Duterte's daughter Sara Duterte-Carpio, should win the vice-presidency, that post for once may become significant.

On the other, liberal side, Leni Robredo had attitudes which support institutional rather than personal rule, and moderate reform policies which appeared much as a continuation of those of Duterte's predecessor, Benigno (Noynoy) Aquino. But even with strong backing from the Liberal party and a supportive Senate, change under her would likely be gradual and more in terms of attitude than policy – except towards human rights and China. The past and its class divides is deeply entrenched in both the business community and elected institutions. Any sudden swings in sentiment before the election might just propel another name to the fore, most likely Manila mayor Francisco (Isko Moreno) Domagoso, a classic combination of mayor and media celebrity, a middle of the road opportunist not expected to change much other than end the crude language and limit the violent tendencies of the Duterte era.

Whatever the result, there was no escaping the need of the country to overcome seven decades of under-performance in social and economic spheres compared with almost all its east and southeast Asian neighbours.

These now cannot all be blamed on the debts of the Marcos years, let alone the former colonial rulers. It also often feels cut off from its Asian region. This is partly the effect of a very parochial media, partly the lingering pull of America and partly the protection from foreign capital accorded to local business interests, even though these feed off an economy significantly driven by the remittances of the millions of Filipinos who have found work overseas. In confronting China's aggression in the South China Sea, it has also yet to capitalize on the 2016 Permanent Court of Arbitration ruling in its favour.

Foreigners – this author first visited in 1973 – as well as Filipinos have long hoped for better results as they see the success of those who have migrated as well or compare Philippine data with those of Thailand, Vietnam or Indonesia in areas including education, manufactures and agriculture. Yet nationals and foreigners alike acknowledge that sometimes chaotic ways and the high level of corruption and dynasticism throughout the political system have been accompanied by greater freedoms, and a tolerance of human foibles, than has become the norm in much of Asia. Until the Covid pandemic closed borders, there was a tourist promotion advertisement which read 'It's more fun in the Philippines'. The 'it's' was not specified but one could say the same about politics in the Philippines. Yes, the democratic process in the Philippines can be fun, but it is also sometimes violent, while providing for endless debate and speculation. Whether it results either in non-elite participation or good government is another matter.

As a frequent visitor to and writer about the Philippines since 1973 I can do no more than offer my thanks to countless, often nameless, people who I encountered as a journalist. It is a puzzle to reflect on the contrast between the intelligence and civility of people – women in particular in the middle ranks of government and business – and the poor standard of government of the nation, whether under Marcos in 1980 or Duterte forty years later. But history and geography explain so much of today's condition so I can only hope this book places today's Philippines in that perspective. As a foreigner I can, perhaps, write more in sorrow than in anger about some of the many things which have gone wrong as well as note those that have offset the failures – many in fields not covered here. But this book is written in the hope and belief that it can become what it should be, a major island nation drawing strength from its geography, its Malay people, the positive legacies of Spanish and US rule and of its Chinese migrants.

It is hard to know where to start or end in acknowledging the debt I owe to people, living and dead, who have helped me in getting to know a little about the country. Here are a few and I apologize to the far greater number who are left out for reasons of space and memory. In no particular order, names local and foreign that come to mind in developing my interest of the country over those decades, several no longer with us, include Leo Gonzaga, Juan Mercado, Sheilah Ocampo, Marites Vitug, Bobi Tiglao, Betty Escoda, Antonio Carpio, Guy Sacerdoti, John Forbes, Ian Gill, Emmy Tagaza, Cris

Yabes, Rodney Tasker, Nellie Sindayan, Cesar Virata, Sandra Burton, Amando Doronila, Keith Richburg, Francis Pangilinan, Aries Rufo, Harvey Stockwin, Patricio Abinales, Lourdes Mercado, Mohamed Ali Dimaporo, Hugh Peyman, Sheila Coronel, Mo Ordonez, Jose Galang, John McBeth, Sixto Roxas, Ambeth Ocampo, Blas Ople, Ramon Guillermo, Peter Edwards, Kit Tatad, Stephen Zuellig, John Nery, Rob Salomon, Mo Ordonez, Reine Arcache, TJS George, Jose de Venecia, Walden Bello, Roberto Romulo and Jessie Lichauco. I also thank the readers of earlier drafts for their advice, and Don Brech for compiling the index.

The book was written when Covid restrictions made travel to and within the country practically impossible. But I hope that any lack of immediacy and recent reportage is compensated by an attempt to put the situation today into the context of history, to see the foundations on which current politics, society and economy have been built. That may give some idea of the way forward and the challenges now faced by a country still demographically young and thus, in theory at least, capable of fundamental change.

Introduction

The Philippines: pieces of a jigsaw state

In March 1521 three ships under Ferdinand Magellan (Magalhaes/ Magallanes), a Portuguese navigator in the service of the king of Spain, landed in the Visayan islands. One ship later completed the first circumnavigation of the globe, an event for the history record books but more importantly it changed that history of the islands, now home to 110 million people. A few decades later, Spain assumed ownership of the archipelago stretching from the Luzon Strait to the Sulu Sea and named it Islas Filipinas. The Spanish left a religion, a few genes and some aspects of culture, but the people were and remain predominantly of Malay/ Austronesian race, language and culture, albeit with other influences from America and China.

The Philippines is unique in many ways; its geology, its fauna, in its history of rule by two successive Western powers, Spain and the United States. It has been a political identity with a singular name for nearly 500 years, much longer than many of its neighbours. It is the only predominantly Christian nation in Asia south of the Caucasus and is fervently Catholic. In the nineteenth century it spawned the first modern nationalists fighting Western imperialism.

However, this singularity does not make for an identity which is readily understood even by its own citizens, let alone by foreigners. It is part of the vast Malay Archipelago and shares a basic language and some culture with its Indonesian and Malaysian neighbours but it is separated from them by 500 years of history and itself divided by fragmented geography and regional loyalties. That history explains its current problems as reflected in its weak post-1945 economic and social performance compared with most of its neighbours, and its continuing high levels of violence. Democracy flourishes, elections are regular, noisy and competitive yet little progress is made towards changing a system dominated by dynasties as seen in the contests in the 2022 election. After the grip of two distant empires, Spanish and American, it now lives under the shadow of another, closer one, China.

Geology divides it into more than 2,000 inhabited islands. Regional rivalries and the widespread but not universal use of English have thwarted the acceptance of Filipino (essentially the Tagalog of Central Luzon) as the national language. Regional languages and loyalties remain strong so that imported languages and the Church seem at times the main unifiers. It is also an administrative jigsaw in that power locally lies not with its geographically coherent seventeen regions but with eighty numerous provinces and cities with province-level powers, some very small.

A basic Malay culture has been so influenced by Spain, the Catholic Church and then by America that its identity is sometimes seen as Latin as much as Asian. Indeed, many Filipinos in California, where they are the second largest Asian community, often self-identify as Latino or Pacific islander not Asian.[1] The Catholic Church, as adapted locally, provides some common bond, other than for the Muslims, but faces its own challenge from evangelicals and populist preachers. Religious division is an underlying historical reality exacerbated by the concentration of Muslims in western Mindanao and Sulu and more recently by extremist Islamism from abroad. Yet the cultural roots and language, even aspects of its politics, remain essentially Malay from Ilocos in the north to Sulu in the south. However, fragmented by religion, local languages and quasi-tribal identities, the Philippines is at once identifiable yet hard to define or describe.

The very notion 'Filipino' began with local born Spaniards, known as *creoles*, and only very gradually spread to Spanish *mestizos*, Chinese *mestizos* and urbanized indigenous people accepted into the dominant *principalia* class.[2] The nationalism of the *ilustrados* (the reformist educated elite) in the late nineteenth century raised national consciousness and the struggles against America and Japan saw mass participation. Independence brought the masses into the Filipino embrace but despite shared urbanization and education, the sense of national identity developed fitfully. Added to the centrifugal forces of geography were the strength of elite links to the US and of many leading businessmen to China. Suggestions to change the colonial name to a Malay one have failed – many late nineteenth revolutionaries preferred 'Katagalugan', which became the name of a short-lived Tagalog republic. More recently 'Maharlika', a word denoting a Tagalog noble warrior class, has been suggested but attracted little support.

Five hundred years on from the arrival of Spain and Catholicism fissures remain. Muslim Mindanao's on and off warfare has been about local rivalries as well as opposition to Manila and Christianity. Meanwhile, non-Muslim parts of the island also continue to see conflicts, mainly over land rights between local ethnic groups, particularly in Mindanao and the broader population whose composition has been changed by decades of migration from the Visayas. That internal colonization continues. Visayan languages now predominate in Mindanao. Generally, regional loyalties and in political terms local patron-client relationships remain important. They remain crucial even if weakened by urbanization and the shared identity of the millions of Filipinos now working overseas or brought together via social media such as Facebook or by international beauty pageants. National politics is still partly driven by the regional appeal of particular candidates. Local identity is mostly stronger than national identity, perhaps a reflection of the lack of esteem of the national government.

After years under a backward Spain and the aegis of friars, American imperialism brought education and new legal and administrative systems. Seventy years ago, the then recently independent Philippines boasted higher literacy levels than most of Asia and the highest income levels of populous Asian countries apart from Japan. It had an admired – at least from a distance – US-inspired legal and democratic system. Today, despite two decades of reasonable economic performance, it is widely seen as having failed to match most of its neighbours in income growth and progress in education. It remains better known for natural disasters, flamboyant leaders, political violence and sporadic insurgencies, and for its major export – its own citizens finding work abroad which they could not find at home.

Its social structure has changed only modestly over time, with huge gaps in income and wealth, the dominance of certain families, particularly in the provinces, the preference for the fairer skins of *mestizos* (European or Chinese) and even place names celebrating colonialists, for example the posh enclaves of Makati – Magallanes, Forbes, Legazpi, Urdaneta and Dasmarinas. Violence is an all too constant ingredient in politics. President Duterte's so-called War on Drugs killed particularly large numbers. Killings of political rivals, critical journalists and of farmer and worker activists had long been common but accelerated dramatically under Duterte. Lawyers abound but the state of law and order varies widely, ever subject to political and pecuniary influences. The state structure is weak for historical and geographical reasons which partly explain the persistence of insurgencies and of dynastic politics at both national and local levels. Senses of nationalism and civic duty appear weak compared to the demands of kinship and client relationships, blurring lines between public and private spheres. These features have especially flourished under the de-centralized political system and weak central bureaucracy bequeathed by America. Trading and sailing have always been essential elements of economic life and smuggling a natural outcome of attempts to tax it.

However, the nation has strengths too. Filipinos may be divided among themselves at home but in the outside world they have an identity and solidarity that is strong and recognized as such. Gender equality is ahead of most of Asia; Filipino workers are valued overseas for their skills and commitment, and command of English carries global benefits. Its Catholicism is sometimes more about ritual than ideology and society has relatively few hang-ups about racial mixing born of centuries of practice and the more recent impact of migration. It is welcoming of foreigners and renowned for its love of music and fiestas. There is a tradition of free speech – and sometimes gaudy rhetoric – and a media which is often too lively for those in power. In the much longer run, a generation or two away, its high fertility rate, which has long been a burden, will in a generation prove a bonus as most of its neighbours face ageing and falling populations. One day the nation may even acquire a name which reflects its Malay core identity.

As a nation, the Philippines needs to be taken more seriously by itself as well as by outsiders. Already it has 110 million people, or ten times as many as a century ago, and still growing by about 1.3 million a year. Its island chain separating the Pacific Ocean from the South China Sea, and hence the Indian Ocean, is strategically vital to bigger powers. Its own West Philippine Sea (the eastern part of the South China Sea) is now largely claimed by China, while the US, Japan and others demand freedom of navigation. Despite its close ties to the US, and its stunning 2014 victory over China's sea claims at the Permanent Court of Arbitration in The Hague, its attitude to China has been equivocal. Now, as in the past, money sometimes trumps patriotism. Its own ethnic Chinese are also sometimes an issue given their prominence in big business, and in the preference (also partly colonial) for fair over the browner skins which are the Filipino norm.

Philippine fortunes have often reflected global power shifts – Spain at the height of its sixteenth century power, the US as it moved on to the imperial world stage in 1898, Japan briefly between 1941 and 1945 until the US became the regional hegemon. Now the question is whether China, with economic as well as military power, will be next, or can this fundamentally Malay people find common cause with their Malay cousins in Indonesia and Malaysia, and their ever-proud Vietnamese neighbours and, helped by outside powers such as the US, Japan and India, keep China in its mainland box?

For the Philippines itself, much may depend on its own social and economic development, in particular broadening the base of power and prosperity in a country where government, local as well as national, has been the domain of dynasties and rent-seeking politicians and where those of *mestizo* origin (Western or Chinese) and appearance are often favoured. Ethnic Chinese dominance of much big business adds to the gap between elites and the rest. Foreign investment has been held back by vested interests cloaking themselves in nationalism. The islands have had numerous changes of rule, foreign and local, but no revolution and only half-hearted efforts at land reform. Communist insurgency still troubles some rural areas but not enough to be a sufficient threat to generate change. Meanwhile, the shared values and identity that the Catholic Church, or at least its saints and symbols, has provided to the majority have made reconciliation of the Muslim minority more difficult.

Filipinos have a reputation for being hard-working and quick to learn new skills but these attributes have mainly benefited the foreign countries to which millions have migrated. Their remittances support the domestic economy but are no substitute for the investment and good governance which would keep them at home. In recent years a surge in Business Process Outsourcing (BPO) has provided a way to use some of these talents but the nation has largely failed to develop a competitive manufacturing sector like its neighbours. Strong and broad family ties and obligations provide a measure of social security but also contribute to the dynastic politics and nepotism which undermine good government.

The past is littered with fake history including a mythical fifteenth century law giving legitimacy to President Marcos' wartime medals. Nationalism is more often rhetorically invoked than put into practice. False dawns have been many and false prophets are a constant threat. Ferdinand Marcos promised martial law would bring order and progress but his regime ended in debt and disillusion. When the famous dynasts failed to deliver prosperity, the people turned to celebrity figures from movies and sports, and then back to a dynast and then an action man with a real gun. President Rodrigo Duterte's vulgar populism promised change by targeting privileged groups, drug users and, supposedly, corruption but little changed other than that his personal rule undermined already weak institutional checks and balances. He also helped the possibility of Marcos' son becoming president.

But things can improve, indeed must do if the nation is not to fall further behind its neighbours and provide for its ever-growing population at a time of increased natural hazards. Global warming is adding to the familiar hazards of annual typhoons, sporadic earthquakes and occasional volcanic eruptions. The way it will change is unpredictable but is unlikely, given the history, to be entirely peaceful and democratic. It is also likely that overseas Filipinos, now numbering about 13 million, will have to play a role beyond keeping the nation afloat with their remittances. Many heroes of Asian revolution and independence learned from their radicalism overseas, not least the Philippines' national hero Jose Rizal, writer, doctor, cautious revolutionary schooled in nineteenth century European liberalism.

This book looks at the Philippines today in the context of its past, at how history has dictated the present and what the future may hold. The first half is a narrative from the earliest times to the Duterte years. The second half looks at specific issues, social, economic, political, religious international, environmental as they are today. The conclusion peers into the future.

Notes

1 Anthony Christian Ocampo, *The Latinos of Asia: How Filipino Americans Break the Rules on Race*, Palo Alto, CA: Stanford University Press, 2016, pp. 166–9.

2 Renato Constantino, *The Philippines: A Past Revisited*, Vol. 1, Quezon City: Tala Publishing Services, 1975, p. 151.

Varied climatic zones

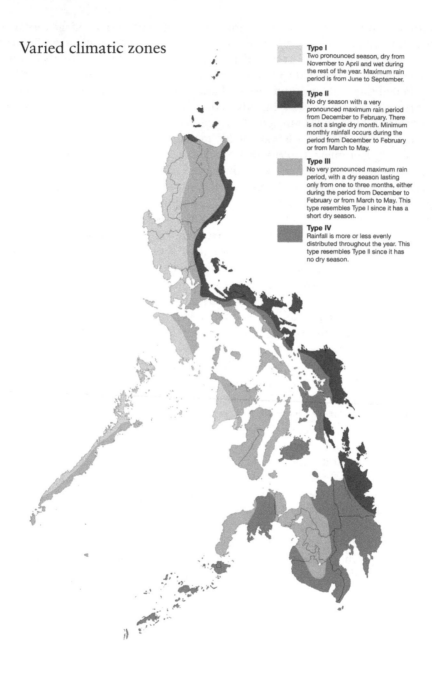

Type I
Two pronounced season, dry from November to April and wet during the rest of the year. Maximum rain period is from June to September.

Type II
No dry season with a very pronounced maximum rain period from December to February. There is not a single dry month. Minimum monthly rainfall occurs during the period from December to February or from March to May.

Type III
No very pronounced maximum rain period, with a dry season lasting only from one to three months, either during the period from December to February or from March to May. This type resembles Type I since it has a short dry season.

Type IV
Rainfall is more or less evenly distributed throughout the year. This type resembles Type II since it has no dry season.

A complex topography

0-100m	
100-200m	
200-500m	
500-1000m	
1000-2000m	
>2000	

The seventeen regions

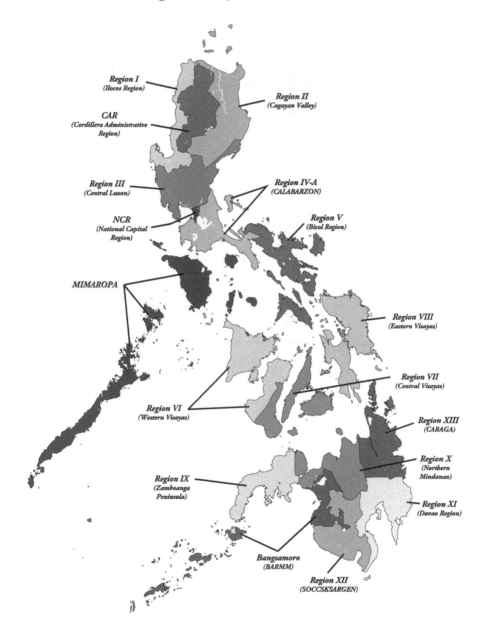

Region I
(Ilocos Region)

CAR
(Cordillera Administrative Region)

Region II
(Cagayan Valley)

Region III
(Central Luzon)

Region IV-A
(CALABARZON)

NCR
(National Capital Region)

Region V
(Bicol Region)

MIMAROPA

Region VIII
(Eastern Visayas)

Region VII
(Central Visayas)

Region VI
(Western Visayas)

Region XIII
(CARAGA)

Region IX
(Zamboanga Peninsula)

Region X
(Northern Mindanao)

Region XI
(Davao Region)

Bangsamoro
(BARMM)

Region XII
(SOCCSKSARGEN)

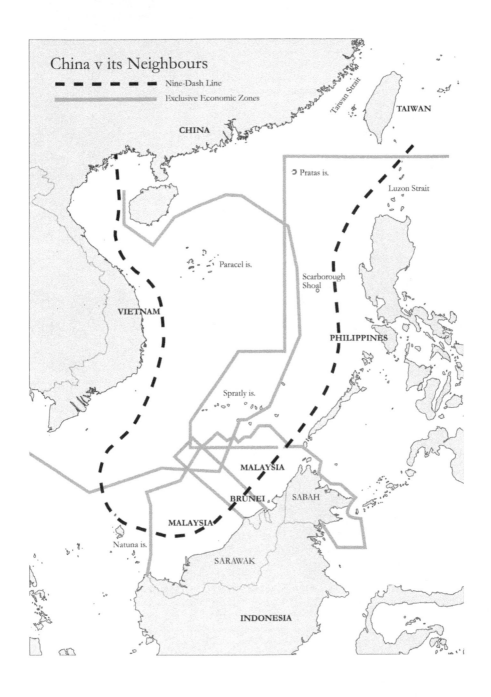

China v its Neighbours

Nine-Dash Line
Exclusive Economic Zones

CHINA

TAIWAN

Taiwan Strait

Pratas is.

Luzon Strait

Paracel is.

Scarborough Shoal

VIETNAM

PHILIPPINES

Spratly is.

MALAYSIA

BRUNEI   SABAH

MALAYSIA

Natuna is.

SARAWAK

INDONESIA

1

Fractured geography, complex identity

A glance at the map might suggest that the islands of what are now the Philippines are just an arbitrary and chance division of the great Asian archipelago which runs from Sumatra to the Maluku Islands in the east and Taiwan in the north. Until the relatively recent colonization of Taiwan by the Chinese this great arc of islands was inhabited largely by people speaking Austronesian – Malayo-Polynesian – languages and sharing many cultural characteristics and linked by mitochondrial haplogroups.

However, the reality is more complicated and makes the Philippines different. Its people are largely of Malay stock but its geology is unique and convoluted. The islands lie on what is named the Philippine Mobile Belt which lies between the vast Eurasian plate and the small Philippine plate, which lies east of the islands between them and the Pacific plate. With small but significant exceptions, the islands are separated by relatively shallow seas but surrounded by deep oceanic trenches: the Manila Trench in the west and north, the Philippine Trench (the earth's deepest) and Luzon Trench in the west and the Cotabato Trench in the south. The exceptions are the Sulu archipelago and Palawan. During the last Ice Age, when sea levels were tens of metres lower, Palawan was joined to Borneo which, like Sumatra and Java, were both part of the Eurasian mainland. Sulu remained separated from Borneo by the Sibutu Passage but Mindanao was joined to Bohol and the eastern Visayas, Cebu to the western Visayas.

The plate intersections, trenches and associated fault lines in turn explain why the whole country is susceptible to earthquakes and volcanoes on an annual basis. In 2019, for example, major earthquakes in southwestern Mindanao killed a total of forty-four people and left hundreds homeless while one off Batanes in the far north near the Luzon Strait killed nine. Tsunamis are another earthquake hazard, killing more than 3,000 in Mindanao in 1976.

Volcanoes such as Taal, fifty kilometres south of Manila, and Mayon in southern Luzon, are intermittently active. The 1991 eruption of Mount Pinatubo, ninety kilometres from Manila, was the second most powerful of the twentieth century, caused massive destruction of property and loss of a large area of fertile land which was inundated by volcanic ash washed down to the plains by summer rains.

The complex geology not only shows in the number of islands and twisting coastline but in the prevalence of hill country over plain. There are no big river basins such as those of Thailand or Vietnam and only Central Luzon has a very extensive area of flat land. The Cagayan Valley of northern Luzon, parts of Negros and Panay, the valleys of southern Mindanao and coastal strips on many islands are also suitable for paddy. The area has been a rice importer since the early twentieth century, particularly as rice has replaced corn and root crops as staples for many. The land is mostly more suited to corn and tree crops with coconuts almost everywhere. Sugar, coffee and tobacco are mostly grown in Luzon and Western Visayas, and bananas, pineapples, oil palm and rubber are mostly grown on plantations in Mindanao. Much land is too steep or now eroded for cultivation – in some cases because of wholesale free-clearing of forests. In 1946, 55 per cent of the land was virgin forest, now only about 3 per cent is forest.

Geography has another effect. The nation runs north-south from 20 degrees to 5 degrees north of the equator, a direct distance of some 1,600 kilometres or, in another context, from Edinburgh to Barcelona or Philadelphia to Miami. In other words, it goes from sub-tropical with its pronounced hot and wet, cool and dry, seasons to an equatorial climate, often with all-year-round rain and cloud cover. Monsoon patterns also make the eastern regions significantly wetter than western ones. Pronounced seasonality, with cooler but sunny months is best for grain crops such as rice. All-year rainfall also tends to leach soils. In the days before motorized vessels, seasonal winds were an important contribution to mobility and trade. Most important was the shift from northeast monsoon in the winter and southwest in the summer. Equatorial regions had less wind but some seasonal east-west shift. Add these factors together and they largely account for the fact that Luzon has 50 per cent of the nation's population but only one third of the land area.

Like most of the islands of eastern Indonesia east of Bali, all but Palawan are in a unique situation, cut off by deep water from the animal life both of the Sunda Shelf to the west, which was long part of the Eurasian landmass, and from the Sahul Shelf on which New Guinea and Australia sit. Thus, it had none of the native big mammals of Eurasia – horses, buffaloes, tigers, etc. – but also no marsupials or monotremes (egg-laying mammals).

As for humans, the earliest known were dark skinned people related to those of Melanesia and Australia. They appear to have been the ancestors of still-surviving small groups known as Aeta, or Negritos, traditionally small-statured, forest-dwelling hunter-gatherers. How they arrived is not clear but most likely, during the last Ice Age, they came across the narrow channel separating Palawan, then joined to the Asian mainland. The earliest evidence of human settlement is from about 30,000 years ago in the Tabon caves on

Palawan. Now on a cliff above the sea, it would then have been well inland. Quite possibly the early inhabitants moved further north to Luzon as a warming climate made the Luzon hill country more habitable than the equatorial forests.

The vast majority of Filipinos today, however, are southern Mongoloid by physical type. Languages – Tagalog, Cebuano, Ilocano and a dozen or so others – are all of the same Austronesian or Malayo-Polynesian family which extends from the eastern Pacific to Madagascar and includes Malay and Javanese. When and how settlement by southern Mongoloids, and when and how they acquired their Austronesian language and culture remains a matter for debate. The most generally accepted theory is that the Austronesian-speaking people originated from the eastern Asia mainland, and the language spread from Taiwan to Luzon about 5,000 years ago and then gradually through the Philippine/Indonesian archipelago, to the Malay peninsula and coastal Vietnam in one direction and the Pacific islands in the other. However, not all agree, some suggesting that migration from south to north was caused by the rise of sea levels which inundated Sundaland, now the southern part of the South China Sea. Linguistic experts, archaeologists, geneticists – human and plant – all have contributed to a debate which involves cultural affinities such as tattoos, pottery designs, burial systems and rice and millet agriculture. Pig genetics, for instance, suggests that the animal spread from southern mainland Asia to Sumatra then Java and ultimately to Polynesia.

Whatever the route, the language could only be carried by seafaring peoples who took it from island to island, one small coastal settlement to the next. That sailing prowess could itself have been the result of the rise in sea level after the Ice Age, forcing people on to boats and to search for land above the waters. The eminent archaeologist, Philippine based Wilhelm G. Solheim II suggested that the outrigger-equipped boats still familiar in Philippine waters, and capable of long inter-island passages, date back 7,000 or more years.[1]

The Tabon caves remained in use by seagoing people who about 3,000 years ago left behind a beautifully decorated burial jar topped by two figures on a boat – they would need boats in the afterlife too. This jar and other objects were identified as part of the Sa Huynh culture which developed across the sea in what is now coastal southern Vietnam and touched on the Spratly (Kalayaan) Islands.

Little is known about the extent of maritime trade in the pre-historic era but enough common objects have been found from Thailand to Taiwan to know it existed. Solheim saw a maritime trading community stretching from Sumatra northeast via the Ryukyu Islands to Japan and Korea, and southeast to the Bismarck Archipelago of New Guinea and beyond. He named its people, mostly but not all Austronesian, the Nusantao – island people. This derives from Nusa, the Sanskrit/Bahasa Indonesia word for island and Tao, the word for people in several Austronesian languages.

FIGURE 1.1 *Manunggul burial jar with figures in boat*, c. 900 BCE. © *Julan Shirwood/Wikimedia Commons.*

It goes without saying that an archipelago, particularly one with few areas of flat coastal land, could only be populated by people arriving on boats and living in large part from the sea. The most common coastal boat was the *balanghai*, normally a twelve- to fifteen-metre vessel with outriggers. A new settlement could begin with two or three families arriving on such a boat. It is the origin of barangay, now the word for an administrative division.

For the Philippines, history, in the sense of written records and accurately dateable objects, is little over 1,000 years old but clearly the islands had been linked by trade for very much longer. They were on the fringe of the Sumatra-based Srivijayan trading empire and then the Mataram kingdom of Java, at its ninth century height when the great temples of Borobudur and Prambanan were built. The oldest surviving written evidence is a copper plate found in Laguna, near Manila, written in old Javanese and recording a settlement of a large debt which had resulted in the enslavement of an important family. It is precisely dated by Sanskrit – 21 April 900 in the modern calendar. Clearly it was a settlement of some sophistication but Mindanao was probably more important for trade at that time, being closer to Java and south of the typhoon belt.

Remains of a thirteen-metre boat dated to the early fourth century have been found at Butuan, the city at the mouth of the Agusan River in northeast Mindanao and a Buddha image of similar age. Nearby Surigao, in particular, has yielded a wealth of exquisite gold ornaments dating from the tenth to the thirteenth centuries, locally made but with themes indicating links to Hindu/Buddhist Java; some have also been found in the Visayas. Butuan was a Hindu kingdom and excavations have yielded artefacts from Persia as well as India. Hindu influence was sufficiently extensive that the Maranao people of north-western Mindanao had a pre-Islamic oral epic, Darangen, which has similarities to the Hindu Ramayana epic. Hindu influence also lived on in titles such as raja and maharlika alongside Malay ones such as datu and lakan, and some place names possibly including the Visayas. There are other Sanskrit-origin words which have survived in common use such as *guro* (teacher) and *diwata* (divine being).

By the tenth century, Butuan was sufficiently active to be sending at least three trade missions to Guangzhou, according to Song dynasty annals. Chinese ceramics from around that time as well as later have been found in Butuan and also near Manila so there was clearly trade to China from Luzon as well as Mindanao.

China received raiders as well as traders from the islands with attacks by 'tattooed ones' and people with skins said to be so dark that the tattoos were barely visible. The first reference to Chinese traders visiting the islands was not until 1225, exchanging ceramics, silks and metal manufactures for cotton, wax, pearls, tortoiseshell and banana-fibre cloth. The Quanzhou-based trade official Chau Ju-kua referred to locations including Mo Yi, on the north coast of Mindoro, and described an established trade in which Chinese paid 'tribute' to local rulers just as traders paid 'tribute' in China. He wrote: 'When trading ships enter the harbour they stop in front of the official plaza, the place for barter and trade, and register their ship'.[2] After providing gifts, including white umbrellas, for the ruler in return for protection they could then trade freely.

By the time Europeans arrived in the sixteenth century, Butuan's importance appears to have declined, overshadowed by the sultanates of western Mindanao and Sulu. According to local annals, Islam first arrived in Sulu in 1380 with a missionary, probably from Melaka, named Makhdum Karim. Ten years later it acquired a Minangkabau ruler from Sumatra, Raja Baguinda. More Muslim merchants and preachers arrived in the early fifteenth century and Sulu became a sultanate in 1457, headed by Sayyid Abubakar who was from Johor. Islam's spread was partly a result of the impact of the Melaka sultanate and the impetus given by its support from China's Ming dynasty at the time of the voyages around southeast Asia and the Indian Ocean by the fleets of Zheng He. Although Zheng He does not seem to have visited any of the Philippines, some of his ships would have. One result was that in 1417 the ruler of Sulu and family members journeyed to Beijing via Quanzhou to be enfeoffed as subjects of the emperor. One died in Shandong and is commemorated there.

Islam also developed a foothold at Maynila on the south bank of the Pasig River, apparently replacing Tondo on the north bank as the main trade centre. The ruler was a sultan with family links to Brunei. However, this may have been a very late development as the Melaka-based Portuguese chronicler Tome Pires wrote of the traders from Luzon: 'They are nearly all heathen [i.e. neither Christian nor Muslim]. They are robust people little thought of in Melaka. They have two or three junks at the most. They take merchandise to Borneo and from there they come to Melaka'.[3]

Political divisions were small, often island-based with activity summed up by one modern author as 'Raiding, Trading and Feasting' to describe the activities of the rajas (a word, Sanskrit in origin, meaning king) and datus (a Malay/Austronesian word meaning local ruler)[4]. These were also hierarchical societies with luxury goods indicating status and leadership by bravery in battle. Debt bondage was common.

However, the lack, except for the brief Chinese references, of pre-European written accounts of the islands and their people has made them fair game for fake history and frauds. Perhaps the most successful of these was the Code of Kalantiaw, a text of six laws dated to 1433 ascribed to a Datu Kalantiaw of the Visayas – Panay or Negros depending on the version. An early Spanish translation of this was 'discovered' in 1913 and quickly became an established fact and source of national pride, featuring in many history book but was subsequently revealed to be a hoax. The truth took a while to be officially admitted and to this day the myth of Kalantiaw is perpetuated in some books and movies and a shrine to him still exists in Panay.

More credible is the Maragtas, written in 1907 and based on oral history and folklore from Panay and includes descriptions of customs and clothes, and tell stories about the arrival of datus from Borneo and their subsequent adventures. So, for most descriptions of the people of the pre-Hispanic Philippines it is necessary, if inadequate, to rely mainly on the works of early

European visitors and residents writing mostly about the Tagalogs and Visayans. Accounts were necessarily biased by European norms but some also displayed intellectual interest which transcended Spanish official and religious norms.

The very first account was by Antonio Pigafetta, an adventurous Italian scholar who accompanied Magellan on the first attempted global circumnavigation. He kept a detailed account of the voyage and was one of only nineteen out of 270 to survive it. Leaving Spain in September 1519, the expedition, depleted by the loss of one ship and a mutiny, landed in the Philippines in March 1521 at the small island of Limasawa, south of Leyte and made a compact with its Raja Kolambu. The first Mass was celebrated there on 31 March. From there they went to Butuan, where Kolambu's brother was raja, and then to Cebu whose Raja Humabon and most of his datus became Christian, but Magelllan got involved in a dispute between Humabon and the datu of neighbouring Mactan known, according to Pigafetta, as Lapu-Lapu.

Magellan and several of his comrades were killed in a battle with Lapu-Lapu's forces. Nothing much is known of Lapu-Lapu or if he was even present at the battle. Lapu-Lapu is a national hero but at the same time, the 1521 landing and celebration of the Catholic Mass on 31 March of that year has been celebrated as the birth of Christianity in the nation.

The Mactan battle also saw the departure from the scene of the man who may have been the first to sail around the world. Having taken part in the 1511 Portuguese conquest of Melaka, Magellan acquired a young slave there, given the name Enrique, who accompanied him back to Europe and on the circumnavigation became his interpreter. Enrique could originally have been from Sumatra, the Malukus or Visayas where port residents would have spoken Malay as well as local languages. He parted company with the Spanish in Cebu after Magellan's death, apparently having been refused release from service. What happened to him thereafter is not known but it is possible that by the time he reached Cebu with Magellan his circumnavigation was complete. One will never know for sure.

After Magellan's death, the expedition visited Bohol, Mindanao and Palawan. Everywhere Pigafetta noted an abundance of foods, the ubiquity of habits ranging from betel chewing to tattooing (which was especially pronounced in Cebu), cockfighting and the male practice of inserting a spike through the glans of the penis. He also noted among other things the Cebu raja's literacy in the local script, the quality of the palm wine and the frequency of parties with music and dancing girls and also drinking bouts. The raja advised that it was the practice of all ships entering his harbour to pay tribute. Only four days earlier, he said, one with slaves and gold on board, indicating that it must have been a Portuguese vessel. With that ship had come a Muslim merchant who, wrote Pigafetta, advised the raja that 'these are the people who conquered Melaka and Calicut'.

Politically, the country was divided into small entities ruled by rajas (a Sanskrit word meaning king) and datus (an Austronesian word for a noble).

Under them, at least in the Tagalog region, was a free but dependent class and serfs known as Alipin. In addition to inherited slavery, debt slavery, which could be the result of a crime or capture in battle, was common but debts could be settled. There was also some mobility between other classes via marriage or service to a superior. The most important socio-political unit was the barrio (or barangay), presided over by a datu who might be subject to a raja or other overlord but would have his own elite retinue who joined in feasting and fighting. They were known as Maharlika in Tagalog and the Timawa in the Visayas – freemen but owing service.

A Spanish official, Antonio de Morga, writing about 1600 noted: 'In each island or province many chiefs were recognized, some more than others, each with his own followers constituting barrios and families who gave them obedience . . . and service in their wars, sailing expeditions, farming, fishing . . .'[5]

Rizal was later to write: 'Thanks to their social condition and number at that time the Spanish domination met very little resistance while Philippine chiefs easily lost their independence and liberty. The people, accustomed to the yoke, did not defend the chiefs from the invader or attempt to struggle for liberties they never possessed'.[6] Both the political fragmentation and the social divides remain familiar.

Likewise, though the people had spiritual beliefs related both to natural phenomena and a supreme being, there was no organized religion. The impact of the Hindus had been superficial and that of the Muslims too recent to take root. Thus, the Spanish religious orders who flooded in behind Spanish conqueror Legazpi, easily found converts. The new religion might not run deep or overwhelm social practices, but its ceremonies and music had immediate appeal.

The early Spanish saw an economy which was simple but thriving. People were well fed with fish, fowl, root crops and bananas. Wet rice was grown in some lowland places but more often rice was an inland dry crop exchanged for sea and other products. A wide variety of crafts were practiced with metal working and boat building especially noted. In sum, the accounts show that the islands were very similar in customs with little difference between highland and lowland peoples.

The people were probably healthier than contemporary Europeans, had varied diets thanks to product exchanges between coastal and inland peoples and they were skilled at a variety of handicrafts. Gold and other jewellery was ubiquitous.

Three things in particular stood out as far as the Spanish were concerned. One was excellence in boat building and navigation, the subject of extensive descriptions by Francisco Alcina, a Jesuit based in the Visayas for thirty-four years and steeped in local languages and customs. In his monumental *History of the Bisayas and its People* published in 1668. Alcina also noted the changes that had taken place in some customs as a result of Spanish influence.

The second was widespread literacy, particularly among women, in local scripts derived from *kawi,* the old Javanese script, itself of Indian origin. The best known was the Tagalog Baybayin but other regions had their own. In their zeal to convert, the priests translated some Christian texts into local scripts. A small book of prayers, sacraments and practices, *Doctrina Christiana*, published by the Dominican missionaries in 1593 was written in Spanish, Baybayin and Romanized Tagalog. Among the populace, writing was used for day-to-day purposes including love letters and poetry rather than law or history. There were several forms of poetry and song, and great subtlety in the use of words, which, according to Alcina, took Europeans a long time to understand.

A third much remarked feature was the degree of sexual freedom, at least by the austere standards of Catholic Spain. De Morga noted: 'They are not very chaste. Either single or married women. While their husbands, fathers or brother are not very jealous about it. When the husband finds the wife in adultery he is easily pacified'. Alcina claimed that it was 'always the women who urged them [men] to have more freedom and less hindrance in their sensuality'.[7] Women were also said to have 'excessive and unbridled relationship with each other . . . more zealous in this regard than men with their concubines'. Divorce was common as was abortion.

Early Spanish accounts were mainly about the lowland settled areas of Luzon and the Visayas. They dealt less with the mountain people of northern Luzon, collectively known as Igorots (mountain people in Tagalog) who included the Ifugao who at Banaue cultivated wet rice on terraces carved out of the lower hillsides, and others such as the Kalinga, Bontoc and Apayo who grew hill rice as well as root crops and hunted. Tribal warfare and headhunting were not uncommon.

The Igorots were Austronesian by language and culture but Luzon's forests and remote parts of the Visayas, Mindanao and Palawan were also home to small groups of earlier peoples, known collectively as Negritos due to their dark skin and wiry hair. Small-statured hunter-gatherers they are the oldest known human inhabitants of the islands, arriving at least 25,000 years ago. The largest group surviving today are the Aeta of Luzon.

Western Mindanao and Sulu were Muslim by the late fifteenth century but before Islam they had much in common with Sulawesi and other islands of eastern Indonesia including Kulintang music, gong instruments sharing many characteristics with those of gamelan ensembles of Java. Both even pre-date Hindu influence which dominated Java and touched Mindanao.

The Islamic region was divided into sultanates based on similar but rival ethnic groups – the Maguindanao of the southwest, the Maranao of the Lake Lanao region, the Tausug of the Sulu Islands and the Yakal and Samal/Baju of other islands of the Sulu archipelago. The latter were sea-based peoples who also inhabited the coast of northeast Borneo, as were the Iranun (Maranao people who had moved to the coast and become formidable sailors). Power often lay with local datus rather than larger sultanates. Islam then was also a relatively relaxed affair and still incorporated traditional beliefs. The rest of inland Mindanao was thinly populated by a variety of related but often rival tribal groups, mainly reliant on shifting, slash and burn cultivation, speaking variations of related Austronesian languages.

Five hundred years on, many of these fissures remain. Muslim Mindanao/ Sulu's on and off warfare has been about local rivalries as well as opposition to Manila. Meanwhile, non-Muslim parts of the island continue to witness conflicts, mainly over land rights between local ethnic groups, collectively known as *lumads* (indigenous people) and today's broader, immigrant-descended population whose Visayan language now predominates.

These indigenous culture issues in Mindanao/Sulu, and the lesser ones in the Cordillera region of northern Luzon, add to the problems of an already complex geography. Tiny island nations apart, there is no country in the world more splintered by islands than the Philippines. While the sea has always provided links, as now air travel does, geography has hindered its ability to take full advantage of modern road and rail transport links between major cities which in other countries have helped forge national integration and identity. As we shall see, political history has sometimes exacerbated these problems despite 500 years of being considered, at least by its rulers, one country, the Philippines, named after its Spanish conqueror.

Notes

1   William G. Solheim II, *Archaeology and Culture in Southeast Asia Unravelling the Nusantao*, Quezon City: University of the Philippines Press, 2006.

2   Chau Ju-kua quoted in Laura Lee Junker, *Raiding, Trading and Feasting: The Political Economy of Philippine Chiefdoms*, Honolulu: University of Hawaii Press, 1998, p. 244.

3   Tome Pires, *Suma Oriental*, Vol. 1, trans. and ed. Armando Cortesao, London: The Hakluyt Society, 1948/New Delhi Asian Educational Services, 2015, pp. 132–3.

4   Junker, *Raiding Trading and Feasting*.

5   Antonio de Morga, *Sucesos de las islas Filipinas*, trans. Henry E.J. Stanley, London: The Hakluyt Society, 1868, p. 296.

6   Jose Rizal, 'Notes on Antonio de Morga', in *Sucesos de las Islas Filipinas*.

7   Francisco Alcina, *Historia de las Islas e Indios de Bisaya*, Vol. 3, trans. Cantius Kobak and Lucio Gutierrez, Manila: University of Santo Tomas, 2002, pp. 421–7.

2

More Church than State

The Magellan expedition's celebration of a Catholic Mass soon after arriving at Limasawa was deeply symbolic, even though Spanish colonization did not begin for another forty-four years. While the earlier Portuguese and the later Dutch and English interlopers in the region sought mostly trade and profit, the implantation of Catholicism was to be Spain's main purpose and achievement.

The Portuguese had been in Melaka since 1511 and had a fort as far southeast as Tidore in the Malukus, the spice centre, by 1522. Only one of Magellan's fleet's ships made it home to Cadiz but with such a valuable cargo of cloves and other spices as to pay for the whole expedition. So, Spain decided to challenge the Portuguese grip on the Malukus with the seven-ship Loaisa expedition which set out in 1525 via the south Atlantic and Pacific. Although named after its nominal leader Jofre de Loaisa, in practice it was headed by Juan Sebastian Elcano who had taken charge of the Magellan expedition after his death. It met with a series of disasters, its remnants ending in the captivity of the Portuguese.

Spain, though the dominant power in Europe, could not compete effectively in the highly profitable spice trade because it approached the region the long way round, from Mexico and Peru rather than via the southern tip of Africa. The Pacific route involved the hazardous passage of what is now the Strait of Magellan, so it was from New Spain (Mexico) that Spain made its next attempt at the conquest in Asia. The fleet of Ruy Lopez de Villalobos came to Samar and Leyte in 1544 and named the archipelago Islas Filipinas in honour of the heir to the Spanish throne, but the expedition failed and Villalobos died in Portuguese captivity.

Spain was deterred by the fact that though sailing from Mexico to the Philippines was straightforward, the return journey was extremely difficult. It was not until 1558 that an expedition under Antonio de Urdaneta, a survivor and chronicler of the Loaisa expedition, was persuaded because of his navigational skills to take part in an exploratory expedition which found a return route to Mexico. This involved sailing northeast from Luzon to about the 38th parallel, picking up westerly winds and, following the North

FIGURE 2.1 *Magellan and his ship* Victoria. © *Getty Images.*

Pacific Drift, sailing due east to the coast of northern California then southeast along the coast to Acapulco. Even this route could take twice as long as the outbound journey. The distance involved in Spain's approach to Manila via the Pacific had a profound negative impact on the Philippines.

It was not until the expedition of Miguel Lopez de Legazpi landed in Cebu in 1565 that the conquest of the islands begin, starting with the Visayas, and a bigger effort only became possible after Urdaneta's discovery. In 1570, Legazpi extended Spain's rule to the kingdom of Maynila, then subject to the Sultan of Brunei and known as Kota Seludong in Malay. Its Sultan Suleiman resisted strongly and gathered some local datus in support, but Spanish force eventually succeeded. Manila, far more developed than Cebu, became Legazpi's capital and Luzon the main centre of Spanish attention. The biggest threat to its hold on Manila came not from the local ruler but by the 1574 invasion by a Chinese pirate warlord named Lim Hong (Limahong to the Spanish) whose fleet of large junks had been driven from the Guangdong coast and attempted to set up in Manila. However, his several thousand strong force was beaten back. Lim Hong escaped but the new rulers of Manila were acknowledged by official dealings with the Ming emperor.

By the late sixteenth century, Spain had a large Asian possession but it was cut off from much Asian trade by the dominance of the Portuguese then the Dutch and English. Focused on their rich American territories, the Spanish were in practice excluded from the Asia-Europe trade. Around 1600, Spain was the world's first global power but it did not have the resources to compete with others for the Asian trade while maintaining the trans-Pacific route and fighting the Ottomans in the Mediterranean. It created and sustained the first trans-Pacific route between Asia and the Americas and the eastward flow of silver from its mines in Peru and Mexico gave a huge boost to trade in general and China, which used silver as its currency, but trade was not in its blood as it was for the Portuguese, Dutch, British and the seafaring peoples of maritime southeast Asia.

For the Portuguese, conversion to Christianity was always secondary to the development of trade. Imperial Spain, on the other hand, saw no obvious trade possibilities in the Philippines, which lay north of the Spice Islands, but a huge opportunity to acquire territory and heathen souls to be brought to the one true faith. From a missionary perspective they were a much easier target than lands already converted to Islam.

Conquest mostly proved to be relatively easy but was far from complete in that it barely touched Mindanao and Sulu, or indeed the highland areas of Luzon. There was sporadic local resistance in which Spanish officials were killed, resulting in harsh retribution. Spanish official Antonio de Morga wrote of the people of Cagayan, 'They have been in insurrection and rebellion twice since they were first reduced to submission'.[1] Some groups retreated to the forest and uplands to maintain their autonomy, but local leaders mostly came to deals with the invaders, in particular accepting conversion.

In Mindanao, Caldera Fort, near Zamboanga, had to be abandoned in the face of attacks by Moros (the word given by Spain to their Muslim foes in Europe which was transplanted to Asia and has survived to today) and Spain was long on the defensive in the western Visayas which were the subject of raids. De Morga reported that a force from Mindanao and Sulu came 'with a large fleet of more than seventy vessels with more than four thousand fighting men'.[2] Raids into southern Luzon occurred sporadically in the early seventeenth century, including the sacking of Tayabas in southwest Luzon in 1635. The raids were focused on seizing captives for sale. Meanwhile, as big a problem for the government was the challenge of marauding Dutch and later English ships.

Officials had very limited resources for governing the territory. Madrid was a year away, wrestling with its even bigger new acquisitions in the Americas and its wars in Europe, including its catastrophic attempt to invade England in 1588. Spain turned to two very different agents for its rule – military/civilian and clerical. Military/civilian rule followed the example set in its American territories – parcelling out territory known as *encomiendas* to soldiers, officials and others who had taken part in the conquest or Spaniards who had otherwise assisted the crown. The *encomenderos* were given the right to tax the people and demand labour in return for providing law, order, justice and development, and funding the spread of Christianity by the friars. It was a system ripe for exploitation, made worse by the fact that the *encomenderos* were mostly a rough bunch of soldiers and fortune seekers.

The clerical arm of the conquerors were the friars, of which there were four orders, Augustine, Dominican, Franciscan and Recollects. Mostly recruited from lower social ranks than other clergy, the friars' missionary zeal made up for any lack of learning. They were obliged to work among the people so were the spearhead of conversion. In addition, the newly-founded Jesuit order also contributed an intellectual heft to the Christianizing effort and were given the diocese of Cebu – hence the presence of Alcina (see chapter 1). The orders of friars each received a specific territory which were divided into *doctrinas*, effectively parishes where they were responsible for conversions, church building and trying to ensure attendance at mass. They were given land but later came to charge churchgoers for their services

The State divided the country into pueblos, administrative areas based on towns. Barangays were sometimes forced to join together to form pueblos, but civil administration tended to be weaker than either the *encomenderos* or the *doctrinas*. Towns were ruled by *alcaldes* who reported directly to the governor. To complicate the power structure further was that the religious orders reported to their superiors in their respective orders, not to the bishops, who in practice were chosen by the State as a papal decree had acknowledged the Spanish king's rights of appointment of clerical positions.

Christianity appears to have taken root quite easily, if mainly because its ceremonies and singing had popular appeal and saints' days provided opportunities for feasts and merriment after Mass. Divorce was ended for converts and abortion probably declined although old social practices, whether related to sexual relations, drinking, gambling or cockfighting, appear to have been little affected. Early missionaries learned the local scripts and translated some Christian texts, but such education as was imparted was in Spanish and Roman script gradually came to replace Baybayin.

On the debit side of early Spanish rule was the demand for labour which had never been in abundance. Populations in settled areas which had never needed stone buildings or galleon-sized ships were dragooned into cutting stone, building churches and providing labour for the friars. The Church built some magnificent, massive baroque stone churches which mostly withstood the islands' frequent earthquakes, but the human cost was high. The population initially probably declined, partly perhaps because of imported diseases, although the archipelago had never been as cut off from the Eurasian continent as had the Americas.

The State demanded the cutting of forests and the building and repair of the huge ships needed for the trans-Pacific trade. Each galleon, 45 to 55 metres long, needed about 2,000 trees. The boatbuilding skills which so impressed the Spanish became a huge burden on the *Indios* (natives), as did the quarrying of stone for churches.

Though local farmers quickly adopted new plants introduced from the Americas, including sweet potatoes, tomatoes, maize and tobacco, the overall early economic impact of Spain appears to have been at best neutral, with the growth of a few towns but the impoverishment of some regions because of labour and tax demands, insurrection or Moro raids.

Apart from the Church, Spain's cultural impact was limited. Unlike in the Americas, few Spanish people moved to the Philippines and the language did not become implanted in the population at large. As for the friars, they, unlike the secular clergy, reported directly to Rome not Madrid.

Despite the best intentions of some Spanish officials and priests, the overall low standard of Spanish rule was exacerbated by the conflicts of interest between State, clerics and *encomenderos*. This was acknowledged at the time by officials on the ground. Already in 1591, the bishop of the Philippines wrote that 'the *encomiendas* are in worse condition than if the Spanish had never come'. Sending solders to exact tribute 'renders impossible the pacification of the country'. The abuses were recognized in Madrid but the king was far away and State resources very limited so little was done, despite some efforts by friars to rein in the *encomenderos*. The communities were also kept apart with Spanish, other than officials, tax collectors and clergy, not allowed outside the Spanish enclaves. Taxes and labour demands, whether by the *encomenderos* or the State or the clergy, were heavy. *Encomiendas* controlled by the government were headed by an *alcalde major* who reported to the governor. The Spanish also partly incorporated pre-conquest systems into their appointing datus as minor officials and heads of villages.

Manila was a different story. As the main focus of Spanish rule and source, it soon acquired walls, stone buildings and a cathedral. The city flourished from the galleon trade established very soon after the conquest. Ships from Mexico brought silver, while traders arrived from China and Japan, and a few from Melaka and elsewhere, to sell luxury goods, spices etc. for silver. The trade was immensely profitable for the Spanish merchants in Manila and the growth of the city attracted thousands of Chinese workers in addition to traders. Chinese generally became known as 'sangleys' – derived from the Hokkien word for trader, a name still reflected today in Sangley Point, the little peninsula jutting out into Manila Bay and the location of a small US-built airport. Some Augustinian friars learned Hokkien and converted some Chinese to Christianity.

By 1603, there were far more Chinese – about 30,000 – than Spanish. Tensions rose to the point that the Chinese, fearing they were about to be forced back to China, revolted and had initial success. However, they were inadequately equipped and had to retreat to a camp in Batangas where they succumbed to a force of some 200 Spanish, 300 Japanese and 1,500 locally recruited men. The Chinese had appealed to their emperor for help but Ming China was unsympathetic to those who betrayed their country by settling abroad. About 20,000 Chinese were massacred. The emperor threatened the Spanish with retribution but did nothing. Trade was interrupted but only briefly.

Another impact observed by de Morga was the shortage of skilled manpower. Due to the influx of low-cost Chinese labour, the *Indios* had 'forgotten husbandry, the rearing of fowls, flocks, cotton and weaving robes as they used to do in the time of their paganism and for a long time after the country had been conquered'.[3]

The Chinese gradually returned to Manila so that they numbered 25,000 by 1636 but they were again the subject of killings in 1639 following a minor rebellion by Chinese relocated to the countryside outside Manila to grow rice. The Chinese and Spanish needed each other but the relationship was always uneasy due to Spanish (and some indigenous) fears of Chinese numbers. Although most were in Manila and major towns and dominated the retail trade and crafts, some did move to rural areas as petty traders and money lenders.

The galleon trade was very profitable for those involved in it and a right to space on one bound to Mexico one was highly valued. Two vessels a year usually made the journey – two out, two in. Losses at sea were quite small – twenty-six out of a total of 108 galleons over the 250 years. Most of these occurred in the vicinity of the archipelago, particularly the tricky passage from Manila to the open Pacific via the San Bernardino Strait between Luzon and Samar. Four vessels were seized by the English.

The flow of silver into China gave a major boost to its money supply and other trade, domestic and foreign. It is sometimes described as the first globalization, though in reality Manila was involved with little other than the galleon/China trade as trade with Europe via the Indian and Atlantic Oceans was controlled by others. Merchants from ports such as Melaka brought goods such as cottons, carpets and spices from India, to join the cargoes of Chinese and Japanese products, but Manila merchants did not go west. The galleons were the property of State which controlled access to space, which enriched officials. A committee headed by the governor and including the head of the *audencia* (supreme court) and representatives of the Church, city council and leading merchants allotted *boletas*, tickets providing a certain amount of cargo space on a galleon. These were not supposed to be traded but gradually the *boletas* became saleable to genuine merchants, at a price. By the eighteenth century, the system had become an income subsidy for a large part of the Spanish population, at the expense of the genuine merchants.[4]

The galleon trade also existed within a bigger restrictive system which aimed to protect other production and trade interests of Spain and its American possessions. These necessarily were sometimes at odds with each other but in any case kept foreigners out of any non-Asian trade. Meanwhile, the Dutch and English grew fat on their Europe-Asia trade with which Spain could not compete effectively.

The galleons did little for the domestic Philippine economy or trade with other parts of Asia. Indeed, it took away the incentive for the local Spanish to develop the economy. There was little trans-Pacific export of local products. Over time some Filipinos settled in Mexico, having arrived as galleon crew. One group brought knowledge of palm wine production which became so popular that the Filipinos were ordered home to protect the Mexican market for Spanish brandy.[5]

A few towns outside Manila such as Cebu, Vigan and Iloilo, acquired cathedrals and some public buildings and stone houses for the Spanish rulers but it was to be well into the eighteenth century before the population began to rise. Manila Spanish lived well off the galleons and elsewhere the officials and *encomenderos* simply collected taxes and labour tribute. The friars also grew fat as they benefited from lands granted by the State or by devout individuals making penance. The friars learned local languages but did not teach the locals Spanish. Thus, they became, and remained, the intermediary between the people and Spanish officials. Some *Indios*, mostly from the pre-Hispanic aristocracy prospered moderately, enjoying enough land to have their own tenants. A few could reach the *principalia* class as *gobernadorcillos*, in charge of small towns, but outside Manila progress – other than gradual increase in conversions – was minimal.

Elsewhere in maritime Asia, the seventeenth century saw a period of prosperity driven by trade as European merchant adventurers flooded the region and local trading sultanates such as Makassar, Patani and Aceh thrived even in the face of Dutch mercantile empire-building. Spain's situation and the galleon trade itself declined steadily in the eighteenth century. Outside Manila, there were few Spanish. For example, in 1760 Capiz (now Roxas City), the second largest town on relatively developed Panay, had sixteen Spanish out of 3,900 people.

Distance and the lack of easy wealth compared with its mineral and land-rich American possessions meant that Madrid had scant interest in the Philippines, which was ruled from Mexico. Hence, the islands became more of a project for the Catholic Church, and the friars in particular, than the State.

Occasional non-Spanish Western visitors were contemptuous of Spanish rule. Geographer and adventurer William Dalrymple, who spent many years in the region for the English East India Company (EIC), suggested that the poor state of the islands was 'entirely due to the indolence and bad government of the islands'.[6] The level of discontent was so high that it would be easy to take them over. The island of Bohol near Cebu was in open revolt and effectively independent between 1744 and 1829.

The British did, in fact, occupy Manila for nearly two years during the Seven Years War, 1756–63, but never extended their power beyond. It was more of a bargaining chip in a European conflict than extension of empire. Manila was returned as part of a deal in which the British acquired Florida and Upper Canada. However, it left its mark including support for a short lived rebellion in Illocos and Pangasinan headed by Diego Silang, a member of the *principalia* class, a charismatic leader with a strong peasant following. The movement died with his assassination by Church and *mestizo* interests but has since been remembered as a proto-nationalist event.

Local revolts against taxes were increasingly common and severely suppressed. The failure of Spanish rule to effectively protect the Visayas, in particular from Moro raids, was an added burden. In the aftermath of the occupation, Madrid was shocked into admitting the abysmal state of the islands where the Indians (Spanish *Indios*, as in English then a generic word for indigenous people) had little respect for the Spanish and were civil only out of fear. French explorer and writer, the Comte de la Perouse regarded the 'Spanish nation with disgust as they see it humiliated by the English, the Dutch, the French and even the Moros'.[7]

Indeed, the Visayas, and even occasionally Luzon, saw raids by fast Iranun and Samal warcraft from coastal western Mindanao and the Sulu archipelago seizing captives for sale in the region's slave markets and forcing coastal communities, often led by priests, to organize their own defences. Although independent operators they were approved by Sulu for providing slaves and keeping the Spanish on the defensive. Populations at best stagnated. The Sulu sultanate remained de facto independent trading with other ports, including Batavia and Singapore. Only in the mid nineteenth century was it forced to acknowledge Spanish sovereignty. This led to the decline of the sultanate and its trading class who were replaced by Chinese.[8] Otherwise, Muslim mainland Mindanao was relatively little touched by Spain and was more pre-occupied with local disputes between sultans and datus than with Spain.

Through the eighteenth century little about Luzon and the Visayas changed other than the gradual decline of the galleon trade. In 1768, the Jesuits were expelled for the dangerous practice of educating the colonized. La Perouse, who visited in 1787, wrote: 'It would be difficult for the most unenlightened society to form a system of government more absurd than that which has regulated these islands for the past two hundred years ... They cultivate the earth like men of understanding, are carpenters, smiths, goldsmiths, weavers masons etc ... Though the Spaniards treat them with contempt ... the vices attributed to the Indians ought rather to be imputed to the government they themselves have established.'[9] The friars, he said, wanted to make Christians not citizens, meanwhile the economy was hindered by 'prohibitions and annoyances of every kind'. Fine tobacco was produced but was made a state monopoly which benefited the State but infuriated the farmers.

A few Filipinos prospered moderately. There were so few Spanish outside Manila that cooperative leading families, datus and the like, occupied senior government posts in the pueblos and were admitted into the *principalia*, the elite entitled to be addressed as Don and Dona. Society was also slowly changing. In 1760, there was the official acceptance of an existing reality – a *mestizo* class. These were mostly the product of marriages between Chinese and local women of the *principalia* class. Numbering 36,000 in 1760, those registered totalled 119,000 by 1810, of which only 10 per cent were Spanish *mestizos*. This class became increasingly important during the nineteenth century. Originally often *compradores* (agents) managing others' estates, some acquired land themselves and hence added wealth to their existing importance in provincial affairs. The racial composition gradually evolved but the class system remained.

A few economic lessons were learned. In 1785, the Royal Company of the Philippines was established to create plantations and to trade direct, tariff-free with Spain via the Cape rather than Mexico. In 1789, foreign ships were allowed to trade but only in Asian goods. India had become as important as China as trade partners, imports to Manila from Bengal and Coromandel in 1809 equalled those from China at 1,150,000 pesetas.[10]

The Philippines was barely touched by the liberalizing revolutionary events in Europe – the American, French, industrial and free trade revolutions. Spain's liberal 1812 constitution might have helped but it was soon replaced by the return of clerical and monarchical rule. Nor, unlike in the Americas, where Mexico declared independence in 1810, was there yet any locally-born class powerful enough to challenge Madrid. However, it could not entirely escape from events nearby, the huge expansion both of capitalist imperialism and the explosion of investment in mines and plantations to feed the new industries. Recognizing the potential for exports, British and American capital emerged to enable large scale processing of sugar by *haciendanos* (owners of large estates). In the 1850s, some ports in addition to Manila were opened to foreigners and some Chinese immigration was permitted, but a British visitor in 1857 still bemoaned the failure to exploit the huge resources of the country 'attributable to the miserable, traditional policy of the mother country'.[11] However, he noted the migration of Chinese into neighbouring countries and expected them also to have a positive impact on the Philippines.

Nonetheless, there was nothing stopping the pressure for political change that came with the plantations and export economy which began in the 1830s and continued to the wars of independence. Sugar output rose tenfold to 250,000 tons between 1835 and 1885 and abaca (a banana-like plant native to the Philippines. Its leaf fibres are used for making hemp and hence ropes) and tobacco by roughly similar percentages. Foreign investors brought steam power to sugar mills. Beginning in the late eighteenth century, the population also expanded rapidly for the first time since the Spanish occupation, rising from an estimated 2 million in 1818 to 6 million by 1888.[12] With the sugar boom, Negros' population increased tenfold between 1850 and 1890.

Wealth from sugar, abaca and tobacco as well as an ever-growing labour force benefited the *mestizo* land-owning class in particular and its upper echelons received education in Spain, a chance to imbibe liberal ideas and learn more about the greater progress of non-Spanish nations – Britain, France, etc. Trade and investment also brought the beginnings of modern banking.

Plantation crop agriculture also brought discontents. Prices, for example of sugar, varied hugely and were a particular burden for small producers previously leading a mainly subsistence life. Smallholder debts led to the acquisition of large estates, notably by Chinese *mestizos* in Pampanga and Tarlac, and Spanish and Chinese *mestizos* in Panay and Negros.

The nineteenth century saw a sustained clash between the religious needs of the Filipinos and the colonialist views of the Spanish Church, the friars in particular. Nationalism had its roots in this conflict.

Tension between the Spanish-led Church and peasant Catholics led to the creation of the all-Filipino Cofradia de San Jose in Central Luzon by Apolinario de la Cruz, better known as Hermano Pule, who had wanted to join the Dominican order but was barred because of his race. Becoming a lay preacher, he and a Filipino priest established the Cofradia de San Jose, attached to a hospital. It gradually attracted several thousand followers and only admitted Spanish and *mestizos* personally approved by Pule. It combined Catholic teaching with some pre-colonial ideas. Refused recognition by both State and Church, it was seen by the governor-general as implicitly political and was violently suppressed. In a battle with followers, troops killed several hundred and Pule and other leaders were captured and executed; Pule was just twenty-seven years old. Madrid was shocked and eventually the Supreme Court admonished the governor-general saying the Cofradia was not political but had merely committed an ecclesiastical offence, but the damage had been done.

The country was in the curious position of having become devout believers in Christ while increasingly despising the Church's principal agents the friars, the mendicants who had grown rich and greedy. In 1858, a British visitor was entertained to a dinner which would have 'satisfied a Parisian gourmand'[13] meanwhile also noting that local Spanish 'newspapers were more pre-occupied with the lives of saints than the most stirring events of the political world'.

At the same time, the Church saw growing divides between its mostly Spanish clergy and both the local priests and their flocks. The government did make efforts to extend primary education with its own schools in addition to the clerical schools but with a focus on teaching Christianity. The friars tended to ignore government demands that they teach Spanish to the *Indios* fearing that it would give them access to new, often secular, ideas.

In 1870, of 792 parishes, 611 were administered by the orders while the rest were controlled by secular priests, most of whom were Filipinos.[14] The confrontation between the two sparked a surge of local identity. Political swings in Madrid exacerbated issues as a liberal governor was replaced by a conservative. A minor uprising in a Cavite shipyard was used by the government, egged on by the friars, to accuse three outspoken local priests – Fathers Burgos, Gomez and Zamora – to be tried for plotting rebellion and executed. Others were imprisoned or exiled to the Marianas. Well-to-do supporters exiled themselves to Spain.

The deaths of the three priests were a landmark. Burgos, the son of a Spanish officer and a local *mestiza*, was highly educated, so too were Gomez and Zamora, *mestizos* educated at the University of Santo Tomas. All deeply resented the inferior position of the non-Spanish clergy.

This episode fuelled the wrath of an upcoming generation of prospering new class of mestizos, elite *Indios* and creoles (local born Spanish) who could be educated in Europe but who at home felt the heavy hand of racist officials and the *Guardia Civil*. From this elite, known as *ilustrados* (the enlightened) emerged the Propagandists, a movement aiming not for independence but for equal treatment as citizens and representation in the *Cortes* (parliament) in Madrid as Cuba and Puerto Rica had been given. They also demanded the ending of the friars' role in government, their replacement by local priests, more mass education, the curtailment of foreign – notably Chinese – economic power and a fairer tax system – the Spanish did not pay tax.

Gathering gradual momentum from 1880, by 1889 the movement was embedded among young *ilustrados* in Spain who published *La Solidaridad,* a fortnightly newspaper. The names of those involved are celebrated by street names throughout the country – Marcelo del Pilar, a lawyer, who wrote tracts in Tagalog as well as Spanish, Mariano Ponce, Juan Luna, a painter, and his brother Antonio, a future general, but most noted even then was Jose Rizal, a *mestizo* from Calamba near Manila whose elder brother had been a friend of Father Burgos. Rizal, a name he adopted, was fluent in several languages, a medical doctor and a writer whose first novel, *Noli Me Tangere* published in 1887, was a searing attack on the regime in Manila and on the friars.

The polymath Rizal's activities ranged from translating Schiller's play *Wilhelm Tell*, about the Swiss national hero, into Tagalog and, while in exile, having a practice as an eye doctor in Hong Kong. He was a man to whom women were attracted. One, Elizabeth Bracken, probably the daughter of a British soldier who was adopted by an American in Hong Kong, became his common law wife after they met in Hong Kong when she was eighteen and he thirty-three. After his death she helped the revolutionary movement before moving back to Hong Kong.

Rizal was particularly interested in the achievements of the pre-Hispanic Filipinos and wrote an influential annotation of de Morga's 1609 work an English translation of which he came to know while in London, which itself had an interesting background,[15] and then had the original and his notes and comments of his German friend Ferdinand Blumentritt published in Spanish in Paris. In 1891 he published his second novel, *El Filbusterismo* (The Subversive), an even more inflammatory attack on the regime than *Noli Me Tangere*. Returning to Manila, he formed La Liga Filipina to promote reform and national identity but after one meeting Rizal was arrested and exiled to Dapitan in northern Mindanao. He was there for four years but this did not stop the rise in anti-government sentiment as it resisted all notions of reform or any meaningful form of equality and representative government. Spanish nationalists clung desperately to the largest remaining piece of their once mighty empire, the friars to their vast lands – the Dominicans had 12,000 hectares of Rizal's home district, Calamba.

FIGURE 2.2 *Jose Rizal. © Wikimedia Commons.*

It was just forty-six years between the death of Herman Pule and Jose Rizal's *Noli Me Tangere* that anti-colonial movement shifted from the peasant populism of Pule though the Burgos period, when educated priests led new ideas, to the more secular nationalist views of the *ilustrados* with their connections to European liberalism.

However, the impetus for action rather than words came not from the *ilustrados* but from lower social ranks not interested in assimilation or being pseudo-Spanish. Following Rizal's exile, a more radical group of its members formed a secret society dedicated to independence and a republic, the Katipunan.[16] Most were lower middle class and freemasons and had the support of del Pilar. New members had initiation rites, a blood compact and acquired a nom de guerre. It also emphasized the equality of women as partners with men – a pointed rejection of patriarchal Catholicism.

Its undercover activities and recruitment among Manila's middle classes went unseen by the authorities until 1896 by which time it was headed by Andres Bonifacio, an educated man but below the ranks of the *ilustrados*. His group expected an armed struggle and had organized acquisition of weapons. Once discovered, the Katipunan declared revolution on 23 August 1896. Many *katipuneros* were quickly arrested and executed but revolt blossomed across Luzon.

Rizal had, earlier that year, rejected an approach from the Katipunan. He preferred a peaceful struggle for freedom. He even volunteered to serve as a doctor with Spanish forces fighting revolutionaries in Cuba, but while en route the authorities changed their mind. Rizal, seen as inspiration of the Philippine revolt, was returned to Manila and after a brief trial for rebellion was executed on 30 December 1896 by firing squad on Bagumbayan Field – now Luneta, within which is Rizal Park.

Rizal's legacy was remarkable but scantily acknowledged outside his own country. Although from a wealthy, *mestizo* background and steeped in European culture, he identified entirely as a Filipino and more broadly as a Malay. He helped develop Tagalog as a literary language and aspired for it to become the national language. He was the first modern nationalist in a region where Western colonialism was reaching its climax but they often ruled partly through compliant traditional elites with little interest in mass action or liberal ideas. Early nationalists in Indonesia and elsewhere were inspired by Rizal.[17] Rizal's surviving colleagues such as Mariano Ponce cooperated with Chinese revolutionary, Sun Yat Sen.

Bonifacio's management of revolt proved less effective than that of Emilio Aguinaldo, a *katipunero* who was mayor of Kawit in Cavite and hence a member of the *principalia* class. He was able to mobilize others of his class and achieve some victories. However, he was soon at loggerheads with Bonifacio for reasons which included class, regional and personal rivalries. Aguinaldo was chosen as leader of the revolutionary government. Bonifacio refused to cooperate with it. He and his brother were arrested, found guilty of treason and executed on 10 May 1897. A long-term result was the domination of the independence movement by socially more conservative forces. Bonifacio was no rural visionary but though highly literate he was not from the same *mestizo* socio-economic class as other leaders.

However, Bonifacio was not alone in that. Aguinaldo's closest adviser, Apolinario Mabini, was from a very poor family who managed to get a good education. Despite being crippled by polio, Mabini came to be regarded as the revolution's policy planner who authored of the Malolos Constitution.

There has been years of debate among historians about the relative roles of the *ilustrados* and traditions of peasant revolt in the nationalist movement. Reynaldo Ileto's ground-breaking *Pasyon and Revolution*[18] saw much of the same rural populism mixed with folk Christianity in nineteenth-century movements such as the Cofradia breakaway religious group led by Hermano Pule and was violently suppressed in 1841 with the loss of several hundred lives. These linked discontents with the passion of Christ and the notion of an earthly redeemer.

Pressured by Spanish reinforcements, Aguinaldo retreated to Biak-na-Bato in Bulacan where a republican constitution, based on a Cuban model, was announced. However, little more than a month later, through the mediation of an opportunistic *ilustrado* poet/politician Pedro Paterno, Aguinaldo signed a treaty with the Spanish Governor-General Primo de Rivera. He and his associates agreed to leave for Hong Kong and be paid a large indemnity, which he said would be used to support continuing agitation for independence. Aguinaldo left on 27 December and in Hong Kong his colleague Agoncillio attempted, without success, to elicit official US support in return for economic advantages. Aguinaldo sought arms for the struggle which continued in his absence. What might have happened next is conjecture because on 15 February an event on the other side of the world aborted the struggle for independence from Spain.

The more radical ideas of Andres Bonifacio and his urban lower middle class followers might, under other circumstances, have left a mark at a time when Marxist-influenced leftist and anti-colonial ideas made an appearance in the decade before the First World War and China's 1911 overthrow of the Qing dynasty proved an inspiration to others. But 15 February 1898 set off a chain of events which radically changed the world, and the Philippines more than most.

Notes

1   Antonio de Morga, *Sucesos de las Islas Filipinas*, trans. Henry E.J. Stanley, London: The Hakluyt Society, 1868, p. 264.

2   Ibid., p. 141.

3   Ibid., p. 241.

4   Benito J. Legarda, Jr., *After the Galleons*, Quezon City: Ateneo de Manila University Press, 2002, pp. 32–40.

5   Ibid., p. 45.

6   Alexander Dalrymple quoted in O.D. Corpuz, *The Roots of the Filipino Nation*, Vol. 1, Quezon City: University of the Philippines Press, 2005, p. 363.

7   Dalrymple quoted in Corpuz, *The Roots of the Filipino Nation*, p. 401.

8   Najeeb Saleeby. *The History of Sulu*, Manila: Bureau of Science, 1908, reprint Filipiniana Book Guild, 1960.

9   Jean-Françoise de Galaup de la Perouse, *The Journal 1785–1788*, Vol. 2, trans. John Dunmore, London: The Hakluyt Society, 1995, p. 238.

10   Manuel Buzeta, *Diccionario Geografico-Estadistico-Historico de las Islas Filipinas*, Madrid, 1850.

11 John Bowring, *A Visit to the Philippine Isles*, London: Elder Smith, 1859.

12 John A. Larkin, *Sugar and the Origins of Modern Philippine Society*, Berkeley, CA: University of California Press, 1993, pp. 47–9.

13 Ibid., p. 42.

14 Luis H. Francia, *A History of the Philippines*, New York, The Overlook Press, 2014, p. 106.

15 The translation had been made by the Hakluyt Society in London at the suggestion of John Bowring, the former governor of Hong Kong and author of *A Visit to the Philippine Isles*. During that visit Bowring had been a guest at Binan in Laguna of Don Jose Alberto, a rich and educated *mestizo* who was an uncle of Rizal who stayed there when he first went to school.

16 In full: *Ang Kataastaasang Kagalagalangan Katipunan ng mga Anak ng Bayan* (Highest, Most Honourable Society of the Sons of the Country).

17 John Nery, *Revolutionary Spirit, Jose Rizal in Southeast Asia*, Singapore: Institute of Southeast Asian Studies, 2011.

18 Reynaldo Ileto, *Pasyon and Revolution Popular Movements in the Philippines 1840–1910*, Quezon City: Ateneo de Manila University Press, 1979.

3

'Uncle Sam's Brown Boys'

On 15 February 1898 the US battleship *Maine*, sent to Cuba ostensibly to protect American lives, exploded in Havana harbour, killing most its crew. The explosion was (wrongly) blamed on Spain and resulted in widespread calls for war, notably in the US press.

For some time, intervention in Cuba had been an issue in US politics. Some called for support for Cuban freedom fighters, others hoped to promote US economic interests there, but there were strong feelings against any kind of foreign involvement or attempt to acquire empire. President McKinley was no warmonger and vacillated, but after trying to force a compromise with Spain he ceded authority to Congress and a law compelled him into war and support for Cuban independence.

The Philippines was not itself an issue, but the growth of US economic interests had toppled the Hawaiian monarchy in 1893 and the islands became a US territory in 1898. Some saw it as inevitable that the US should look across the Pacific, given the economic potential seen in China and noting the rise of Japanese power. Others in the US feared such involvement as being costly and dangerous, but expansionism was the stronger force at a time when America's wealth and population were growing apace.

A fleet commanded by Admiral Dewey sailed from Hong Kong – leaving Aguinaldo behind – and demolished the Spanish fleet off Cavite in Manila Bay. Aguinaldo soon returned to his country on another US ship and on 14 June declared Philippine independence at a ceremony at his house in Cavite. Dewey did not attend. By then Filipino insurgents were in control of much of the country and surrounded Manila but did not press an attack. Dewey played for time and the arrival of a large US force.

American President McKinley had scant knowledge of or interests in the islands other than as bargaining chip with Spain, but once there and basking in Dewey's victory over a decrepit Spanish fleet, attitudes changed. With the arrival of thousands of US troops, and hearing of events in Cuba, the governor in Manila indicated a willingness to surrender to 'white people not to niggers'. A staged battle then took place to save the Spanish honour and the US took the city. Had he not deliberately cut the cable link to Hong Kong, Dewey would have known that by then an armistice had been agreed,

with Spain yielding Cuba and Puerto Rico, and leaving the future of the
Philippines to be decided at a peace conference.

Aguinaldo meanwhile was trying to create his own facts and he drew up
a constitution (the Malolos Constitution). It incorporated an elected
assembly but with a narrow franchise which reflected the interests of the
mestizo nationalist elite. Aguinaldo became president and Mabini prime
minister. Independent Philippines had a government of sorts but was ignored
by the Americans. In Washington, McKinley now determined to hold the
territory. There were good business prospects and if the US moved out some
other power – most notably Germany, which had recently acquired almost
all the small islands in the Pacific apart from Guam – would try to move in.

Aguinaldo's government and its chief negotiator, Felipe Agoncillo, were
denied representation in Paris where Spain and the US met to draw up a
treaty. Signed on 10 December 1898 it handed the Philippines and the
Marianas Islands to the US, in US eyes giving it the right to govern. McKinley
had to deal with strenuous opposition in the Senate which needed to ratify
the treaty. Some opposed on party lines, others against the concept of
acquiring foreign territories. The Anti-Imperialist League, including writer
Mark Twain and industrialist Andrew Carnegie, campaigned against it.
The treaty was eventually passed by just one vote, but by then open conflict
had broken out in the outskirts of Manila where Philippine trenches ringed
US forces.

The Americans launched a full-scale attack, using artillery and gunboats as
well as well-armed infantry, gradually controlling the area around Manila and
then forcing Aguinaldo to retreat north from Malolos. With several leading
ilustrados deserting to the Americans in return for positions in the
administration, Aguinaldo made overtures for a truce and the possibility of
some more limited form of independence, but the US commander, General
Otis, was not listening and his troops were in no mood for compromise
with people they treated with the same degree of contempt as they had for
native Americans. With Filipinos forced to resort to guerrilla tactics, they were
treated as bandits not soldiers. Torture was widely used to extract information.

The killing of US troops by Filipinos, as at Balangiga in Samar, led to
the local US commander ordering: 'I want no prisoners. I wish you to kill
and burn, the more you kill and burn the more you will please me'. The
troops also looted the church, taking its three bells back to the US as
trophies. (The bells remained a source of friction with the US until they were
returned in 2018.)

The Filipinos suffered a series of setbacks. Mabini was captured and
General Gregorio del Pilar killed, while the volatile but very capable General
Antonio Luna, who had proved an effective general and hence a possible
rival to Aguinaldo, was assassinated by troops from Cavite. Aguinaldo
denied involvement but the death was symptomatic of the divides between
those committed to the war with the US and those looking for compromise.
Aguinaldo opted for guerrilla tactics but after he was captured in Isabela

FIGURE 3.1 *Emilio Aguinaldo and his army.* © Getty images.

province he then declared allegiance to the US. Nevertheless, fighting continued well into 1902 and pockets of resistance in Southern Tagalog and Negros continued until 1906. Altogether, the Philippine-American War caused the deaths of about 4,000 US troops, 20,000 Philippine soldiers and perhaps twice that many non-combatants.

Initially, the Moro region had been kept out of the war thanks to a deal with the Sultan of Sulu who recognized US sovereignty in return for non-interference. It did not last. A massacre at Bud Daju in Sulu in 1906 became a symbol of oppression, but despite the solidarity supposedly provided by Islam, common cause among sultans and datus was lacking. Army rule throughout Mindanao continued until 1916 but the datus' status was respected.

The extent of popular resistance in the Philippines generally did however make US officials aware of the need to show that their presence could bring benefits. News of massacres also led to pressures on the government in Washington to show they could as promised 'uplift and civilize' their new possession. Removing military governor Arthur MacArthur, McKinley assigned this task to William Howard Taft, a federal judge and future president. Taft had no respect for the Filipinos but was determined to do his energetic best to educate the 'little brown brothers' as he termed them. He was at least eager to create a civilian government and improve education. Taft was a large man by any definition, 182 centimetres tall weighing about 130 kilos. Photographs of him at this time meeting the diminutive Sultan

Kiram in Sulu in 1901 and riding a carabao became an occasion for some mirth.

The injection of American ways proved less problematic than it might have been given the war and the racism of white America. It was made easier by the cooperation of much of the elite. As a successful lawyer and politician, Taft knew how to make attractive offers. The law-making Philippine Commission created in 1900 initially had a few local members. Early collaborators included two former members of Aguinaldo's Malolos government, Gregorio Araneta, who became Solicitor-General in 1901, and Benito Legarda. Another was and T.H. Pardo de Tavera, a leading *ilustrado* intellectual and former anti-Spain activist. They formed a group, the *Federalistas*, seeking eventual US statehood. They persisted in this despite being brushed off by the US Secretary for War, Elihu Root, who noted that Filipinos would 'add another serious race problem to the one we already have'.[1]

For all the nationalist fervour of the masses, landowners were more often interested in preserving the social status quo that the US offered. The Americans negotiated a deal with the Vatican to buy the friars' 150,000 hectares of land. Rather than giving the land to the tenants, they sold it to those already rich — names such as Lopez, Elizalde and Lacson in Negros and Cojuangco in Tarlac. This was good politics at the time but created enduring social problems. The American Sugar Refining Company also got a large sugar estate in Cebu, but that caused such consternation among nationalists that limits were later put on land sales to Americans.

For all their low opinion of the natives, the Americans, with their anti-colonial history, needed to show they were not just another colonizer like the Dutch, French or British. Taft also knew that a display of benign paternalism was needed to ward off critics back home. Americans also had a strong streak of missionary-style idealism allied to their belief in the superiority of American values as shown by the nation's success. Americanization was spearheaded by a policy to inculcate English as rapidly as possible making schooling and the teaching of English compulsory. This was to be both an avenue for advancement for Filipinos and a way of making them more like Americans and hence easier to govern.

In August 1901, a ship named the USS *Thomas* arrived in Manila carrying 500 young Americans to begin the huge task of teaching English language and American ways throughout the archipelago. Later known as Thomasites, they were the vanguard of idealism, even though many struggled against a lack of interest in a very American syllabus, but they were followed by many more – doctors, engineers, health workers, agriculturalists, etc. Young Americans flocked to the standard of uplifting the Filipinos. The better side of American rule was shown by free public schools run by the State not the Church, though it was not compulsory and in the early days attendance was spasmodic. There was a big gap between Philippine mass culture and their earnest, American teachers but gradually education gained traction. A few Filipinos went to college in the US on scholarships.

Although some of the elite objected to the side-lining of Spanish, the spread of English was made easier by the emphasis on literacy. By 1920, more people were literate in English than Spanish or local languages, though the old elite continued to write mainly in Spanish. Investment in public health was another priority which previously had little attention. Manila got a sewage system and cholera was largely wiped out as a result. The death rate fell sharply and the population increased from 7.5 million in 1903 to 10 million in 1918 and 16 million in 1939.

The Americans also brought a commitment to engaging local elites in government. This was partly out of necessity – there was no existing civil service infrastructure. The US was accustomed to de-centralized government and giving status to the elites made government easier and cheaper. The US thus further enhanced the status of existing leading, mostly *mestizo*, families who had both prospered in the nineteenth century and then led the nationalist movement. The US bottom-up approach to government, and the link between the judicial and political systems, left deep marks and contrasted with trends in countries such as Thailand where the focus of rulers was on strengthening central bureaucracy. Emphasis on English, although of benefit for education, was also a barrier to the development of Tagalog as the national language.

US rule in practice weakened the position of the Catholic Church. In 1902, followers of Gregorio Aglipay, a former Catholic priest from Ilocos who had supported the war against the US, formed the Independent Philippine Church. It conducted services in vernacular languages, allowed priests to marry, admitted freemasons and rejected the doctrine of the Trinity. Another breakaway church, the Iglesia ni Cristo (INC), was founded in 1914 by Felix Manalo who claimed divine revelation. It was also unitarian and allowed priests to marry. However, despite its association with friar abuses, the Catholic Church still had the institutional weight and money. The new churches did not attract the elite and though protestant sects arrived the Catholics with their rituals and feast days were too well dug-in to lose many followers.

Co-opting elites enabled the US to move ahead with a form of representative government. The Philippine Organic Act of 1902 provided for a two-chamber legislature, with the Philippine Commission as upper chamber and an Assembly as lower one, to be elected. The first Assembly elections were in 1907 but the franchise was very narrow – property ownership as well as literacy limiting registered voters to 104,000. It did, however, represent an elite divided between those, in principle, hankering for independence – the Nacionalista Party, and those – the Progresista (formerly Federalista) Party – looking for a federal relationship with or statehood within the US. With fifty-nine out of eighty seats, the Nacionalistas and their allies won easily.

Two names emerged from that election which were to dominate politics for more than thirty years. One was Manuel Quezon, handsome, eloquent *mestizo* of complex but mostly Spanish parentage who had been an officer in Aguinaldo's army before surrendering in 1900. He then became a successful lawyer and was found useful by the Americans who recognized his sharp brain, magnetic personality and lack of scruples. Elected mayor of Tayabas in 1906, he became leader of the majority in the first Assembly.

The other was Sergio Osmena, illegitimate son of a rich *mestizo* Chinese family from Cebu. He served briefly with Aguinaldo before starting a newspaper in Cebu, where he became governor in 1906, then Speaker of the Assembly in 1907. Unpretentious, diligent and a devout Catholic, he was mostly to be in Quezon's shadow and in 1923 was replaced as speaker by a Quezon protégé, Manuel Roxas, but his skills complemented those of Quezon.

In 1909, Quezon became one of the two Philippine Commissioners to the US Congress, pushing to increase localization of government and influencing President Wilson to appoint the liberal-minded Francis B. Harrison as governor who arrived in Manila in 1913 declaring: 'Every step we take will be taken with a view to the ultimate independence of the islands'. He replaced Americans with Filipino officials who he made a majority of the nine-member Commission. The 1916 Jones Act provided increased autonomy with a two-chamber legislature, a Senate replacing the Commission. Independence was promised as soon as an undefined 'stable government' was achieved. For the time, political progress could partly compensate for racial division. Locals, however distinguished, were kept out of white homes and clubs, and American men kept local mistresses while officially frowning on racial mixing. (Filipinos could go to work in the US, mainly Hawaii and California, but in the US were barred from marrying whites.)

The 1920s saw a slowdown in political progress with tension between Quezon and Governor Leonard Wood, a retired general appointed by President Harding. Following a mission by Osmena and Roxas, and subsequently by Quezon, the 1934 Tydings-McDuffie Act granted the Philippines Commonwealth (self-governing) status to be followed by independence in ten years. A convention headed by lawyer Senator Claro M. Recto, a Quezon ally, then drew up a constitution modelled on the US with votes for all literate men aged twenty-one, with women to follow in two years. Quezon and Osmena re-formed an alliance as president and vice-president respectively with Quezon facing an ageing Aguinaldo and the independent church's Gregorio Aglipay. They won very easily but only 1 million out of about 4 million adult men voted. Quezon remarked: 'I would rather have a country run like hell by Filipinos than a country run like heaven by the Americans'.

The emotional appeal for independence was strong, particularly among the new political class. Others were more sceptical as to whether it would do anything for the masses in a society which remained divided between a mostly *mestizo* boss class and the *tao* (common people). There was also a fear that US withdrawal would lay the nation open either to Japanese expansionism or an unstoppable flood of cheap labour from China. The Tydings-McDuffie Act also held several problems for the country. Filipinos in the US became aliens with an annual migration limit of fifty. Those already there could, as Asian aliens, not leave and return. They were already there in significant numbers – at least 50,000 – in both Hawaii and California, mostly as farm workers. Their lives were vividly described in the semi-autobiographical novel *America is in the Heart* by Carlos Bulosan,[2] was a farm boy from Pampanga who went to California and became a union activist and prolific writer.

Filipinos in the US faced racial hostility and exploitation not only by employees but by Filipino recruitment agencies and by longer established, better organized Chinese and Japanese immigrant groups. Nonetheless, few accepted the offer of one-way repatriation provided after the Tydings-McDuffie Act. As the title of Bulosan's book suggested, America was still a dream. When the Second World War came, Filipinos in the US formed two segregated regiments which served in New Guinea and the Philippines. Service was a path to citizenship but in California they were not allowed to marry outside their community as inter-racial marriage was illegal there until 1948.

Tydings-McDuffie provided for a continuing US military presence. Command of the Philippine army would remain for ten years and thereafter be subject to negotiation. Nationalists wanted to be rid of the Americans but there were strong concerns that the country could not defend itself. The bigger issue, however, was economic. Sugar planters in particular but also the abaca and tobacco interests feared losing access to the US market. By then the country's foreign trade had become far too tied to America for comfort so the fear of losing preferential access after independence was real, a very logical fear and shared by many who publicly avowed nationalism.

Taft had believed, both as governor of the Philippines and US president, in the value for both parties of free trade between the US and its new territory. He fought for the 1909 tariff reform, ensured that the US market was fully open for Philippine sugar, abaca, tobacco and coconut oil and copra – in the case of sugar against the interests of US beet growers. High tariffs were applied to non-US goods entering the Philippines. Thus, by the 1930s, the US accounted for about 80 per cent of its exports and two-thirds of Philippine imports. This version of 'free trade' protected the sugar barons but gave them no incentive to increase productivity while providing no barrier behind which manufacturing could develop.

US investment did come but not as fast as had been hoped. Docks were much improved, and some 800 kilometres of railway were constructed – though much less than promised by the companies which won the franchises. Road building progressed slowly due to the scarcity of manpower as well as money. Little US investment went into plantations due to a limit of 2,500 acres (1,000 hectares) which was imposed after nationalist uproar at the intended award of half a million acres of public land in Mindanao to the Firestone tyre company. There were some small plantations, including in Basilan, and gold mining prospered in Luzon, particularly after 1934 when President Roosevelt raised its price from $20 to $35 an ounce. The country also saw an influx of Japanese, first as labourers, then as merchants and farmers developing small abaca plantations in Mindanao. The expansion of plantation agriculture drove trade and profits but rice production failed to keep up with demand and the Philippines became a net rice importer.

Domestic trade developed as roads improved and a few farmers were helped by the establishment of local banks, but landowning peasants were a minority and absentee landlords often paid little attention to their lands. The 1930s global depression was especially hard on tenants growing cash crops, despite US market access. It is estimated that in 1938 two-thirds of the workforce were share-croppers or day labourers.[3] Unrest simmered and two leftist parties were formed to represent worker and peasant interests, the Partido Obrera de Filipinas founded in 1924 and in 1930 the Partido Komunista ng Pilipinas which was declared illegal in 1932 but continued underground. Another influence, albeit briefly, was the Sakdalista movement of Benigno Ramos. He had been a Quezon colleague but became a critic, demanding land re-distribution as well as independence. The Sakdalistas had early appeal but with the failure of a 1935 uprising supported by peasants in the Tagalog region it was doomed. Ramos left for Japan and a pro-Japanese future but the seeds of discontent did not die. The Commonwealth passed legislation to give some protection to workers and tenant farmers, and a National Rice and Corn Corporation was created to undercut middlemen. Unions were given the right to organize but there was no significant social change.

The new political class was mostly the same rival leading families at province or town level for whom democracy was their duelling stage. Quezon was a masterful manipulator of the system. It was no coincidence that he developed a good relationship with the equally self-assured Douglas MacArthur, son of Arthur MacArthur. As a young officer, Douglas had served in Manila in 1903–5 and became acquainted with Quezon and Osmena. In 1918, thanks to his exploits in the First World War, he became the youngest general in the US army, and served in Manila again from 1922 to 1924, by which time Quezon was President of the Senate. After years in Washington, Quezon influenced MacArthur's return to Manila as commander of the US infantry brigade in the Philippines from 1928 to 1930. There MacArthur acquired a sixteen-year-old *mestiza* companion, Isabel Rosario Cooper, known as Dimples. He later took Dimples back to Washington, hiding her in an apartment until the threat of exposure saw him pay her $15,000 in severance and for the letters he had sent her.

On the formation of the Commonwealth, Quezon saw the need for an army, and in 1935 he enabled the appointment of his friend MacArthur to train it. The role of adviser evolved into the grandiose title of Field Marshal. MacArthur was a political conservative and a believer in the importance of the US presence in Asia. Racism, however, was not among his many faults which explained his ability to get along with Quezon and others, and eventually be seen as a national hero by many in the Philippines.

The extension of America across the Pacific had made it a global power befitting its economic might, but also increased its vulnerability. The new possession needed to be defended, with Japan, after its 1903 defeat of Russia, the most likely competitor in the region. However, it was envisaged that naval capability would suffice for the Philippines' defence. That view prevailed even after 1918 when Japan, in return for naval assistance to Britain, was awarded several German possessions, the tiny but strategic chain of islands across the north-western Pacific – the Marianas, and the Caroline (now Micronesia) and Marshall islands. By the mid-1930s, Japan's domestic politics and international outlook had changed with expansionist objectives in China becoming all too clear. The Philippines needed its own forces, however inadequate, as well as on the US shield. MacArthur had a plan for a force of some 10,000 regulars supported when needed by a lightly-trained mass militia, a job he gave to a sceptical subordinate, Dwight Eisenhower, whose best efforts produced only a fraction of the number envisaged. In July 1941, MacArthur returned to the US military as Commander of US Army Forces in the Far East, bringing the new Philippine troops under his command.

Quezon, meanwhile, had luxuriated in his position of president of an almost-sovereign state, travelling to China and Japan as a representative of Asian nationalism. He used his political dominance to try to expand the power of the Sate and reduce the reliance on the patronage system.[4] Given more time he might have succeeded, but as tensions between the US and Japan rose, Quezon also became acutely conscious of the weakness of an independent Philippines. 'It could not be defended even if every last Filipino were armed with a modern weapon,' he told a crowd. He visited Tokyo hoping for a post-independence commitment to its neutrality but was politely ignored.

At home, Quezon and his colleagues basked in wide approval. Progress included votes for women and the encouragement of the use of Tagalog, now defined as Pilipino. In 1938, the Nacionalistas won 94 per cent of the seats in the Assembly. Using his popularity to prolong his reign, Quezon then proposed that instead of one term of six years, there should be two terms of four years each. This, and a proposal for a two-chamber legislature, was approved by a plebiscite and was followed by legislative, local and presidential elections in November 1941. Voters totalled 1.57 million out of an adult population of 7.5 million. Quezon and Osmena were re-elected with 81 per cent and 92 per cent of votes respectively but had scant time to savour victory.

The nineteen years of constitutional development had enhanced a version of democracy but done little for national unity as far as Muslim areas were concerned. The 1935 Assembly had just two Muslim members. Its first

FIGURE 3.2 *President Manuel L. Quezon and wife Aurora at Mass, 1940.* © *Wikimedia Commons.*

elected, Senator Alauya Alonto, Sultan of Ramain in Lanao, had long been cooperating with Quezon and been a delegate to the Constitutional Convention, but many Muslims resented the newly educated Christian Filipino officials sent south and distrusted education delivered by non-Muslims. There was scant sense of loyalty to Quezon's nation-in-the-making and some disquiet at the movement of land-hungry Visayans into Mindanao. At the grass roots level, there was little friction. Muslims and Christians alike included earlier beliefs in their practices, both enjoyed festivals and music, and Muslim women generally did not wear the hijab. Nonetheless, forty years of American overlordship had done little to enhance Muslim-Christian common identity or to undermine the role of traditional rulers averse to education and development.

As for the largely Christianized majority of Filipinos, attitudes to the Americans were conflicted between resentment and admiration, nationalism and opportunism, greed and fear. Those were even more to the fore with the traumas which lay immediately ahead of the 1941 election.

Notes

1 Quoted in Stanley Karnow, *In Our Image: America's Empire in the Philippines*, New York: Random House, 1989, p. 231.

2 Carlos Bulosan, *America is in the Heart*. First published in 1946 but only became well-known after re-publication by University of Washington Press,

Seattle, in 1974. Bulosan first became known for a 1943 essay "Freedom from Want" in the *Saturday Evening Post*, illustrated by the famed Norman Rockwell. He died in poverty of tuberculosis in Seattle in 1956, aged 45.

3 Luis H. Francia, *A History of the Philippines*, New York: Overlook Press, 2014, p. 174.

4 Patricio N. Abinales and Donna J. Amoroso, *State and Society in the Philippines,* revised edition, New York: Rowman and Littlefield, 2017, p. 153.

4

Choices of evils

Japan's occupation of the Philippines lasted only thirty months but left not merely a trail of destruction and misery but as many myths and as much opportunism as heroism. It also, in the end, raised the reputation of America among Filipinos and in practice ended the efforts of Quezon to centralize power.

There had been a long build-up to the war which hit the Philippines on 8 December 1941. Japan's occupation of Manchuria in 1934 had been followed by the invasion of China in 1937, but the longer the war in China lasted, the more Japan needed resources. After the outbreak of war in Europe and the German occupation of France and the Netherlands in 1940, the vulnerability of the Europeans' Asian empires was clear. Japan moved troops into northern Vietnam, then ships to Cam Ranh Bay, prompting a US oil embargo and freeze on Japanese assets in July 1941.

The German invasion of Russia in June further changed the picture. Japan could help Germany by attacking the Soviets, or push into resource-rich Southeast Asia, or make a deal with the US in return for oil. The US, worried about the situation in Europe, engaged in negotiation but insisted on Japan's withdrawal from China. The appointment of Douglas MacArthur as commander of the US Army in the Far East indicated Washington's concern and a large build-up of troops and weapons got underway. However, MacArthur was overconfident both in his own forces and with his prediction that the Japanese would not be ready for an offensive until the following April.

Even when the Japanese launched their assault on the Philippines a few hours after their 6 December attack on the US navy at Pearl Harbour in Hawaii, MacArthur was slow to respond. Most of the newly reinforced US Air Force was destroyed on the ground at Clark Field. Japanese troop landings in the Lingayen Gulf, 100 kilometres northwest of Manila, soon had the Americans and their bigger but inexperienced locally raised forces falling steadily back.

The Japanese entered Manila and MacArthur's forces retreated to the Bataan Peninsula. MacArthur, with President Quezon and Vice-President Osmena, was at a redoubt at Corregidor, an island off Bataan at the northern entrance to Manila Bay. Quezon asked President Roosevelt to offer immediate independence so the Philippines could declare neutrality and 'save my country from further devastation as the battleground of two great powers'. MacArthur initially termed this 'the sound course to follow' as he could not count on the loyalty of Filipinos who had 'violent resentment of the US'.[1] Both were persuaded to 'stand and fight'. Despite MacArthur's defeatism, Roosevelt needed a hero, so MacArthur was given a Congressional Medal of Honor, newspapers ran invented stories about the 'Lion of Luzon'. MacArthur was then ordered to Australia to take charge of US military forces in the Pacific but famously promised 'I will return': Quezon and Osmena were evacuated to the US to lead a 'government in exile'.

A three-month battle for Bataan ended in early April with the surrender of some 75,000 troops, 60,000 Filipinos, 15,000 from the US. The Bataan defence and the subsequent 'death march', which saw thousands die from exhaustion, disease and starvation as they were forced to walk some 100 kilometres to a camp in Tarlac, is deeply etched in the Philippine memory. The shared Filipino and American suffering did much to forge an emotional bond with America which had not previously existed, while Japanese behaviour was to make people forget the brutalities of the American conquest. It was also to provide Filipinos with tales of heroism which bolstered national self-esteem and later provided a platform for future leaders such as Ferdinand Marcos.

At the time however, Filipino elites were divided as to how to deal with their new masters. Jorge Vargas, Quezon's secretary had earlier been appointed mayor of Manila, which had been declared an open city, and stayed to negotiate as best he could with the victorious Japanese. As in other colonial countries in the region occupied by Japan, views of the Japanese changed over time in response both to their behaviour and the course of the war. Unlike the European colonies, the Philippines was on the cusp of independence so their claim to be Asian 'liberators' from white man rule was less persuasive than for the local elites of Burma (Myanmar) or of the Dutch East Indies (Indonesia). Nonetheless, many saw the need for accommodation with the realities. Others were positively enthusiastic.

Nor were the Japanese lacking in admirers despite their invasion of China. Their military and industrial successes were proof that Asians were not the inferiors of the white bosses. 'Asia for the Asians' had appeal, even if the reality was to prove rather different. In the Philippines, the Japanese had shown themselves to be diligent, disciplined and beneficial to the economy. There were about three times as many Japanese civilians in the country as Americans. In Mindanao in particular, they had invested in hemp plantations, sawmills and fishing. Davao had Japanese schools and shops. In pre-war Philippines, some journalists were paid to write in favour of Japan and a few went to study there, including Jose S. Laurel III, son of Jose P. Laurel Jr, a Yale law graduate who was a Senator and then Supreme Court justice. A pan-Asianist admirer of Japan, Laurel was to become President of the

Japanese-sponsored Republic declared in October 1943. Until then Vargas was the principal intermediary with the Japanese governor-general Masaharu Homma as Presiding Officer of the Philippine Executive Commission. Vargas saw his role as trying to ameliorate the conditions of occupation following, he claimed, Quezon's instructions. He ended the war as the puppet republic's ambassador in Tokyo. Jurist and senator, Claro Recto, who became Commissioner for Education and then for Foreign Affairs, proclaimed that Japanese victories represented 'the rebirth of the powerful oriental civilisation and the awakening of mighty Asia under the unselfish leadership of the Japanese Empire'.[2] Chief Justice, Jose Abad Santos, who had been named acting president by Quezon, was made of sterner stuff. Captured in Cebu he refused to cooperate and was executed.

At least initially, few of the elite saw reason to confront the Japanese. A majority of senators joined the Executive Commission; others kept a low profile. A few were enthusiastic, including Laurel who admired Japanese order and devotion to the nation. Laurel could reasonably claim that some cooperation with Japan was necessary for the good of the people. Accepting the Presidency of the supposedly independent republic, however, was another matter given that the elected president and vice-president had a government-in-exile in Washington.

Another key collaborator was Benigno Aquino, a lawyer and landowner from Tarlac, who had been Secretary for Agriculture under Quezon. The Japanese made Aquino head of a new appointed assembly, known by the acronym Kalibapi (the Association for Service to the New Philippines). Also banging the drum for Japan was the MaKaPili, the Patriotic Society of Filipinos, led by former Sakdal leader Benigno Ramos. Former revolutionary general, Artemio Ricarte, who had always refused allegiance to the US, returned in late 1944 after thirty years in exile in Hong Kong and then Japan. Even Emilio Aguinaldo resurfaced, urging close cooperation with Japan.

Spanish citizens, who were still numerous and influential as priests or from the old elite, were divided. Many had supported the Falangists during the Spanish Civil War and were thus prone to be sympathetic to Japan, but Andres Soriano of the giant A. Soriano Corporation stuck with Quezon as a member of his cabinet even though he had been the local leader of Spain's Falangists. Others played an equivocal role. Manuel Roxas, who Quezon originally favoured as vice-president over Osmena, was captured by the Japanese and became an adviser to Laurel. The Japanese hoped to make him president in 1943 rather than Laurel but he declined. Late in the war Roxas may have provided intelligence to the Americans.

Whatever its notion of Asia for Asians, the occupation had several problems which fed on each other. The first was the arrogant and often brutal behaviour of the Japanese military for whom easy-going Filipino ways were alien. There was also a demand for comfort women for the soldiery, for which there was little local consent. Second was the quest for raw materials by Japan, combined with the inevitable shortages of a wartime economy shorn of foreign trade. The Japanese needed local resources to feed a 400,000-man army in the Philippines. Food shortages and unemployment were caused by Japanese demands for materials and the collapse of export industries which had been focused on the US market. A third factor was that antipathy towards the Americans was found more among the elite than lower down the social order where the US was associated with progress and aspiration. In exile, Quezon and Osmena provided a focus for resistance, there was pride in the Filipinos' sacrifices in Bataan, and before long an expectation that the Americans would return.

Guerrilla activity developed, in many cases led by former soldiers, and provided some support brought by American submarines. As only Americans could defeat the Japanese, many Filipinos now longed for their return, past sins forgiven. They provided information and help to the Americans while appearing to be loyal to the puppet government. As resistance grew, so did reprisals and fear of the *kempeitai*, the Japanese military police. Disorder reigned too with some supposedly anti-Japanese activity becoming a cover for settling feuds between rival families. The resistance spawned many heroes but also, in the aftermath, many bogus claims to it.

The most significant resistance, at least in the longer term, was provided by the Hukbong Bayan Laban na Hapon – the People's Anti-Japanese Army – or Huks in Central Luzon, heart of rice and sugar cultivation, and of big haciendas. Feudal and paternalist tenancy systems, which at least provided stability for families, had been significantly replaced by sharecropping and small farmers, reduced by debt, into becoming wage labourers. As anti-landlord as it was anti-Japanese, some of the movement's leaders drew inspiration from Mao Zedong. The movement was headed by Luis Taruc, a protégé of early nationalist and convert to Marxism, Pedro Abad Santos, brother of the Chief Justice. Taruc, who had been a full-time peasant organizer for the Socialist, then Communist, Party since 1934, was the leader of several thousand members from the sharecropper and landless workers, mainly in Bulacan, Nueva Ecija, Pampanga and Tarlac. The Huks were, however, predominantly a peasant organization born of injustice more than ideology. Various peasant movements had grown rapidly in the late 1930s, notably the Kalipunang Pambansa Magsasaka sa Filipinas (the National Society of Peasants in the Philippines) with a cross-province association organizing self-help efforts, supporting strikes, seizing grain stores, opposing evictions and publicizing landlord excesses. In frequent conflict with the pro-landlord police and local authorities, some of its leaders were jailed for insurrection. Big landowners used armed men against their tenants, so peasant groups sought arms in response. Quezon tried to mollify them by promising remedies and attempted some reforms but the situation in Central Luzon was increasingly unstable when war came. Thus, by the time the Japanese arrived to add to their woes, there was an institutional peasant basis for resistance with some ideological sinews provided by the

Communist Party. As well as guerrilla warfare, the Huks organized to hide their crops from the Japanese. Just as the Japanese invasion helped the development of China's rural revolutionary movement, so did its Philippine counterpart emerge stronger after the war with its additional privations.

Japan's attempt to use naval power to thwart MacArthur's return to the Philippines in October 1944 resulted in the Battle of Leyte Gulf, the most destructive in naval history with the loss of half of Japan's fleet. It caused the commander in the Philippines, General Yamashita, who had originally planned to focus on the defence of Luzon, to fight in Leyte. The two-month battle cost 4,000 US dead but the Japanese many times more thanks to superior US fire power, much of it from ships. The US invasion of Luzon began at Lingayen Gulf to the north, then Nasugbu to the south of Manila. Yamashita did not defend the beaches and, aiming to preserve his forces drew them north leaving Manila apparently within easy grasp. Indeed, the Americans had no problem securing the release of their internees at the Santo Tomas campus and Bilibid Prison, and on 6 February MacArthur declared the city liberated. It was not. The Japanese naval commander in the city, Rear-Admiral Iwabuchi with about 12,000 men ignored Yamashita and elected to fight. MacArthur was equally keen for a fight, seeking a clear victory with scant regard of the civilian cost.

The US had not been prepared for urban warfare, nor did it provide an escape route for the Japanese. What followed was a month of slaughter which cost the lives of upwards of (very approximately) 100,000 civilians, 8,000 Japanese, and a little more than 1,000 US soldiers. It also destroyed almost the whole of the centre of the city, notably Intramuros and the area

FIGURE 4.1 *Manila after the battle, 1945.* © *US Government/Wikimedia Commons.*

south of the Pasig River. Many civilians were killed by Japanese troops but most were casualties from the US artillery pounding the buildings.

The story of the Battle of Manila has mostly been told with reference to US accounts suggesting that without the battle the civilian deaths would have been higher. That is a dubious claim but in most Philippine perceptions the Japanese were the main villains in the destruction of the 'Jewel of the Orient' an elegant city with its Tagalog, Spanish and American histories. What is not clear is whether MacArthur consulted Osmena (president following Quezon's death in 1944) or other Filipinos over tactics which could have saved Filipino lives. Likewise, nothing was heard from Laurel or Aquino who, like Yamashita, were in Baguio. After Manila was taken, US defeated Japanese forces in the Visayas and Mindanao paving the way for the Philippines to become a key to the planned invasion of Japan. Yamashita, however, held out in northern Luzon until the Japanese surrender in August 1945.

Post-war tales of Japanese atrocities and Filipino suffering during the occupation helped provide a focus for the nation in the early years of independence, which finally occurred on 4 July 1946. Yet not far under the surface of this massaged history was the reality that the elite recognized. There was little instinct for retribution against collaborators. Aquino was charged with treason but released on bail and died the following year. Laurel was likewise charged with treason but never tried. In 1948, as President, Manuel Roxas, whose own cooperation with the Japanese remained questionable, declared an amnesty. Only five years later, Laurel stood unsuccessfully for president as the Nacionalista Party candidate winning 37 per cent of the vote. The victor was Elpidio Quirino who, despite the deaths of many family members in the Battle of Manila, pardoned the Japanese convicted of war crimes. Vargas went from the puppet republic's ambassador in Tokyo in 1945 to head of the National Planning Commission in 1946.

Whatever mixture of class solidarity, family relationships, Catholic notions of forgiveness or common nationalism, the quick post-war healing was in sharp contrast to experiences in many other countries occupied during the 1937–45 wars. There were also cross currents. Lingering Spanish and Church sentiments were in favour of the Spanish dictator, General Franco, as a bastion against atheistic communism and hence highly critical of the anti-clericalism of leftist nationalists. Those with Chinese affiliation, on the other hand, were influenced against Japan by its invasion of China. Nationalists came in different colours with some interested in sustaining the status quo but without the Americans. Only those on the far left were consistent in being anti both Japanese and US imperialism and even they were sometimes divided between middle class Marxist revolutionaries and rice farmers fighting landlords.

Under the circumstances, Roxas and Quirino wiping the slate clean was good politics given the extent of collaboration among the elite. Meanwhile, the collaboration of the old nationalists such as Laurel, Aquino and Recto with Japan weakened the popular appeal of the anti-American sentiments of the older generation. The younger generation was now brought up on stories of the liberation by America and on tales of Filipino heroism in the fight against Japan.

The most vivid of the imaginary tales was to be provided by a young lawyer from Illocos Norte, Ferdinand Marcos. Marcos was from a moderately influential local family whose father, Mariano, had been a representative of the province but was defeated in 1935 by a rival who was then killed. Ferdinand was found guilty of the murder, but the conviction was eventually overturned by the Supreme Court Associate Justice Jose Laurel, in a decision smacking of political influence. Joining the army after the invasion, Marcos was captured at Bataan but soon released, rejoining the returning American forces in December 1944.

For the period between these dates, he was to create a largely fictional war record featuring his leadership of a guerrilla and intelligence band named Ang Mga Maharlika for which he claimed to have received many medals. In reality, Maharlika seems to have been a smuggling and trading outfit but Marcos' version of history for long was an integral part of his political persona and was widely accepted. The truth only came out later, including the likelihood that he repaid the debt to Laurel with help when Laurel was president under the Japanese. In short, there are many reasons other than their sufferings why Filipinos were eager to forget the years of Japanese occupation.

Notes

1 Quoted in Karnow, *In Our Image*, p. 296.
2 Quoted in David Joel Steinberg, *Philippine Collaboration in World War II*, Ann Arbor: University of Michigan Press, 1967, p. 50.

5

Old wine in new bottles

With the war ending and Osmena heading the government, independence could not be far behind, but Douglas MacArthur remained the main decision-maker. There was supposed to be the round-up and prosecution of collaborators but although some were charged in 1946, the effort soon stalled. Vengeance was more easily satiated by the prosecution for war crimes – during the Battle of Manila – of Yamashita. A military court verdict for punishment by execution was upheld by the US Supreme Court but two justices opposed, one, Justice Frank Murphy, writing of an 'uncurbed spirit of revenge masked in formal legal procedure'. MacArthur set the example in April 1945 by not only forgetting the role of his pre-war favourite, Roxas, who had worked with him as liaison officer before his capture by the Japanese. MacArthur even contrived a role for him in the liberation. A *mestizo* from Capiz, Panay was from a leading family related to the Zobels and Ayalas, Roxas was seen by him to have the image and military background to lead.

MacArthur blatantly ignored or frustrated Osmena, meanwhile the legislature, which had been elected in 1941 but had never met, was convened. It had numerous members who had cooperated with the Japanese and chose Roxas as the president of the Senate and chair of the appointments committee. US observers noted the bitterness of many who had actually fought the Japanese while leading collaborators developed 'a well organized propaganda campaign to persuade the world'[1] of their patriotic motives in doing so.

By the war's end, the economy was chaotic and food in short supply. However, its agricultural base could recover quickly given a modicum of order and transport facilities. One immediate loss, however, was the repatriation of the Japanese planters from Davao, but new settlers soon moved in. It was to be a decade before Japanese reparations were agreed but American money and equipment for more immediate reconstruction was to add to the US reputation as liberator in the immediate aftermath of the war and for collaborators to cover their tracks as best they could.

By the time MacArthur left to become Governor of Japan in August 1945 his unofficial support for the self-promoting Roxas was eclipsing the more plodding Osmena who declined to campaign in the 1946 election because his record was well-known. Thus, it was the collaborationist who won a majority – 54 per cent of votes – partly with smears about Osmena's age, Chinese origin and supposed 'Communist' inclinations for accepting Huk support. Roxas' running mate, Elpidio Quirino, a lawyer from Ilocos, also won and his new Liberal party gained House and Senate majorities. Total votes of 2.5 million were about 30 per cent of those eligible in a contest about personalities and local interests not policies.

One close collaborator, Teofilo Sison, who had been in Quezon's government had been tried and found guilty of treason offences. Soon after his inauguration, however, Roxas issued an amnesty proclamation claiming that collaborators had acted 'in the sincere belief that it was their patriotic duty . . . for the well being of their countrymen who were then at the mercy of the enemy'.[2] That may have been true in some cases but the wartime Laurel government appointed by Japan had certainly made life easier for the occupiers.

For many countries, wars bring about deep socio-political change, but very little changed in the Philippines because of the continuity between so many of the pre-war occupation and post-war individuals and their interests. Another American might have cleaned out the old and compromised politicians but MacArthur with his pre-war links to them had no interest in the kind of measures – land reform and curbing the *zaibatsu* (conglomerates) – he pursued in Japan. In the Philippines, there was a reversion to a pre-1942 world in three ways making it seem a poster child of so-called 'neo-colonialism'. Firstly, and in the long run most important, was that it entrenched existing, mostly *mestizo*, elites who were generally able to ensure that universal suffrage was a competition between families and personalities not policies or even parties, were needed as a bastion against the very same rural leftist movements that they had helped create by ignoring the injustices felt by the rural majority, particularly in Central Luzon. Symbolically, Philippine independence from the US formally occurred on 4 July, the same day as American independence in 1776.

The US and the elite, however much it espoused nationalism, needed each other. The electoral system was also costly so access to the spoils of office was indispensable. Seventy-five years on, many of the same names are found in the lists of senators, congressmen and presidents. Dynasties are even more common at provincial level. Nor was this just socio-economic. There was a racial element too, still reflected not just in politics but in the winners of Miss Philippines contests.

An even more immediate post-war issue was the economic tie to the US. Against strong opposition from the US State Department, a mix of special domestic interest groups, old-time imperialists and some businesses seeking a captive market pushed through the US Congress the 1946 Philippine Trade Act, designed to rig relations in US favour before independence. The Philippines would not get its promised and desperately needed reconstruction aid – a legislated promise of $1.24 billion– unless it accepted the provisions of the Trade Act which included the rights of Americans to own mines and natural resources, and continued US free trade access while Filipino coconut oil faced a quota and restriction on any new product that might come into 'substantial competition' with US producers.

Roxas reluctantly persuaded his majority in the legislature to accept this charter of dependence before independence because afterwards it would be deemed an international treaty needing two-thirds approval by Congress. He still needed to change the constitution after independence to give equal ownership rights to Americans. That was achieved by depriving many elected members, including Huk leader Luis Taruc, of their seats on concocted grounds, and holding a referendum to approve it in which only about 6 per cent of adults participated

The third issue was the US military bases. Not all the US top brass wanted to keep them: Eisenhower, then chief of staff, thought they would cause unnecessary friction. Guam or Okinawa were better bases, but as the Cold War loomed the military was reluctant to give up facilities which it already occupied. Roxas was not eager to see them depart either as he saw a need for help against the Huks. Thus, in 1947, he agreed to a ninety-nine-year presence at Subic Bay and Clark Air Base on conditions which gave the US jurisdiction over Filipinos at the bases while denying the Philippines judicial rights over US forces. There was also a Joint Military Assistance Agreement (JUSMAG) which provided for day-to-day collaboration.

In short, the economic and bases agreements described not only Roxas' American loyalties but the broader sense of the dependence of a battered nation on a US then at the zenith of its global power.

The Huk challenge grew more serious with its abandonment of the electoral system after the exclusion of Taruc and other left-leaning representatives. Having found their own strength against the Japanese and being further alienated from the mostly absentee landlord class by its record of collaboration, they were set on resistance. By 1949, they had at least 10,000 under arms and broad support among the rural people of Central Luzon. It was a tenant and rural worker uprising led by the Communist party's military commander, Taruc, but with an identity of its own. There was also a significant involvement of women – dubbed 'Amazons' in the local media – in operations, but not leadership. Recruits included young unmarried women who often had relationships with married cadres, the tension between ethics and biology creating problems for the leadership.[3]

Roxas died of a heart attack in 1948 and was succeeded by Vice-President Quirino who won the election in 1949. A moderate but ineffective president, Quirino pardoned Japanese war criminals even though his wife and three children had been killed in the Battle of Manila. The Huk threat increased just at the time when US fear of international communism was rising to fever pitch. Quezon's widow and a daughter were killed in a Huk ambush. Frustrated by what it saw as the corruption and incompetence of the Quirino administration, the US engineered the appointment of Ramon Magsaysay as Secretary of Defence. An elected representative from a non-elite family who had distinguished himself in US-directed guerrilla action against Japan, he was an inspired choice. Magsaysay in turn was advised by US intelligence officer, Edward Lansdale, a gregarious former advertising executive who had been in the Philippines since 1945. He had a genuine interest in the country, travelling widely, including through Huk-dominated territory – the lowland plains of Bulacan, Pampanga, Tarlac and Nueva Ecija which lie between the forested hills of Zambales to the west and the Sierra Madre to the northeast and with Mount Arayat in the middle.

Peasant discontent in Central Luzon had been brewing for decades with the breakdown of patron-client relationships between landlord and tenant. The wealth and power gap had long been wide but traditionally tenants had security of tenure, received benefits at feast days, weddings and funerals and interest-free loans when crops failed. However, that relationship broke down as landlords became profit-focused businessmen and peasants beholden to money-lenders. Many tenants were evicted, landlords moved to the towns leaving agents (*katiwala*) to collect rents. They grew rich on the sale of rice and sugar surpluses while peasants faced insecurity and debt, their crop shares barely providing enough food for their growing families. By 1948 in Pampanga, no fewer than 88 per cent of farms were tenanted, some tenants of larger farms paying cash (*inquilinos*) to landlords then sub-letting part of their land on a crop-share basis.

Once there had been plenty of undeveloped land but with the rapid expansion of the population land was increasingly scarce in Central Luzon and the sugar lands of the Visayas, leading to demands for a larger crop share for peasant families. There was also a steep rise in the number of landless labourers. In response, cooperation developed between peasants in barrios across the region. Their experience against the Japanese was brought into play once it became clear that the democratic area had little place for advocates of peasant grievances. However, it was not as politically radical as often presented by the government (and its US allies). The people wanted security for their families, humane treatment, a fair share of their labours, not necessarily ownership of land, which had its own problems.[4] They wanted the end of oppression of their cooperative efforts. These were not unreasonable demands as both Magsaysay and Lansdale recognized.

Magsaysay was dynamic, reorganizing and enlarging the army, improving discipline and reducing corruption. He exuded a man of the people image, meeting peasants and joining troops on operations. His close links to the US was not an issue for most Filipinos, Huk-leaning peasants included, who were still grateful to The US for helping rid them of the Japanese. He acknowledged peasant grievances and talked of land reform, increased crop shares and offers of free land in Mindanao. Copious US funds brought clinics, roads and services to poor villages. Lansdale was a behind campaigns to discredit the Huks, frighten their peasant supporters with psywar propaganda and use money and the media to highlight the positive. Those measures were at least as important as the military ones. Gradually, the tide turned against the rebellion which remained focused on Central Luzon despite Huk efforts to develop movements in Bicol, the Visayas and Mindanao.

By the time Magsaysay became president, the Huks were weakening, their forest camps threatened by Magsaysay's troops. They were short of arms and divided ideologically between urban mostly well-born idealist Communists, several of whom were arrested, including the party boss, Jose Lava, as well as Taruc and his men in the field.[5] Many peasants felt they had been heard and that conditions were being ameliorated. The rebellion faded, particularly after Taruc's surrender following negotiations with Magsaysay's envoy and a young well-connected journalist, Benigno Aquino Jr. The son of a leading collaborator he was to use the resulting fame to propel his own political ambitions.

Magsaysay was very much America's man in foreign policy, the Manila Conference of 1954 creating the South East Asia Treaty Organization – a US-led anti-Communist alliance. He also declined to join such giants of anti-colonialism as Nehru, Nasser and Sukarno at the Afro-Asian Bandung Conference in 1955, though he did agree to send foreign secretary Carlos Romulo. Magsaysay's clout in Washington enabled the nation to re-visit some of the provisions of the odious 1946 Trade Act. Jose Laurel represented the Philippines in negotiating what was known as the 1955 Laurel-Langley Agreement. This freed the Philippines to set its exchange rate against the US dollar and significantly improved trade access to the US through preferential tariffs and quotas. In particular, it benefitted sugar producers now able to sell in the US at a higher price than the world market. Parity rights for Americans were maintained but the Agreement was to expire in 1974. Also in 1955, the Philippines finally reached a reparations agreement with Japan, providing $550 million and a promise of another $250 million in private sector investment.

The flow of US money was the first key to a rapid recovery of the economy, even if it was mostly evident in Manila and a few other cities. Japanese reparations followed with private US investment arriving to take advantage of its privileges. The nation was seen as the most likely to prosper in the region because of its mix of education, access to the US and relatively stable political outlook. Indeed, from 1950, when its GDP per head was already higher than Japan, Taiwan, Korea and Thailand, it had the region's highest annual GDP growth rate of 6.5 per cent.

Magsaysay died in a plane crash in Cebu in March 1957 and was automatically succeeded by Vice-President Carlos Garcia. He had served as Foreign Secretary under Magsaysay and was identified as a pro-American anti-communist, chairing the 1954 Manila Conference which saw the creation of the South East Asia Treaty Organization. One of his first acts in office was to sign a law making the Communist Party illegal, but in other respects he was a staunch nationalist who resented foreign commercial domination, a reference to the local Chinese as well as to the US interests. Garcia was elected President in late 1957 as a Nacionalista with 41 per cent in an election with several prominent candidates, but his running mate, Jose Laurel, the son of the president appointed by Japan, lost the vice-presidency to Diosdado Macapagal of the main opposition Liberal party. The Nacionalistas controlled Congress, with a representative from Ilocos, Ferdinand Marcos, as the minority leader.

The argument between the two main parties increasingly focused on economic policy. Garcia adopted a Filipino First agenda intended to develop local production by curtailing imports and rationing access to foreign exchange, aiming to divert dollars from consumption to investment by Filipinos. He aimed to combine private and public capital to supplant US and Chinese capital. Projects included a partnership between the government-owned National Shipyard and Steel Corporation and the private Jacinto family who owned a rolling mill in Iligan with interests to develop an integrated steel industry there. Some US-owned assets were bought by Filipinos, notably the Manila Electric Company (MERALCO) by Eugenio Lopez of one of the richest *hacendero* families of Iloilo and brother of Fernando Lopez, vice-president under Quirino and later also under Marcos.

The creation of an indigenous capitalist class was a natural goal and one pursued elsewhere in Asia. However, it rested on three pillars: one was the landowning elite who used their resources, wealth and political clout to expand their economic role but were not natural entrepreneurs; the second was the Chinese who, evading laws to deter them, managed the shift from middle-man role to into newer manufacturing industries; the third was the state, supposedly in command but without institutional roots, short of funds and at the beck and call of politicians and rent seekers. The policies did have the effect of bringing more local investment into protected manufacturing. The anti-Chinese Retail Nationalization Act in the longer run helped the Chinese by forcing them out of retailing into manufacturing, whose percentage of GDP rose from 10.7 per cent in 1948 to 17 per cent in 1960.[6]

With industry protected behind high tariff walls, businesses old and new prospered. New business groups emerged on the back of access to state funds, including the Development Bank of the Philippines (formerly the Rehabilitation Finance Corporation) and Philippine National Bank. With foreign banks barred from opening new branches, private sector banks became especially profitable. Politically influenced access to foreign exchange was an open invitation to corruption as allocations could be sold on the black market and help fund political campaigns, and luxury imports. Kickbacks gave them access to government deposits and businesses with access expanded on the back of easier credit, though a strong Central Bank was a restraint on overall credit growth. Tight foreign exchange controls were opposed by the exporters, notably the sugar barons who wanted to retain their earnings. The corruption and exchange control issue became a cause of Garcia's downfall in the 1961 election, losing 45–55 per cent to Diosdado Macapagal.

Not long afterwards, exchange controls were loosened and the peso devalued, falling from 2.0 to the dollar to 3.9. Devaluation led to a boom in some exports, notably copper and timber, while tariff increases helped the manufacturer, but the more fundamental social and economic issues remained. Fewer controls meant less graft and Macapagal himself was seen as relatively clean, but scandals inevitably erupted which went close to other members of his government.

Macapagal made yet another attempt to use legislation to improve the lot of tenant farmers. Previous laws to regulate landlord/tenant relations and improve security of tenure had had too many holes or been evaded by landlords and by the provincial authorities they dominated. The 1963 Agricultural Land Reform Code, among other improvements, abolished share-cropping in favour of fixed rents and gave tenants pre-emptive rights, but again the original bill was much watered down by exemptions and exceptions.

The 1960s spawned what came to be described by the writer Paul Hutchcroft as 'booty capitalism'. One indirect result of the end of the peg to the dollar was the proliferation of family-owned banks linked to existing businesses. The Central Bank had always helped local bank development but under governor Andres Castillo (1961–7) it liberalized licences, further helped finance their balance sheets and assured wide loan margins. By 1965, private bank assets were 56 per cent of the total against only 36 per cent in 1955. Banks were family affairs and also had to contend with family quarrels.

Macapagal tried to appeal to nationalist sentiment with a claim to North Borneo (Sabah) on the basis that it had previously been part of the Sulu sultanate. He also proposed attempting to realize Rizal's dream of a confederation of all Malay peoples, Maphilindo – Malaysia, Philippines and Indonesia, – but confrontation between Malaysia and Indonesia over the Borneo states, and Macapagal's claim on Sabah assured that this grand idea went nowhere. There was also a revival of anti-US sentiment and a narrative critical of the supremacy of the English language. One minor result was the shift of national day from 4 July to 12 June, the day of Aguinaldo's 1898 proclamation of independence from Spain, but the language issue failed to gain traction.

In spite of nationalist and leftist sentiments among media and populace, mainstream politics remained dominated by personality contests between rival but always shifting elite groups. Macapagal succumbed to the smartest and most devious of them all. Ferdinand Marcos had been a representative from Ilocos Norte since 1949, trading on a war record which subsequently proved largely fictional. Standing as a Liberal he topped the 1955 Senate election, becoming minority leader until the Liberals won a majority in 1963 when he became Senate President. In 1954, despite having children by

Carmen Ortega, a beauty queen from an influential Ilocos family, Marcos married Imelda Romualdez. An unsophisticated beauty from a relatively impoverished side of the leading Leyte clan, Imelda was initially just a dutiful consort, but after treatment in New York for a nervous breakdown she emerged as a self-confident figure. By the time of the 1965 campaign, she had blossomed into a popular adornment to campaign rallies, captivating the public with her singing as well as her striking looks in a *terno* (a long, shapely uniquely Philippine dress with butterfly-wing sleeves). The family name also helped bring some votes from the Visayas, traditionally Osmena family territory.

Marcos' trading skills learned during the war were in evidence as a representative and then senator. He proved a master at milking the system, in particular by controlling tobacco imports and influencing foreign exchange access. He also had useful Chinese business connections originating in links to the Chua family, the most influential Chinese family in Ilocos Norte who came from his own home town, Batac.

In 1965, Marcos switched parties to the Nacionalistas and won their nomination contest against then Vice-President Emmanuel Pelaez and former Vice-President Fernando Lopez. With the immensely rich Lopez clan desperate to get rid of Macapagal, Lopez swallowed his pride and, succumbing to the charms of Marcos' wife Imelda, agreed to again run for vice-president. Marcos beat Macapagal with 55 per cent of the vote and Lopez narrowly beat his opponent, Gerardo Roxas, son of former president Manuel Roxas.

Gerardo was the husband of Judy Araneta from another Spanish-Mestizo Negros sugar family whose grandfather, Gregorio Araneta, had helped draft the Malolos Constitution but became one of the first Filipinos to join the US regime. One relative was close to President Quezon, another in Magsaysay's government and another owned sugar mills and other business in Negros. J. Amado Araneta built Araneta City, a vast commercial hub in Manila and location of the Araneta Coliseum which, when completed in 1960, was the largest such covered stadium in the world. Another relative, Gregorio Araneta III married President Marcos' daughter Irene in 1981. In 1957, Salvador Z. Araneta was a founder, with Jose Concepcion, of RFM Corporation, a major listed food and beverage company now run by Jose Concepcion III. A third founder was Albino Z. SyCip of Fujian. One of this Chinese financier's sons included Washington SyCip who founded the accounting firm SGV, which was particularly prominent during the Marcos years and remains the largest such firm in the country. The Aranetas also had Negros family links to Jose Arroyo, husband of President Arroyo. These details matter in the world of Philippine political and business family links and feuds.

Marcos was already a known quantity for cunning and resolve. The Americans were a little wary but saw him as a tough and eloquent leader and he had support from some of the team who had worked with Lansdale.

His inaugural address drew attention to government and national woes: venality, disorder, slothful civil service, lack of resources, etc. His rise had, of course, been an illustration of some of those ills, marked by violence, bribery and ballot stuffing, but as a shrewd operator he recognized that America's war in Vietnam provided leverage with Washington. Making offers of help in the form of engineering battalions, he extracted large sums from President Lyndon Johnson desperate to have Asian allies.

In reality, the Philippine contribution in Vietnam was minimal, but in addition to direct support – which the US called aid but Marcos described as rent for the bases – the Philippines, and notably the cities of Central Luzon near the Clark and Subic bases, prospered from the Vietnam War military surge. Up until 1973, hundreds of thousands of cash-rich servicemen were to enjoy rest and recreation (R&R) in the bars and massage parlours of Manila, Angeles City (near the Clark Air Base) and Olongapo (adjoining Subic Bay).

The country was also given a boost being chosen as headquarters of the newly established Asian Development Bank which opened for business on Manila's bayfront Roxas Boulevard in 1966. These benefits, however, could not disguise the fact that by then the nation was falling behind its southeast Asian peers, Thailand and Malaysia, as well as Korea and Taiwan. For the 1960s as a whole, GDP growth averaged just 5.1 per cent. Unlike its neighbours, agricultural productivity improved only slowly and manufacturing failed to provide enough jobs for the expanding workforce.

One indirect but long-lasting boost to the economy came in 1975 when Marcos made it easy for Chinese immigrants and their offspring to become citizens. He did this partly in response to the thawing of US-China ties and to steer the allegiance of tens of thousands of Chinese away from Taiwan or Beijing to the Philippines. These new citizens thus gained access to the large parts of the economy from which they had been excluded.

The late 1960s were also a period of growing radicalism and anti-Americanism in many parts of the world, resulting in part from the Vietnam War. It barely touched the mainstream parties in the Philippines but from it emerged Jose Maria (Jo Ma) Sison, born in 1939 and the son of a collaborationist *mestizo* landowner and former governor of Pangasinan. A university lecturer in literature, in 1964 he formed the Patriotic Youth group adopting Maoist principles. Rejecting the Moscow alignment of the Lava-led Communist Party he eventually formed a new Communist Party of the Philippines (CPP) which soon eclipsed the older one. Sison linked up with a remnant Huk faction led by a young peasant activist from Tarlac, Bernabe Buscayno, alias Komander Dante, to form the New People's Army (NPA). (Sison, who has lived in exile in the Netherlands since 1986 married Julieta de Lima, a relative of Senator Leila de Lima, later jailed by President Duterte. The de Limas are a leading family of Iriga City in Bicol.)

The 1969 election saw spending on a monumental scale which, combined with 'guns and goons' of his allies among the provincial warlords with their private armies, helped assure that Marcos become the first president to be re-elected. But the cost was a currency crisis, sharp devaluation of the peso and a surge of inflation which ignited popular discontent both in Manila and among the tenant farmers of Central Luzon. The year 1969 proved a prelude to what became dubbed 'The Conjugal Dictatorship.[7]

Notes

1 Quoted in Karnow, *In Our Image*, p. 328.

2 Quoted in Steinberg, *Philippine Collaboration in World War II*.

3 Vina A. Lanzona, *Amazons of the Huk Rebellion*, Madison, WI: University of Wisconsin Press, 2009

4 Benedict J. Kerkvliet, *The Huk Rebellion: A Study of Peasant Revolt in the Philippines*, New York: Roman and Littlefield, 2002. This outstanding work is the most comprehensive and non-ideological account.

5 There were five leftist Lava brothers, all highly educated. Three, Jose, Jesus and Vicente, were at different times General Secretary of the Communist Party

6 Paul D. Hutchcroft, *Booty Capitalism: The Politics of Banking in the Philippines*, Ithaca: Cornell University Press, 1998, p. 74.

7 Title of a book on the Marcos pair published in 1976 by Primitivo Mijares, former Marcos spokesperson who defected in 1975. Mijares disappeared not long afterwards and his son was murdered. The book is widely regarded as self-serving and inaccurate but Mijares' fate was clearly a warning to others.

6

Marcos: power corrupts absolutely

Presidential term limits are fine on paper but unless a constitution and supporting institutions are deeply ingrained, they may count for little when challenged by a decisive president. So it was with Ferdinand Marcos who, for nearly fourteen years, succeeded in turning the obvious problems that the nation faced in 1972 into an opportunity to hi-jack the constitution, using martial law powers to impose personal rule and change the constitution.

Excuses for declaring a state of emergency in 1972 were not lacking. Political violence had become commonplace thanks to the availability of weapons and the arming of security guards by politicians. Marcos was too deeply involved in such politics, and dependent on colleagues' votes in Congress, to address the issue. Labour and peasant unrest combined with a resurgence of anti-Americanism due to the Vietnam War, to foster the growth of JoMa Sison's Maoist-oriented Communist Party and the New People's Army (NPA). Early 1970 saw what was called the 'First Quarter Storm', a series of violent clashes in Manila in which several students were killed.

In contrast to so much bitter public strife, Imelda Marcos pursued her yearning not just to be level with the cream of Manila society but to be recognized internationally as a patron of the arts. The first grand and costly project was the Cultural Center of the Philippines, a striking building on the edge of Manila Bay, designed by local architect Leandro Locsin and completed in 1969. The opening was attended by Ronald Reagan, then governor of California. Imelda's ambition was to leave indelible marks and to be part of the international celebrity set along with movie stars, conductors and heiresses. Imelda's 'edifice complex' continued to generate costly projects throughout her 'reign'.

The combined ambitions of the husband and wife were clear enough but the Lopez and Laurel clans deserted Marcos, their defections causing Marcos to lose his Senate majority.[1] Opposition leader, Ninoy Aquino, sensed victory in the 1973 elections, even though Imelda ran in Marcos' place as he could not run for a third term. However, even as early as May 1971, a US State Department internal document noted: 'He has already decided to try to

FIGURE 6.1 *President Ferdinand Marcos and Imelda Marcos, thirtieth wedding anniversary, 1984.* © *Getty Images.*

extend himself in office by one means or another after his present term expires'.

In Manila, violence escalated. August 1971 saw grenades thrown into a Liberal Party rally in Plaza Miranda seriously injuring many, including Jovito Salonga who had topped the Senate poll in 1965 and would do so again in November when most Marcos-aligned candidates lost. The Liberals blamed Marcos who blamed the Communists. Many years later it became clear that it was the NPA was to blame but suspicions were that Marcos was planning martial law and looking for excuses. A staged attack on a convoy accompanying Defence Secretary Juan Ponce Enrile was to prove that. Nature also provided a pretext with floods in August 1972 devastating Central Luzon and driving up grain prices.

One route to staying in office had appeared to have been through amendments to the 1935 Constitution via a Constitutional Convention. Congress had voted for such a convention and delegates – 320 – were elected in November 1970, but by the time the Convention sat in 1971 the tide of sentiment had turned against Marcos, and it passed a resolution against allowing a third term. Other options were slow and complicated. It was easier, he determined, to short-cut the system, confident that the military, via Enrile, would not challenge the president, and nor would Washington, where President Nixon was embroiled in his own re-election campaign and Paris peace talks on Vietnam were at a crucial stage.

Marcos struck on 23 September, declaring a state of emergency to deal with an alleged plot. Aquino and his deputy, Diokno, were first to be seized, followed by several hundred and eventually several thousand others. Politicians' private militias were disarmed, half a million weapons were seized, Congress was suspended, almost all media outlets were closed and a curfew was imposed.

Instead of denouncing it as an assault on democracy, Americans mostly supported it as a necessary step to make government more effective. There was bi-partisan support in the US Congress and the American Chamber of Commerce in Manila with Marcos seen as restoring order and business confidence. Locally, for many, martial law initially brought a sense of relief from strife. Elected by the people though it may have been, for now few mourned the Congress though there was also much unease about the arrests of legislators and the closure of media.

Marcos kept the support of the technocrats who had given his government an impression of professional competence. Names included Cesar Virata as Finance Secretary, Arturo Tanco as Agriculture Secretary, the venerable Carlos P. Romulo continuing as Foreign Secretary as he had been under Magsaysay, and Alejandro Melchor as Executive Secretary. These officials believed that although some corruption was inevitable, the pre-existing political system had been monumentally corrupt while incapable of bringing development. Marcos offered a chance for themselves and the country to move forward. However, their technical skills were not matched by wider political influence, so they were dependent on Marcos.

Initially, there was widespread acceptance of the coup as peace and quiet seemed to reign. The World Bank's interest in lending perked up, US military aid increased and Marcos moved to restore retail trading rights for Americans which had earlier been removed by a Marcos-friendly Supreme Court. He well understood that a reliable ally was more important for Washington than the democratic institutions which the Americans had bequeathed to the Philippines. Furthermore, many of those opposed to Marcos were nationalists or leftists who, at least rhetorically, raged against US imperialism.

Business interests generally were enthused, despite Marcos' rhetoric against 'oligarchs' and in particular his seizure of Lopez interests – Meralco, media assets and Negros sugar estates. He promised serious efforts at land reform and the creation of a new Department of Agrarian Reform, but only for tenanted rice and corn land of more than seven hectares.

As a lawyer, he set his seizure of power in constitutional forms. The 1970 Constitutional Convention, minus the jailed oppositionists, reassembled and passed a new constitution providing for a single chamber national assembly which would elect a president and prime minister. He, meanwhile, would remain as president able to rule by decree as a result of a decision by a packed Supreme Court. A new party, the Kilusan Bagong Lipunan (New Society Movement: KBL), was created to promote the so-called New Society.

Despite a rice supply crisis in 1973 which saw Imelda at Makati's Intercontinental Hotel encouraging her countrymen to eat a rice and corn mix, a year after the declaration of martial law, optimism in business and foreign circles was high. The *Far Eastern Economic Review* ran a long article entitled 'Asia's Next Miracle?'[2] sensing euphoria in some quarters. It noted foreign enthusiasm for the new opportunities offered by the Board of Investments, and the benefits of improved law and order. Foreign exchange reserves doubled within a year. The Board of Investments, under technocrat Vicente Paterno, reported being swamped with enquiries while technocrat Gerardo Sicat, head of the National Economic Development Authority, claimed 'a 10 per cent rate of growth for our country is not a matter of impossibility'.

However, the article noted that Marcos had had a huge stroke of luck with strong export commodity prices increasing incomes and drastically improving an always precarious trade balance. This would probably not last. The top export was logs, which were a rapidly diminishing asset, followed by sugar which was protected by a US preference which was soon to expire, followed by coconut products and copper, both highly cyclical.

Looking ahead, the article noted that agricultural productivity was weak, timber exports were destroying irreplaceable forests, over-protected manufacturing limited the progress of export manufacturing, the Philippines having largely missed the first big wave of Japanese export of textile and electronics manufacturing. The high-rise Makati business district looked sophisticated enough with an active inter-bank market and the arrival of foreign brokers, mostly interested in mining stocks, but the nation generally was poorly served by banks still regarded with suspicion due to previous failures.

Marcos' good fortune appeared to end in late 1973 when the quadrupling of oil prices drove the world into recession. However, the Philippines was still well supported by other commodity prices. By then, too, the still positive aspects of martial law, as seen from the perspective of foreign business, plus US support plus the technocrats saw the Philippines easily able to borrow the dollars being recycled from the now giant surpluses of the oil exporters. Foreign bankers flocked to Manila to set up offshore banking units. These provided an avenue for lending dollars to the country but protected local banks from foreign competition for peso business.

The foreign banks – including the World Bank and the Asian Development Bank – turned a blind eye to the percentages required to be deposited in the offshore accounts of Marcos and friends or milked from contracts.

Alongside this old way of doing business with Philippine politicians, Marcos used his decree-making powers to attempt to enlarge the economic and administrative power of the executive and the Manila ministries. This suited the technocrats who could set budgets and development policies without bothering about local political interests.

Agricultural production continued to rise under technocrat Agriculture Secretary Tanco thanks to investment in irrigation, the provision of rural credit as well as the continuing Green Revolution's new seeds plus fertilizer and insecticides. A campaign known as Masagana 99 aimed at raising average rice yields from 40 to 99 cavans[3] per hectare. The programme was later criticized for driving farmers into debt, causing the collapse of rural banks, and encouraging the over-use of environmentally damaging methods. However, it was nevertheless seen as a success in raising output.

Agrarian reform did make some progress in turning tenants into owners, but reform was insufficient to stem the gradual growth of NPA activity in Central Luzon, Bicol and parts of Mindanao. However, it also saw a rise in landless peasants working as wage earners, and the conversion of rice land into sugar and other crops excluded from reform.

Government control of the grain and sugar trade through the National Grains Authority was supposed to help supply and price stability. In reality, it acted as a barrier to the increased productivity required to meet local demand at a time of a general decline in global agricultural prices. US preference for sugar gradually diminished. Meanwhile, rice was protected at above international prices which hurt consumers, while the producers were hurt by tariffs on imported fertilizer and machinery, and by inefficient distribution systems.

There were ambitious plans to develop heavy industries, including the National Steel Corporation which took over Iligan Steel in 1974 and later acquired the Elizalde group cold-rolling and tin-plating assets. This was the forerunner of several attempts to use government money to force-feed industrialization because the local private sector lacked the capital and know-how. The plans peaked with the announcement of eleven major industrial projects including petrochemicals, diesel engines and smelters for copper, aluminium and nickel. Most never got off the ground but technocrat Industry Minister, Roberto Ongpin, went on to become one of the nation's richest men.

Foreign interest in the Philippines was expressed in the entry of some export manufacturing investment, and the first attempts to move from auto assembly to eventually making the most of the components locally. Commodity exports continued to grow too, at least in volume. The change in foreign attitudes was reflected in the choice of Manila to host the 1986 meetings of the World Bank and International Monetary Fund. A week of banker dealing and partying impressed the delegates who were housed in newly completed five-star hotels and attended meeting at the vast and elegant Philippine International Convention Center (PICC). It helped ensure that money could continue to flow in despite rumblings of political dissent and problems evident to those who looked beyond the glitz. The economy was growing at 6 per cent but exports had peaked in 1974 and investment in export manufacturing investments had been disappointing. It was a 'country with a debt problem that is major but not unmanageable'.[4]

The World Bank/IMF event was also a sign of much of what was wrong. The luxury hotels and the PICC had cost several hundred million dollars but had no chance of being economically viable in a city with relatively few tourists or conventions. Much of the rise in investment spending in the 1970s likewise went on grandiose projects with scant return. Another example was the two-kilometre San Juanico Bridge linking Tacloban (Imelda's home town) in Leyte to Samar. It was built with Japanese development assistance but seen as a birthday present to Imelda.

Even positive moves such as the creation of Metro-Manila to bring greater order to the various cities and municipalities comprising the national capital had drawbacks. Imelda Marcos became its first governor, resulting in diversion of funds into more grandiose buildings as well as drainage and public transport projects.

Also missed by most delegates to the World Bank/IMF meeting was an ominous sign of the sleazy side of the regime. Only a month before the meeting, Marcos himself had played a role in a driving up the price of a minor speculative oil stock, Seafront Petroleum, presenting a tiny gas find as a major discovery.[5] The beneficiary was Herminio Disini, a relative of Imelda's whose business interests were being promoted by Marcos as he sought not so much to replace old oligarchs but add new ones – his cronies – who provided him with cash. Disini's Herdis group had acquired a cigarette filter monopoly, forest concessions, enterprises acquired through 'behest' (of the president) loans from state banks and kickbacks as agent for Westinghouse in a deal to build a nuclear power station in Bataan.

In contrast to South Korea, where President Park Chung-hee offered official backing to a few who had shown drive in establishing new export industries, Marcos focused on handing out monopolies and easy profits to those who would kick them back to him. Thus, Lucio Tan, once a small cigarette manufacturer in Ilocos, was enabled to establish the dominance of his Fortune Tobacco by manipulation of the tax code. Tan then reinvested those profits which did not go to Marcos, into banking and brewing. Ilocano contemporary and golfing partner, Rudolfo Cuenca, chairman of the Construction and Development Corporation of the Philippines (CDCP), made a fortune from inflated government contracts. (Cuenca later wrote a candid account of those years.) Law school friend, Roberto Benedicto, received a sugar export monopoly and chairmanship of the Philippine National Bank. Imelda's brother, Benjamin 'Kokoy' Romualdez, acquired stakes in a wide variety of companies, as well as ambassadorial positions. Most stunning was the Coconut Levy, a tax on coconut production, mostly by smallholders. The levy was paid into the United Coconut Planters Bank which was supposed to be used to help develop the industry but in practice it was used to expand the business interests of Marcos' long-term political ally from Tarlac, Eduardo 'Danding' Cojuangco.

Some genuine entrepreneurs also helped, such as Ricardo Silverio's Delta Motors, the best local effort at car manufacturing until it went bust in 1984. Against that example of entrepreneurship, however, was a long list of relatives and front-men who made many millions each: various Marcos and Romualdez family members, banana baron Antonio Floirendo, energy minister Geronimo Velasco, luxury goods importer Bienvenido Tantoco, government pharmaceuticals supplier Jose Yao Campos and mining rights acquirer Manuel Elizalde. Various cronies had bank interests whose profligate lending was enabled by Central Bank discounting facilities or given logging concessions.

Politically, most of the country was quiet for the first years of martial law. Local politicians were left alone but there was no national stage on which they could play. Central power was increased by the amalgamation of the Philippine Constabulary and local police forces into the Philippine National Police. A few young idealists fled to the hills and the NPA after the imposition of martial law and the urban intelligentsia muttered dissent but there was no sign of any general opposition movement gaining a hold. Aquino remained in jail and in 1977 was sentenced to death by a military tribunal, but US pressure ensured that this would not be carried out and after the US secured a new bases agreement in 1979, he was allowed to leave the country for medical attention.

An interim National Assembly (Batasang Pambansa) was finally established in 1978 but consisted largely of KBL members, though a Visayan opposition group headed by Hilario Davide, later chief justice, remarkably beat a KBL candidate backed by the Osmenas and other big local families. In Manila, evidence at local polling stations[6] suggested there were far more votes for opposition candidates than were officially reported.

The military, meanwhile, was ever more focused on internal strife, initially mostly in Muslim Mindanao/Sulu. Demand for a separate Moro state had existed before martial law partly, driven by conflict between Muslims and Christian settlers from the Visayas. Tensions were magnified in 1968 when Tausugs from Sulu, recruited into the army as part of a secret plan, code named Jabidah, were massacred by the military at a camp in Corregidor. With martial law came an attempt to disarm Muslims and the militias of the local datus. The Sulu-based, Tausug-led Moro National Liberation Front (MNLF) under Nur Misuari found allies among the Maranao, and Maguindanao of mainland Mindanao took to armed rebellion. They received some informal support from Malaysian Sabah, partly in sympathy with fellow-Muslims and partly in response to Marcos' continued claim on Sabah. Newly oil-rich Arab states also took an interest. By 1975, rebels dominated the countryside and cities such as Marawi, and Cotabato could only be accessed by army-protected convoys.

Eventually the military gained the upper hand and a semblance of peace was established using Libya as an intermediary with Muslims promised autonomy in the so-called Tripoli Agreement. However, the Moros split in 1977, some, led by the Moro Islamic Liberation Front (MILF) of Hashim Salamat continued the fight and then the MNLF did so too. The MILF was Maguindanao-based and less secular than the MNLF in outlook. Intermittent lower scale actions became the norm.

The Moro issues were geographically contained and far from Manila. The NPA was another matter. Its original base area was close to Manila but it also realized the need for de-centralizing its activities if it were to prosper in the martial law era when it could no longer do deals with local politicians and was vulnerable to concerted military action. Although Sison and Buscayno were caught and jailed, the NPA gradually gathered recruits and arms mostly captured from the military. In addition to Central Luzon, it was active in the Cordillera, Bicol, Samar, Negros and central and southern Mindanao. By the early 1980s, it was estimated that about 15 per cent of the population lived in areas controlled or heavily influenced by the NPA and where businesses routinely paid taxes to it for protection.

The Catholic Church hierarchy, fearful of secular nationalism and socialism had originally been quietly supportive of Marcos, but with the appointment of Jaime Sin as archbishop (later Cardinal) of Manila in 1974, a more critical attitude prevailed. At the same time, priests in some areas, being aware of the suffering of the poor, became sympathetic towards the NPA.

However, the fundamental cause of the eventual collapse of the regime was economic failure driven by debts, domestic and foreign, incurred in supporting the Marcos family, the crony companies, and Imelda's ongoing passion for show and monuments. The technocrats like the foreign bankers for long continued to believe that, for all its faults, it was no more corrupt but more efficient than the Old Society. They would oppose wrong-headed policies but apart from Alex Melchor, never went so far in criticism as to be removed. After the 1976 World Bank meeting extravaganza, GDP growth slowed to a modest 5 per cent in a country with 2 per cent annual population increase. The years 1979 to 1980 saw another global oil crisis with the price per barrel doubling within a year. This hit at least as hard for the Philippines as the 1973/74 crisis because other commodity prices did not follow and the country was already too deeply in debt to offset its negative impact.

A bigger problem was the local banking industry's excessive loans to cronies. In 1981, the mid-sized group of Chinese financier Dewey Dee, which thrived on the crony fringe, collapsed leaving huge debts, including to the Herdis group. As the house of cards then gradually collapsed, Herdis, then Cuenca's CDCP and Silverio's Delta Group had to be taken over by the government. The technocrats were seen to have gained ground against the cronies and some banks were closed, but crony debt, much in dollars borrowed from the Development Bank, was in effect nationalized.

Even this weight on an already struggling economy might have been bearable but for the shock of August 1983. Deciding to return to the Philippines, Aquino was shot dead on the tarmac at Manila Airport. A crudely executed assassination by members of the armed forces was almost certainly planned by General Ver, army chief of staff and ultimate Marcos loyalist, though whether on his own initiative or that of Marcos, then undergoing kidney dialysis treatment, or Imelda is unclear.

The killing dramatically changed attitudes to the regime, particularly in Washington. Locally, there had been sporadic small bombing incidents by the Light a Fire movement linked to exiles in the US, but the banality of the murder

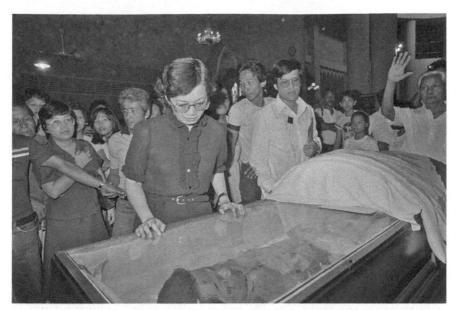

FIGURE 6.2 *Corazon Aquino views her assassinated husband Benigno 'Ninoy' Aquino, August 1983. © Getty Images.*

by bullet, so reminiscent of Old Society politics, and the crudity of a cover-up attempt, shocked even those who had no time for Aquino. Before it, Marcos still had the majority of the population behind him. That changed dramatically.

Eventually, Marcos was pressured into appointing an independent inquiry. A majority report said there had been a military conspiracy including Ver, but all were cleared by a court of Marcos appointees. All this time, money left the country, the economy contracted by 7 per cent in 1984 and 1985, the NPA grew and the Catholic Church became openly critical and hostile, particularly via its Radio Veritas. Deprived dynasts vented anger at the new dynasts. The formerly quiescent Manila middle class began to be aroused, with office workers and civil servants now willing to join protests.

Shamed by the assassination and upset by the lack of professionalism shown by Marcos-loyalists generals, some young military officers had formed a Reform the Armed Forces Movement (RAM). They kept in informal touch with Ramos and the ever-opportunistic Enrile, who worried that should Marcos, who by now had had two kidney transplants, die, Imelda and Ver would try to seize power.

Sick though he was, Marcos was in no mood to resign despite rising distaste for him in Washington spurred by the continued rise in NPA activity and the diversion of military aid into crony pockets. In a defiant gesture of response to US pressure, he called a snap presidential election against an opposition now headed by Aquino's widow, Corazon (Cory), a dutiful wife with zero political experience. He was confident of his ability to fix the result through the official vote-counter, the Commission on Elections (COMELEC). However, it was now faced with an alternative National Commission on Free Elections (NAMFREL) assembled by opposition, middle class and Church groups.

COMELEC declared Marcos the winner, NAMFREL declared Aquino. The RAM then attempted a coup in which Enrile and Ramos joined. Opposition and Church called on people to mass on EDSA (Epifanio de los Santos) Avenue to shield the mutineers at Camp Aguinaldo, the military headquarters and Camp Crame, headquarters of Ramos' Philippine Constabulary. Two days of standoff and growing military defections saw Marcos unwilling to use full force, as urged by Ver, and eventually accepted US advice to leave quickly, a US helicopter taking him from Malacanang Palace to Clark Air Base and then to Hawaii. The era was over.

Marcos' failure is best defined not by his democratic or elite critics but by comparison with his autocratic peers. In Indonesia, President Suharto gave a centralized administration to an even more far-flung archipelago and lifted its economy from the low to the lower-middle income ranks. The ruthless modernizing drive of President Park Chung-hee set South Korea well on the way to world top ranks. The Philippines, meanwhile, declined relative to almost all its neighbours. Both Suharto and Park transformed their societies so that politics afterwards was very different and more democratic. Philippine politics reverted to pre-1972 conditions, the same players, issues and problems of peace and order.

FIGURE 6.3 *Monument to 1986 EDSA uprising, Epifanio de los Santos Avenue, Manila.* © *Getty Images.*

The GDP growth for the ten years from the 1976 World Bank meeting tells the story of failure, mostly attributable to the regime than to external events. Indeed, this decade was a period of rapid growth for most of the Philippines' southeast Asian neighbours, and of world trade. From 8.8 per cent in 1976, partly boosted by the meeting, it fell to minus 7 per cent in both 1984 and 1985.

1973	8.9
1974	3.5
1975	5.6
1976	8.8
1977	5.6
1978	5.2
1979	5.6
1980	5.1
1981	3.4
1982	3.6
1983	1.8
1984	7.3
1985	7.2

Taking twenty Marcos years together – 1965–84 – per capita income in the Philippines rose at an annual rate of just 2.6 per cent compared with 4.9 per cent in Indonesia, 4.5 per cent in Malaysia and 4.2 per cent in Thailand.[7]

Notes

1 Quoted in Sandra Burton, *Impossible Dream: The Marcoses, The Aquinos and the Unfinished Revolution*, New York: Warner Books, 1989, p. 81.

2 Philip Bowring in *Far Eastern Economic Review*, 2 September 1973.

3 One cavan is approximately 100 litres or 45 kilograms of paddy (unhusked rice).

4 Philip Bowring in *Far Eastern Economic Review*, 8 October 1976.

5 Andrew Davenport and Lindsay Vincent in *Far Eastern Economic Review*, 1 October 1976.

6 The author was in Manila and visited several polling stations.

7 *World Development Report* 1986, World Bank/Oxford University Press.

7

Ladders and snakes

There was euphoria at the end of the Marcos regime. At home and abroad his overthrow was hailed as a People Power Revolution – despite its foundation stone, a military mutiny. Filipinos could regain lost freedoms and illegally acquired assets could return to the nation or their pre-martial law owners. There could be a new start, with a constitution, a congress and independent judges, plus retribution against those who had stolen.

However, a new start was easier said than done as the new politics began with the return of the old, pre-martial names such as Jovito Salonga, Salvador Laurel, the Aquino clan and many more. In the frame were two key martial law figures, Enrile and Ramos, and, in the background, the RAM officers. Diverse elements who had come together on EDSA wanted their say in the future – the Church, the Manila middle class, the Makati business elite, the non-Communist leftists and the nationalist, anti-American intelligentsia. There were the links, obligations and rivalries of province, family, law school as well as past Nacionalista and Liberal Party divides.

President Corazon Aquino enjoyed immense personal respect. She was sincerely dedicated to reform, honesty and liberal causes and had some instinct for politics but not for matters of administration or keeping her ministers focused and honest. She was not a commanding figure but one who tried to navigate between competing interests. Meanwhile, Marcos loyalists and beneficiaries, with plenty of money behind them, impeded the task of recovering ill-gotten gains.

Aquino delivered on promises of freedom of speech and set up a commission to draft a new constitution. Narrowly defeating a proposal for a parliamentary system, the new constitution, approved by plebiscite in early 1987, was strikingly similar to that of 1935, with two houses and the separate election of the president and vice-president for a single six-year term. It left the president with much executive authority and control of 'discretionary', otherwise known as pork-barrel, funds. The Supreme Court had powers to examine the constitutionality of laws. The House of Representatives was to include 20 per cent elected by functional groups, not districts. Known as the Party List, this was intended to give broader representation to farmer, worker and professional interest groups. There was a formal but imprecise commitment to agrarian reform, significant restrictions on foreign investment and rhetorical commitment to more equitable wealth distribution and the ending of political dynasties.

Elections under the new constitution largely saw a return of the pre-martial law dynasties and would ensure that agrarian reform made little progress in practice. The worst of Marcos' excesses, such as the coconut levy and sugar monopoly, were ended and the Presidential Commission on Good Government (PCGG) set about recovering stolen assets, but the social structure remained very much in place.

Aquino gave an amnesty to the NPA which had encouraged many to abandon the armed struggle. The Communist movement was also harmed by paranoia which saw the assassination of cadres feared, usually wrongly, to be government agents, but the military still saw it as a major threat and violently suppressed a farmers' demonstration at Mendiola near Malacanang in early 1987, killing about twelve and injuring fifty. The farmers, supported by students and others, were demanding faster progress on agrarian reform. The killings forever cast doubt on whether entrenched land-owning interests, including the Aquinos, would ever accept radical reform which thereafter shadowed Cory's presidency. The events at Mendiola immediately caused the National Democratic Front (NDF), representing the CPP, the NPA and associated leftists, to break off talks with the government. In retrospect, the killings at Mendiola were to end, for decades, the prospect of the left being fully integrated into democratic politics.

More immediate threats to Aquino came from the military itself. Ramos stood firm against coup attempts in 1986 and 1987 by disgruntled RAM officers led by Gregorio Honasan, one in which Enrile was implicated. The second, which caused more than fifty deaths, followed the release of CPP head, Sison. These shocks pushed Aquino towards the much firmer anti-Communist agenda demanded by the rebel officers. The NPA ceasefire ended and a new, often dirty, war between the military and the left unfolded, as vigilante groups re-appeared – similar to the Civilian Home Defence Force of the Marcos era. The coup attempts and the lenient treatment of the plotters, indicated that Aquino's popularity had not translated into real power.

Elections in 1987 under the new constitution saw victory for only two opposition senators, the ever-ambitious Enrile and the movie star Joseph Estrada. The House mostly saw the return of local dynasts. In terms of parties, the government's Lakas ng Bayan coalition won the majority of House seats. The old Liberal and Nacionalista dominance disappeared as several new parties emerged and many independents were elected. A pattern for the future was being set in which self-interest and personality politics prevailed over a stable party system. The left got a small voice via the Partido ng Bayan (later Bayan Muna) through the Party List system.

A relatively radical land reform bill was drafted, which included sugar and coconut lands, but it was viewed as both too difficult and costly to implement. It also faced strong opposition from landed interests in Congress, and particularly from the sugar barons of Negros. A modified version was passed but it excluded sugar and coconut lands and had other loopholes. Implementation was hampered by lack of funds and Aquino failed to take a lead by breaking up her family's huge Hacienda Luisita in Tarlac.

More generally, significant economic reform was soon off the agenda as orthodox economists and the central bank governor focused on reviving the existing system. Aquino inherited an indebted economy barely kept semi-stable by the Marcos technocrats. An early question was whether to repudiate foreign debts on the grounds of corrupt kickbacks to Marcos. The country had a strong case but it would have meant taking on US banking interests and the World Bank and IMF whose continued help were viewed as indispensable. It would also discourage future direct foreign investment.

The government was reasonably accused of not taking a stronger line in debt negotiations. It was a heavy burden on the economy for a decade, for a time eating up half government revenue. Tax collection remained feeble due to continued widespread evasion. Cancellation of the Bataan nuclear power project, then close to completion, left the nation with a huge bill and a power shortage. The foreign investment which was hoped would follow EDSA took long to arrive partly because of new constitutional restrictions on it. Debt service kept interest rates high, depressing domestic demand for goods and services and leading to failures of industries.

In reaction to the Marcos years, the government was suspicious of State intervention and liberalized the tariff regime which eventually helped attract investment in export industries, but it took a long time. Overall GDP growth was modest and there was little progress in poverty reduction.

Although ministerial decision-making remained overly influenced by interest groups and patronage, some government agencies showed a high degree of apolitical professionalism reflecting the growth of the educated middle class. Professional women also became prominent, in contrast to the age of Imelda and her entourage.

However, resolving the issues of ill-gotten wealth proved inordinately difficult and control of sequestered assets such as shares in Philippine Airlines and the beverage and food giant San Miguel shares led to infighting and corruption. The PCGG was very active initially under chairman Senator Salonga sequestering many companies, making settlements with a few cronies including Floirendo, Benedicto and Yao Campos, for the return of some of their loot. Legal actions for recovery were launched in New York and Switzerland but courts in neither country were helpful and the process was slow. The Marcos money had been well disguised and was defended by batteries of lawyers. Marcos and Imelda were charged in New York with fraud and racketeering but his death in September 1989 facilitated her subsequent acquittal.

Among the elite, once the Lopez and Osmenas and a few more sequestered families had got their assets back, outrage and the urge for broader restitution faltered. This was a forgiving society where family and other bonds proved more powerful than principles. Some of the prime beneficiaries of Marcos, notably Lucio Tan and 'Danding' Cojuangco, kept their wealth offshore or safely hidden. They were even on the lookout for new local opportunities, spurred by the decline of the peso from fourteen to the dollar in 1985 to twenty-eight in 1990 making acquisitions cheap for those with dollars. Gradually, Marcos era figures made their way back with Cojuangco returning in 1989 and Imelda in 1990.

The post-Marcos sense of freedoms was enough to keep most of the nation quiet, with popular participation in barangay mayoral and provincial elections, even if dynastic politics and vote buying flourished. International goodwill for the new post-EDSA democracy helped. Foreign aid flowed strongly, much of it through NGOs and community organizations. Supplemented by the efforts of local NGOs, this brought some progress in public welfare despite the shortage of government funds.

However, it was slow going for the economy as a whole because of the debt burden even though exports and remittances grew steadily. Output, and indeed, economic morale suffered from frequent 'brownouts' with government indecision on new power plants and the Bataan cancellation. Loose monetary policy and a rise in oil prices caused by the Gulf War triggered a steep drop in the peso in 1990.

GDP percentage growth under Aquino

1986	3.4
1987	4.3
1988	6.7
1989	6.2
1990	3.0
1991	−0.5
1992	0.3

Aquino's term concluded with a series of disasters. A 1990 earthquake killed about 1,500 in Luzon then in June 1991 came the eruption of Mount Pinatubo, the second biggest global eruption of the twentieth century. Apart from the immediate destruction of homes and the loss of life, tens of thousands of hectares of prime agricultural land and villages were inundated with *lahars* (ash washed down from the volcano slopes) by rains from a typhoon which killed several thousand.

Cory also suffered her biggest political defeat and one which had enormous long-term consequences. The Senate rejected an extension of the

FIGURE 7.1 *Bacolor church, buried by* lahar *after the eruption of Mount Pinatubo, 1991.* © *Getty Images.*

US bases agreement. She had once been opposed to extension but as President, and with Ramos by her side, she fought for renewal, but a combination of old nationalist sentiments about 'US imperialism' with opposition from the ever-opportunistic Enrile and Marcos-admirer Estrada saw it defeated by twelve votes to eleven. The vote was all about sentiments rather than security issues. The withdrawal of US military spending added to the country's economic woes.

Aquino did, however, enjoy one final success before leaving office as someone who was respected for her honesty and the democratic space she had enabled. After some hesitation she backed Ramos as her successor. He won with only 23.5% of the vote, not far ahead of Miriam Defensor-Santiago, a fast-talking but erratic lawyer, and a resurrected Danding Cojuangco third. Even Imelda got 10%. Old party candidates Jovito Salonga, Ramon Mitra and Salvador Laurel were left far behind. Although an essentially conservative figure, Cory's support for Ramos brought with it liberal and anti-Marcos voters. At the same time, reflecting of a new type of populist politics, newcomers with media recognition competed with political elite names for the vice-presidency and Senate seats. Thus, former movie star Estrada easily won the race for vice-president, defeating an Osmena and two Magsaysays.

Ramos was a hands-on president who moved quickly to resolve power issues, albeit at a high price, and set about economic liberalization in a new attempt to attract foreign capital. He was acutely aware of how far the

Philippines had fallen behind some neighbours which he attributed to a system which enabled 'persons with political influence to extract wealth without effort'. In concert with his national security adviser, General Jose Almonte, aimed to use the state to challenge oligopoly domination through trade liberalization linked to World Trade Organization (WTO) and the Association of Southeast Asian Nations (ASEAN) agreements, and privatization of government enterprises.

The Philippines never came close to 'tiger economy' status but it did revive under Ramos as private investment recovered and improvements made in the banking system following a complete reconstruction of the Central Bank. A fixed exchange rate gave an impression of stability, though it tended to encourage foreign borrowing. Ramos also made the first major attack on monopoly with competition allowed in relation to telecoms. By 1998, new entrants into telecoms were offering an international gateway, fixed line, mobile phone, internet, satellite TV and other services. The telecom revolution was to spur the Business Process Outsourcing (BPO) industry and to have political consequences. However, privatization also gave opportunities for the existing elite to expand, such as with Lucio Tan's acquisition of Philippine Airlines.

Tariff cuts also killed some long-protected local manufacturing. The fragmented Philippines could not compete with more centralized and better positioned countries such as Thailand in terms car production. Nor did it have the money from oil and gas to subsidize heavy industry like Malaysia. Wage costs in the formal sector were much higher than China and Vietnam. Food was more expensive and the wage gap between formal and informal sectors high. Smuggling remained another problem for local industry and kidnappings of mostly ethnic Chinese businessmen also hurt investment.

On the plus side, partial decentralization of some government revenue and functions helped the growth of some secondary cities such as Cebu and General Santos City. More generally, however, corruption was simply decentralized. Ramos still found pork politics essential for dealing with Congress, and his 'strong state' was little more effective in collecting due taxes than its predecessors. A new agreement with the MNLF for the creation of the Autonomous Region of Muslim Mindanao (ARMM) reduced violence in Mindanao, though a new group of jihadists and kidnappers, the Sulu-based Abu Sayyaf, emerged. Agriculture made very modest progress, with ongoing debate as to whether the slow land reform process was aiding or impeding farming. Poverty and social welfare issues also took a lower priority than it had under Aquino. However, Ramos was insistent on rights to family planning, his 1993 initiative paving the way for the Reproductive Health Act nineteen years later.

The Ramos era ended with the 1997/98 Asian financial crisis. Relative to its neighbours, the Philippines survived it well with only a small dip in GDP in 1998. Ten austere years of post-Marcos recovery had meant that its foreign debts were small and its banking system in better shape. The latter part of the Ramos era has seen a rising current account deficit and loose monetary policy with the peso falling from twenty-eight to forty to the dollar during the Asian crisis, but this was a smaller drop than several Asian currencies and did not cause significant defaults.

GDP percentage growth under Ramos

1993	2.1
1994	4.4
1995	5.8
1996	5.2
1997	−0.5
1998	3.1

Ramos also had to deal with a predictable response to the ending of the bases agreement – a Chinese surge to fill an apparent power vacuum. At the end of 1994, China occupied Mischief Reef, 135 nautical miles from the Palawan coast, claimed by the Philippines and well within its 200 nautical mile exclusive economic zone (EEZ). The Philippines protested noisily but otherwise did nothing. A proposal to build lighthouses on the Scarborough (Panatag) Shoal off the Luzon coast, and other features, to assert Philippine rights was stalled in cabinet. The chief opponent was Secretary of Foreign Affairs, Domingo Siazon. According to Almonte, Siazon did not want to offend China because he had hopes of being chosen the next UN Secretary General.[1]

Ramos' other big failure was to groom an electable successor. The elite considered former movie star Estrada, who had easily won the vice-presidency, ill-suited for the job. Ideas were floated for 'charter change' – a change to a parliamentary system which would likely enable Ramos to be chosen as prime minister. Ramos' own position was equivocal. In the event nothing happened. His party, Lakas, chose Speaker of the House, Jose de Venecia, an effective but colourless businessman/politician over Ramos' own choice, former armed forces chief of staff, Renato de Villa. As it was, Estrada won by a large margin with 39 per cent in a ten-person race. Lakas' candidate for vice-president, Gloria Macapagal-Arroyo, daughter of the former president, won the post.

Estrada's popularity was based on his years as a screen and then television star in roles where he was always the good guy getting justice for the underdogs. In real life, he was a very likeable but slightly roguish figure with a common touch and given to partying. Even his name Erap was 'pare', the local slang for 'friend' or 'pal' spelled backwards. The urban poor believed his claim that he represented them, even though he was backed by Marcos' cronies Cojuangco and Lucio Tan. It was a persona which in the era of mass communication could trump dynastic names. The 1998 election saw success for other entertainment and sports celebrities. In Estrada's case, the reality fell well short of the image. He was too nice to his friends not to be corrupt and insufficiently tough to stay ahead of his political enemies. He had been elected without needing a party as diverse interest groups rallied around his banner, but what could have been a strength became his fatal flaw.

In terms of policy, not very much changed. The economy gradually recovered from the Asian financial crisis, the BPO sector and remittances resumed strong growth. Estrada promised more liberalization and though little happened there was no backsliding. At the macro level, the economy was healthy enough even if there was no real improvement in poverty and social issues. He embarked on offensives against the MILF in Mindanao and Abu Sayyaf in Sulu and brought American military forces back to provide training and support. Foreign policy, such as it was, remained unchanged, as did its minister, Siazon.

Estrada's problem was that he conducted national government in the same way as the city mayor that he had been (of San Juan, part of Manila). Assuming a deciding role in all contracts of over 50 million pesos, he handed out contracts to all manner of friends and relations as well as businessmen seeking reciprocal favours from Malacanang. Cojuangco was enabled to reclaim San Miguel shares originally acquired from the coconut levy fund, and several favours given to Lucio Tan.

Such sleaze was seen by many as the norm but other behaviour was viewed as singularly un-presidential. Estrada became known not just for indolence but also for late night drinking and gambling sessions, and the use of friends' houses for trysts with his various mistresses. He was finally undone by the personal treason of a drinking buddy, Luis 'Chavit' Singson, governor of Ilocos Sur, who announced that he had given Estrada millions in illegal gambling profits.

This revelation was cue for an impeachment case which failed by one vote in the Senate preventing the submission of key evidence. A coalition of Church, NGOs, Manila middle class and the left then organized another People Power event known as EDSA 2 with vast crowds demanding his removal. The military and Supreme Court then backed the president's ouster and Macapagal-Arroyo became president in January 2001, but for the urban poor who had faith in Estrada this was just elite revenge.

Estrada's subsequent indictment for a range of offences saw more vast crowds back on EDSA in his support. EDSA 3, as it was called, took place over several days. It was eventually dispersed by force after Arroyo declared a state of rebellion; several were killed and many injured. EDSA 2 and EDSA 3 between them showed that a bigger problem than Estrada was the weakness of the constitutional system and the gap between the masses on one side and the middle-class reformists on the other. The left, which had failed to back EDSA 1 took another wrong turn and backed EDSA 2, which showed its lack of rapport with the urban poor. EDSA 2 may have been well intentioned but left no lasting improvement in governance while showing how institutions could be manipulated. (Estrada was convicted of plunder in 2007 but almost immediately pardoned by Arroyo.)

The overall winner of EDSAs 2 and 3 was the socio-economic status quo. The Marcos-era cronies were left unscathed and elections in May 2001 saw Estrada's wife, his chief of police, Panfilo Lacson, Enrile's close associate Edgardo Angara and former mutineer Gregorio Honasan all elected to the Senate. With the EDSA 2 coalition split and the Marcos forces still strong, Arroyo needed to marshal disparate forces in Congress, primarily via the 'pork barrel' – discretionary presidential payments to congressional districts. Even Singson was rewarded with the position of deputy National Security Adviser!

Arroyo, an economist, brought an appearance of professionalism to the presidency. The economy prospered modestly. After the sharp drop to forty to the dollar at the time of EDSA 2, the peso achieved relative stability which was to last two decades, a tribute to the management after the central bank's reconstruction and to underlying conservatism of policy makers. A coup attempt by junior officers in 2003, led by naval lieutenant and later senator Antonio Trillanes IV, fell flat, eliciting no support from the public or superior officers. Arroyo tried hard to find an accommodation in Muslim Mindanao to ward off the new jihadist threat of al-Qaeda in the aftermath of the 9/11 attacks on the US in 2001. However, local opposition and the Supreme Court blocked Arroyo's attempt to secure peace by expanding the ARMM.

Arroyo enthusiastically joined the post-9/11 US 'War on Terror' and expanded military cooperation under the Visiting Forces Agreement, but she also fell for Chinese charms, agreeing to a joint venture with China's National Offshore Oil Corporation (CNOOC) for exploration of areas within the Philippine EEZ. The Joint Marine Seismic Undertaking (JMSU) was essentially a backdoor deal with China done without reference to the Department of Foreign Affairs. The agreement lapsed after 2008 when leftists in Congress, arguing it was unconstitutional, took the deal to the Supreme Court which sat on it despite Arroyo's pleas for a quick approval.[2]

Establishment forces were happy enough about Arroyo's performance to back her for a full term in the 2004 elections, which saw her up against another movie star anxious to emulate his friend, Estrada. Fernando Poe had the advantage of a glamorous film star wife, Susan Roces, but not quite the Estrada image of invincibility. Also in the race were Lacson, now a senator though accused of extra-judicial killings under Estrada, reformist senator Raul Roco and wealthy evangelist Eddie Villanueva.

Arroyo was declared winner with 39.9 per cent of the vote to Poe's 36.5 per cent. Cries of rigging of the vote count were seen as backed by taped exchanges between Arroyo and the election commissioner Virgilio Garcillano, known as the 'Hello Garci' tapes. In reality, her victory may have owed more to her cultivation of local power wielders such as the soon-to-be notorious Ampatuan clan of Maguindanao. The 'Hello Garci' taint never went away and various other scandals touched the administration but there was insufficient backing for impeachment and the public was disillusioned with EDSA-style action.

The country as a whole showed a huge divergence between adherence to constitutionality and the pursuit of power by other means. Voices in the Senate were quite diverse even if more focused on personal promotion than policy principles, and in 2007 included former mutineers, Honasan and Trillanes. The House had a few genuine leftists, members of the National Democratic Front, elected through the Party List. Sometimes informal coalitions formed to pass useful and reformist laws, but overall, the quality of government under Arroyo was significantly worse than under Ramos; despite promises of reform, she was a willing participant of it. Her husband, 'Mike' Arroyo, was also implicated.

Against this background, two city mayors became noted for being effective. Rodrigo Duterte in Davao combined dynastic clout with shrewd alliances and ruthlessness against political enemies as well as criminals and claimed his city the leader in order and development. The other was Jesse Robredo whose achievements in Naga City made him head of the national association of city mayors. Robredo was from a modest family and seen as a model of a new breed of non-dynastic leaders. Duterte on the other hand reflected the reality that there was continued, widespread resort to extra-judicial force. The NPA remained active in several rural locations tying down much of the military. National and local authorities engaged in a programme of assassination of leftist organizers. In 2006 alone more than 800 extra-judicial killings were reported, mostly of CPP and NDF sympathizers including union organizers, student and NGO activists and journalists. The killings had a devastating effect on the CPP but meanwhile the non-communist left failed to make progress. There was limited electoral support for nationally focused leftist programmes and the number of Party List seats was insufficient for them to gain traction in the House. Gradually, traditional political forces took over most of these seats.

Political bosses in some areas maintained private armies which generally had understandings with the military and the police. The reality of these warlords was laid bare by the 2009 killing by Maguindanao's Ampatuan clan of some fifty-eight people, mostly journalists and the family and supporters of their political rivals, the Mangudadatu family. Despite compelling evidence, it was to be another decade before the some of the perpetrators were found guilty.

Taken overall, the economy performed steadily and with a rising trend over time but ending with the hit from the 2008 global financial crisis.

Government debts from the past declined only slowly, meanwhile revenues persistently failed to grow to the point that there was significant money available for infrastructure or social development. The customs and revenue department were notoriously corrupt so collections fell 20–40 per cent below what was due. Meanwhile, a major percentage of direct payments from the central budget for provincial level projects determined by local legislators were diverted into politicians' pockets.

Graft was not the only problem resulting in tax revenue as a percent of GDP falling from 19 per cent of GDP to 12 per cent between 1997 and 2002. Exemptions decided by Congress or as investment incentives given but never withdrawn, plus a failure to adjust tax rates, utility charges etc. for inflation all contributed to a feeble tax effort. Generally, the rich benefited, the poor lost out through a lack of health, education and infrastructure spending.

Satisfactory headline GDP and dollar earning numbers were increasingly supported by continued rises in remittances and in BPO services, both owing mainly to individual efforts not government policy. Remittances rose from $6 billion in 2001 to $18 billion in 2010. Over the same ten years, the working age population rose by a total of 25 per cent or close to 2 per cent a year. Overall workforce participation was stable at 61 per cent but women's employment percentage increased.

As the end of her term approached, Arroyo, like Ramos, toyed with the idea of a change to a parliamentary system which could keep her in power, but a scandal involving her husband over a telecom contract with the Chinese firm ZTE was followed by the 2008 global financial crisis which provided a sharp if short shock to the economy. Then, as the 2010 election loomed, the political game changed again. The sainted Cory Aquino died in August 2009, a reminder both of the fight against dictatorship, and that not all politicians were liars and thieves.

GDP real growth percentage

2001	2.9
2002	3.6
2003	4.9
2004	6.7
2005	4.7
2006	5.2
2007	6.6
2008	4.1
2009	1.1

Notes

1 Jose Almonte quoted in Marites Danguilan Vitug, *Rock Solid: How the Philippines Won its Maritime Case Against China*, Quezon City: Ateneo de Manila University Press, 2019, p. 18.

2 Ibid., pp. 70–6.

8

Straight paths and road blocks

An outpouring of nostalgia for Cory's selflessness and honesty led directly to the hope that her son, Benigno Aquino III, otherwise known as Noynoy, a Liberal party senator of limited ambition, could restore a measure of ethics to a position sullied by presidents Estrada and Arroyo. The Liberal Party's prospective candidate, Manuel (Mar) Roxas, grandson of an earlier president, stepped aside for Noynoy and sought the vice-presidency.

Noynoy won easily with 42 per cent of the vote but the disgraced Estrada showed the depth of his popularity by coming in second with 26 per cent. Arroyo's choice, her defence secretary, Gilberto Teodoro, polled only 11 per cent. Concern for ethics, however, did not extend to the vice-presidency where Makati city boss, Jejomar Binay, beat Roxas despite his history of alleged malfeasance and dynasty-building.

Buoyed by his victory and the apparent desire for cleaner government, President Aquino set about prosecuting some of the most egregious episodes of the Arroyo-era malfeasance. Most spectacular was the impeachment of Renato Corona, Chief Justice appointed by Arroyo in a dubiously constitutional move at the end of her term. Failing to reveal his assets, only three senators voted against impeachment.

Arroyo-appointed ombudsman, Merceditas Gutierrez, was also impeached by the House for failure to proceed on many cases but she quit before any trial. An army general, Carlos Garcia, was court-martialled and given an eleven-year sentence for plunder. Arroyo was charged with plunder of state assets to support her candidates in the 2007 elections. From 2012 to 2016, she was under detention in various hospitals before being acquitted of the plunder charges by the Supreme Court soon after Duterte's election.

These actions against the corrupt enthused the urban middle class and foreign opinion. The Philippine position in Transparency International's ranking of the extent of corruption perceptions improved from 139 out of 175 countries in 2009 to ninety-five in 2015. The Aquino administration was credited with recruiting more professionals rather than politicians for posts in government and on quasi-government bodies. Finance Minister for his whole term was Cesar Purisima – who had quit Arroyo's government over 'Hello Garci' – and Leila de Lima, former chair of the Human Rights

Commission which had investigated Duterte's Davao Death Squads, was Justice Secretary. Jesse Robredo was an effective and popular Secretary for Home Affairs until he was killed in a plane crash in 2012.

Makati Business Club surveys showed that at least some departments appeared well run, though not the police, the appeals court or the customs department. Revenue collection improved as the Bureau of Internal Revenue (BIR) initiated more cases of tax evasion, though the process to convict was very slow. Tax revenue as a percentage of GDP rose from 14.8 in 2010 to 17.0 in 2016. The customs department continued to resist efforts at reform. Collections rose in the latter half of the Aquino term, though large discrepancies remained between Philippine and exporting country data.

Nor could the government's own claims to be clean always stand close examination. Whatever the intentions of the president, the political system demanded pay offs to legislators. Elections in 2010 and again in 2013 showed that the dynasties were continuing to tighten their grip on the House and on elections to provincial governors and mayors. Un-reformist names in both houses included Enrile, Estrada, Marcos, Arroyo, Singson.

To achieve a working majority in the House, representatives had to be rewarded. Funds for distribution to legislators had long existed. Officially known as the Priority Development Assistance Fund (PDAF), but more commonly known as the 'pork barrel'. Disbursement was in the hands of the president – who also had a separate fund at his disposal. It was believed that anything between 20 per cent and 50 per cent of these funds went into legislators' pockets. Back in 1996, the *Inquirer* newspaper had reported allegations of the extent such kickback of funds meant for schools, roads etc. Nothing changed until 2013 when the *Inquirer* published details of a system run by businesswoman, Janet Napoles, to create non-existent projects which would be awarded millions in PDAF. Included in this scheme were senators Enrile, Revilla, Estrada, Marcos and Honasan. Following a Commission on Audit investigation a few were charged with plunder, including Enrile who stayed out of jail despite this supposedly being a non-bailable offence. Revilla and Estrada were held until winning appeals to the Supreme Court under Duterte. The PDAF itself was declared unlawful by the Supreme Court but the practice continued in other forms.

The Napoles scam made headlines but only optimists believed that the Philippines was making a large step forward in governance. Many saw the arrests as being politically inspired. Pork-fund abuse was too widespread to be focused only on the Napoles list and the scandal also touched Aquino supporters. Reformist and technocratic concepts clashed with the realities of politics based on networks of obligations and the cost of competing in the political arena. Collusion between the executive and legislature negated the latter's oversight role but it was too important to funding the political class to be discarded altogether.

Aquino was guilty of over-indulgence towards his friends and relatives, bad judgement and lack of steel undermining some of the progress made.

Several ministers were kept on despite poor performance. Agriculture Secretary Proceso Alcala was accused of backing dubious projects, and Transportation and Communications Secretary Joseph Abaya of sheer incompetence; as senior Liberal Party figures, both survived.

Preference for pals over process led to Aquino's biggest disaster. A major achievement had been the framework agreement for the Bangsamoro region which was signed with the MILF. With details on important issues such as relations with the Manila government and disarmament of forces, it enjoyed support from Malaysia, the US and Indonesia. It was now under consideration in Congress.

Then on 25 January 2015, the nation was shocked by the Mamasapano massacre in Maguindanao in which forty members of the police Special Action Force (SAF) were killed. The SAF operation had been intended to capture a Malaysian Islamist given refuge by the Bangsamoro Islamic Freedom Fighters (BIFF), a breakaway group from the MILF. Poor intelligence resulted in the SAF force being confronted by the MILF as well as BIFF fighters. The botched raid had been overseen by Aquino's friend, police chief Alan Purisima, even though he was already under suspension by the Ombudsman over suspicions of graft. Neither Purisima nor the president informed, let alone consulted, the military. The episode saw Aquino's hitherto high approval rating collapse, progress on the Bangsamoro Basic Law put on hold and anti-Muslim sentiment in congress increase. Relations between police and military were further strained.

Aquino was more successful on social issues, albeit the pace was slower than the headlines suggested. Most significant was the passage of the Reproductive Health (RH) Act, which the government backed though, Aquino was ambivalent. The law required the government to provide assistance for 'all effective natural and modern methods' of contraception. While abortion remained illegal, care had to be provided for women who had had such abortions – a cause of many deaths.

The use of pills and condoms had long been the norm among many middle class people but a lack of knowledge of, access to and affordability of such methods among lower income groups was limited and seen as the main cause of the continuing high rate of fertility. Although it had been declining slowly, at 3.8 births per woman in 2000 to 3.2 in 2010, it was the highest of all Asian countries east of Pakistan and made it doubly hard for the nation to reduce poverty and raise educational levels.

The bill was promoted primarily as an anti-poverty measure, proponents noting that the poorest had more children than they desired. It was opposed by the Church and by others arguing that providing contraception was not the business of government and that poverty had other causes, notably bad government. The bill was eventually comfortably in passed 2012 but was then held up in the Supreme Court until 2014 when it was declared constitutional apart from some implementing clauses struck down for impinging on rights of conscience.

Measuring the impact of the RH Act is difficult because a steady downturn in fertility was already in place due to factors including numbers of women working overseas, urbanization and the decline of Catholic Church influence. Implementation was also limited by the lack of funds and by the lack of effort of local health officials. A fertility fall from 2.9 in 2015 to 2.5 in 2019 suggests it did bring some benefit.

What did not change was the high rate of births outside marriage. Indeed, it increased from 38 per cent of births in 2008 to 54 per cent in 2019, with particularly high levels in the National Capital Region and the Eastern Visayas. Although divorce was not permitted – other than for Muslims – *de facto* separations and informal liaisons were very common and, as in the past, there was little stigma attached. Indeed, despite more women being in work, and contraception more easily available, the children were regarded as more a blessing than burden. Divorce was expected to be agreed eventually and a bill providing for it passed the House committee stage in 2020. However, whether, if enacted, it will make much difference to social practices remains to be seen.

The Aquino government claimed some success in reducing poverty and particularly in its most negative consequences on nutrition, health and education. Its main weapon was a conditional cash transfer programme known as Pantawid Pamilyang Pilipino (PPP). Started under Arroyo with World Bank assistance, it was massively expanded under Aquino and by 2015 was reaching 4 million of the poorest families. The cash provided was estimated at 11 per cent of household income but could be spent only on public health, education and social services. It definitively increased school attendance, especially of girls in Mindanao, vaccinations and pre- and post-natal care. It continued under Duterte.

On a conventional basis, the economy under Noynoy performed steadily, averaging 6.1 per cent growth between 2011 and 2016. Foreign exchange reserves rose modestly and current account surpluses brought the ratio of external debt to GDP down to a very comfortable 19 per cent. Efforts to improve revenue collection were partially successful with tax to GDP ratio rising to 15.2 per cent while conservative budgeting saw the government deficit kept under 2 per cent of GDP. Total export growth (including services) was lower than under Arroyo but still averaged 30 per cent. Capital formation rose from 20 per cent to 24 per cent of GDP as corporate profits and foreign investment increased.

However, the government's own efforts to improve infrastructure took too long to be realized. Improved revenue went mostly to social and defence spending so that government consumption rose from 9.7 per cent to 11.2 per cent of GDP. Familiar problems with project implementation remained. These included the weak capacity of government departments, conflicts between central and local governments, diversion of funds to 'pork' projects, land acquisition problems and delays caused by court challenges. Increased anti-corruption scrutiny was also an issue. Project preparation was however to make it easier for Aquino's successor to show early results from his 'Build, Build, Build' programme.

For many in the major cities, and foreign observers in particular, the Aquino years seemed to bring a combination of steady growth and improved governance. However, a broader attack on poverty required faster and better distributed economic growth. Judging by the sprouting of high-rise condominiums and retail malls in Manila and to a lesser extent Cebu, the BPO industry was creating a new class of educated middle-income earners, but evidence for a broader expansion of the middle-income groups was lacking.

The view from the grass roots was that overall not much had changed in terms of poverty levels and deprivation. Agriculture continued to struggle in spite or because of continued protection. Debate continued over whether there had been too little or too much agrarian reform, but debate did not change the reality of low productivity. The rising population and near static land supply pushed urban migration but the lack of formal employment kept huge numbers of migrants in low income informal work. Inadequate job creation drove ever greater numbers to work overseas. Remittances boosted consumer demand for the food and beverage and construction sectors, but industry's contribution to the economy slipped from 32.6 per cent to 30.7 per cent. Even under stable domestic and international circumstances, it was evident that given Philippines' population growth rate, the extent of corruption, the economic ownership structure, and regional and ethnic divisions the road out of poverty would be long.

The most noteworthy decision of the Aquino years, and one likely to have a lasting impact on the whole region, was the decision to take China to the Permanent Court of Arbitration in The Hague over its claims and activities in the South China Sea. A sweeping victory there was soon set aside by his successor but would remain a decisive judgement not just for the Philippines but for the other littoral states of the South China Sea which faced similar claims by China on their Exclusive Economic Zones and the sea's islands, rocks and shoals.

However, the 2016 victory in the courts followed a defeat which had showed how ill-prepared the country was for China's challenge and how gullible or cowardly it had been in allowing China to land on its very doorstep. The year 2012 was supposedly a 'Year of Friendly Exchange' between the two countries, but it was also a year of change in China between the eras of Hu Jintao and Xi Jinping when nationalist credentials needed to be on display. In April, Chinese coastguard and fishing vessels which had been mustering at Scarborough (Panatag) Shoal began to harass Philippine fishing boats and an archaeological research vessel. A Philippine navy cutter came to help but in a conciliatory gesture was then withdrawn in favour of coastguard and fisheries department vessels. The Philippine ships endured two months of harassment and dangerous manoeuvres by the larger and faster Chinese vessels until in June, with typhoon season approaching, the US appeared to broker an arrangement for both sides to withdraw. The Philippines did but the Chinese immediately returned, denying there ever had been an agreement. The Panatag Shoal was lost to the Philippines.

Philippine willingness to fight, albeit against overwhelming odds, had been shown wanting. A military which had lost hundreds of men every year against the NPA and the Moros had not suffered a single casualty in the loss of an important shoal. For sure, military odds in facing China were overwhelming but China's diplomacy could ill afford a small war against a weak neighbour with history and most of ASEAN on its side.

Philippine diplomacy had often been shown looking for compromise when none was ever likely or suggesting that China's attitude would change once the political transition had passed. The comparison between the Philippines and a robust Vietnam vis à vis China was all too evident. The US was also shown to be a doubtful ally, with Assistant Secretary of State for East Asia, Kurt Campbell proving all too keen to talk up a supposed deal with China which lacked any kind of force behind it.

The Panatag Shoal did not lie within the limits of the Treaty of Paris map defining the territory passed by Spain to the US in 1898 but it could be viewed as being within the archipelago described in the Treaty of Washington the same year, but was not mentioned by name and thus did not qualify as territory under the US-Philippine Mutual Defence Treaty. However, it had been recognized as Philippine territory by the US in 1938 correspondence, and had appeared, as Panacot, as part of the Philippines on the celebrated, highly detailed 1734 Murillo Velarde map created by a Spanish cartographer. It was clearly well within the Philippine EEZ and accepted as such by the US despite the US not having ratified the United Nations Convention on the Law of the Sea (UNCLOS). The Treaty also covered island territories, armed forces and public vessels in the Pacific, which was said to include the South China Sea. The US had specially excluded the Philippines' Spratly Island claims from the Mutual Defence Treaty but Panatag was not a Spratly Island. Campbell's equivocal role was especially puzzling given that as a former naval officer he would have been aware of the proximity of Panatag to Subic Bay to which the US had access under the Visiting Forces Agreement.

The loss of Panatag did, however, shock a few important Filipinos into looking for a way to fight back against China. The lead was taken by Foreign Secretary, Albert del Rosario, and Associate Justice of the Supreme Court, Antonio Carpio, who had been studying the issue since 1995 when he was legal adviser to President Ramos at the time of China's Mischief Reef occupation. Long sceptical of ASEAN efforts to create a viable code of conduct between disputants, in 2011 Carpio had proposed taking the issue to the Permanent Court of Arbitration, relying on the definitions and rules of the UNCLOS, particularly as related to EEZs, definitions of islands and the applications of the archipelagic principle.

When del Rosario became Foreign Secretary in 2011, he was immediately faced with Chinese harassment of both of Philippine fishermen operating in the Kalayaan region (most but not all of the Spratly Islands) and of oil search operations on the Reed Bank. Attendance at ASEAN meetings convinced him of the uselessness of an organization which could only proceed with consensus and where China relied on its Cambodian and Lao surrogates to neutralize any complaints against it.

President Aquino started out with a benign view of China's rise but was soon disillusioned by his failure to buy the lives of Filipino drug dealers on death row in China with a Filipino boycott of the Nobel award ceremony for Chinese dissident writer, Liu Xiaobo. Next came the Chinese moves on Recto (Reed) Bank which he declared was 'as much part of the Philippines as Recto Avenue', a major Manila road.[1]

Thus, after the loss of Panatag, an alliance between the detailed legal positions produced by Carpio and his team with del Rosario's desperate need for a counter to China's weight in power and money had little difficulty persuading President Aquino that the Philippines should bring the case to the international legal arena. That duly happened in January 2013. China predictably refused to engage showing a contempt for the UNCLOS process which it had previously supported.

Nonetheless, the Philippines which needed to prove its case to a court was obliged to consider arguments representing China's position, even if not made by China itself. While the court spent the next three-and-a-half years considering the issues, China continued to harass Filipino fishing and supply boats and 'create facts' with reclamation to expand the features it had previously seized. These incidents were recorded and passed to the court, contributing to its conclusions about China's behaviour.

The judgement was not to come until July 2016, a few days after the end of the Aquino term (see Chapter 21). It was a stunning victory for the Philippines, and by implication for Vietnam, Malaysia, Indonesia and Brunei because it established key points of common interest.

- It rejected China's 'historic' claims. China had never exercised exclusive control of the sea or its resources. The nine-dash line, which encloses most of the EEZs of Philippines, Malaysia and Vietnam, was incompatible with the EEZ rights accorded by UNCLOS.

- None of the islands and rocks could support a self-sustaining population. Hence, whether occupied by China or others, they were not entitled to their own EEZs, only to twelve-mile territorial seas. (Although it was not mentioned in the Philippine claim as outside its EEZ, this judgement also included Taiwan-occupied Itu Aba.)

- China had violated Philippine rights within its EEZ by forcibly interfering with fishing and oil exploration. The Philippines and China both had traditional fishing rights at the Scarborough Shoal but China had interfered with these rights and created dangers of ship collisions.

- Chinese building of artificial islands had damaged coral reefs and the eco-system and its fishermen had harvested endangered species.
- China had aggravated disputes by continuing reclamation and construction while issues were supposed to be subject to dispute resolution proceedings.

The court did not address the issues of ownership of the islands and rocks as UNCLOS only pertains to the seas and their resources. However, by rejecting their rights to EEZs of their own, the decision in principle meant that disputes should only relate to the boundaries of the respective EEZs. These are quite small in the overall context – perhaps 2 per cent of the total area. Against the urging of some of its own officials, the Philippines team, led by Carpio, had included Taiwan-occupied Itu Aba, the largest island. This was a risk due to its size, but the tribunal ruled that none of the islands and rocks were big enough to claim an EEZ. For Taiwan, the position of the then-ruling Kuomintang party was somewhat different from that of Beijing. Although it was a Kuomintang government in China which had drawn early versions of the nine-dash line, it now said it claimed the islands but not the sea itself.

In the long wait for the international court decision, the issue of the sea had long been forgotten by the populace. In 2016, they voted for a sharp change of course, a change which came as a shock for those who felt that the Aquino administration had provided steadier and cleaner government than any since Ramos. Indeed, the slogan of the Liberal Party and its presidential candidate Mar Roxas 'Continue the Straight Path' summed up its sense of self-worth and complaisance. The people wanted more, something new and exciting.

As it was, they were initially presented with familiar faces. Mar Roxas was respected but lacked popular appeal and more than any other represented the establishment. Grace Poe had celebrity name appeal but not much else. Then there were two alliances which merely showed cynicism. Supposed corruption fighter and perennial candidate Miriam Defensor-Santiago teamed up with Marcos' son, Bongbong. The hypothetical anti-corruption former coup-maker Honasan joined forces with Jejomar Binay, the boss of Makati who had defeated Roxas in the election for the vice-presidency in 2010, but had since been indicted for corruption.

Binay started as front runner but faded under the pressure of the corruption allegations, apparently leaving the race to Roxas and Poe. Rodrigo Duterte spotted an obvious opening. His name was well known from many years as mayor of Davao, he was noted as a man of action, and he was new to the national scene. He was from Mindanao but his family background was from Cebu. He may have had a reputation for brutality but he was seen to be an anti-elitist by using crude language and displaying a gun-toting image of a ruthless but effective cop. He won because he was the exceptional candidate in a large but mediocre field, receiving 39 per cent of the vote against 23 per cent for Roxas, 21 per cent for Poe and 12 per cent for Binay.

Note

1   Vitug, *Rock Solid*, p. 153.

9

Man with a gun

Rodrigo Duterte was no celluloid image, he was the real thing. His campaign for president had actually highlighted his role as a killer of drug dealers and other allegedly low-life people in Davao. He had, it was said, cleaned up Davao and would do the same for the nation, vanquishing the twin scourges of drugs and corruption, and confront the old oligarchy. His claims for his Davao achievements were a half-truth and secured more by fear than good governance but that barely mattered. The people, seemingly inured to violence in politics, mostly found President Duterte's reality to their liking. All classes would set aside the things about him they disliked and focus on those they liked.

Thus, his crude, profanity-strewn language attacking even the Pope and President Obama could show him as a populist and anti-elitist without suggesting any socialist tendencies which could frighten the wealthy. His animus against the US, based more on supposed personal slights than ideology, allowed many on the left and traditional nationalists to forget his support for the Marcos family; his misogyny and mistresses could be admired by the machismo males without alienating the female Overseas Filipino workers (OFWs) looking for a national leader; his attacks on the Catholic Church could be brushed off by devout churchgoers who focused on his promise to be the champion of the poor; his claim to represent the interests of the provinces against 'imperial' Manila by adopting a federal constitution was well received from Ilocos to Cebu and Davao without bothering the people of the capital.

Such support was reflected in his popularity on taking office and the durability of it despite outrage at his campaign of killing from critics ranging from local bishops to numerous foreign leaders and non-governmental organizations. Indeed, such criticisms seemed to reinforce his image as a strong leader who would put the Philippines on the world map with its killing spree. Within days of taking office, he in practice set aside the Philippines' national victory at the Court of Arbitration in The Hague. This surrender was seen as the price to be paid for the huge gains to prosperity that Chinese money would bring.

Duterte's focus on the evil of drugs was shrewd politics, an agenda which no one would argue against in principle. However, the facts did not support

Duterte's claims that the nation was being overrun by addiction. The number of users had, according to official figures, declined sharply from a peak in around 2004, thanks to enforcement and rehabilitation efforts. He claimed then that there were more than 3 million users – more than twice the latest official 1.2 million estimate. Then in 2017, he fired Drug Board chairman Benjamin Reyes for saying that the official figure for 2016 was 1.7 million when Duterte was claiming 4 million, a total not high given the size of the population. Most were from the lowest income groups.

Duterte's sincerity in making drugs the villain was hypocritical as he had been a user of fentanyl, a synthetic opioid far stronger than shabu, a methamphetamine which, being cheap, was the local drug of choice. The Philippine drug problem was reckoned to be unexceptional by regional standards. Revenue from drugs, gambling and smuggling were too important a source of money for many politicians to abandon. However, allegations of involvement in the trade were a weapon against politicians who displeased Duterte.

He was barely at Malacanang before the national equivalent of the Davao Death Squads was in action. Hundreds were killed by the police in supposed shoot-outs during arrests and many more hypothetical drug pushers gunned down by masked men on motor bikes. National police chief Ronald (Bato) dela Rosa, who had been Duterte's police chief in Davao, launched Operation Tokhang, a composite word use to describe police knocking on doors to root out and 'neutralize' drug personalities. This involved one-sided shoot-outs and the planting of evidence. Almost invariably, the victims were low-level pushers, users or innocent people, not the high-level dealers. Poor neighbourhoods were mostly targeted, not the gated communities of the rich.

The overall death rate from extra-judicial killings (EJKs) was soon in the thousands, almost all low-level pushers or users. Within months, EJK deaths far exceeded those of fifteen years of Marcos' authoritarian rule. Duterte's rude ripostes to critical foreigners – calling Obama a 'son of a whore' during an ASEAN summit – merely added to his tough guy image. Leaders of ASEAN nations were aghast at speech so alien to Asian diplomacy but said nothing.

Foreign observers could remember similar EJKs of supposed drug dealers in Thailand under elected prime minister Thaksin Shinawatra. In that case, after killing a few thousand even Thaksin quietly abandoned the policy. It was denounced by his military junta successors who said half those killed had nothing to do with drugs. The military admitted in 2016 that methamphetamine use was too widespread to be wiped out, but such facts could not stand in the way of a Philippine killing spree.

The killings were temporarily curtailed following a few 'mistakes' including that of an innocent teenager and a five-year-old struck by a stray bullet in a one-sided shoot-out, but few were shocked when a retired Davao Death Squad policeman admitted that cash payments were made for killings.

In Manila, 85 per cent of those brought to hospitals by police were dead on arrival. It was barely a surprise when anti-drug police superintendent Raphael Dumlao had been behind the kidnap and murder by police (even after payment of a ransom) of a Korean businessman at the national police headquarters at Camp Crame.

Early 2017 saw the arrest of the most prominent local critic of the killings, senator and former Justice Secretary under Noynoy Aquino, Leila de Lima. As head of the Commission on Human Rights, in 2009 de Lima had launched an inquiry into the Davao Death Squads. As Justice Secretary she had attempted to clean up the running of Manila's most notorious New Bilibid Prison. In 2014, raids ordered by de Lima of prosperous inmates – mainly from the drug business – were found to have luxurious quarters and ready access to luxuries, guns, drugs and girls.

Duterte turned the tables of 'justice' on de Lima, with accusations that she was in the drug business. The allegations were seen by critics as prime examples both of the ruthlessness of Duterte and the susceptibility of the justice system to manipulation. At home, de Lima continued to be supported by a few fellow senators and by Vice-President Leni Robredo, while overseas she was honoured, including by Amnesty International and the European Parliament, but this had scant impact on a wider public still admiring 'Duterte Harry'.

The International Criminal Court (ICC) took notice of the killings in 2016. In 2018, it followed this up with details of allegations regarding EJK and its intention to pursue the matter. This prompted Duterte, wrapping defence of his own brutal actions in nationalism, withdrawing the nation from the ICC effective in March 2019. Events up to that date were still covered and in December 2020 the ICC prosecutor announced that there was 'evidence of crimes against humanity' which were being followed up.

Despite international opprobrium, the killings went on, including mayors named by Duterte in his lists of supposed drug lords. The actual numbers remain uncertain. Official sources in 2019 gave 5,552 between July 2016 and November 2019, although another official source claimed up to 6,700. This excludes the thousands more killed other than in police raids, most often by gunmen on motor bikes and frequently following semi-official suggestions that a person had drug connections. The total could be as high as 27,000 according to the Commission on Human Rights. Whatever the number is it very high relative to total intentional homicides of around 9,000 a year.[1]

Killing rates varied widely, probably more in accordance with the zeal of the province's police chief than the extent of drug business. The killing programme was supposed to wipe out the drug problem in a matter of months but it was still in full swing three-and-a-half years later, slowed only by the Covid-19 pandemic and lockdowns in 2020. Nor was there much evidence that the mass killings were slowing consumption.[2] Shabu seizure varied from year to year and though arrests reached 60,000 in 2019, prices remained fairly stable, though with some decline in purity. In most cases, those arrested were dealt with leniently, suggesting that killings were most often motivated by political factors, personal grudges or ambitious police. The UN reported that methamphetamine traffic fell in the first half of 2020 but then rose strongly as new routes were found.

The drug war was cover for killings of political, personal or business rivals so no one can tell how many unsolved murders were drug related. The unsolved murder rate included peasant and *lumad* activists, leftists targeted by 'red tagging' (the identification of liberal and anti-government individuals or groups as pro-Communist and thus potential targets for retribution), environmentalists and journalists. By comparison, extrajudicial killings during the Marcos dictatorship were few, quiet and targeted. Duterte seemed to relish the numbers and promote his most willing executioners.

When the US withdrew the visitor visa of dela Rosa because of the EJKs, Duterte responded by announcing the cancellation of the Visiting Forces Agreement. In a bizarre twist in late 2019, Duterte appointed his most prominent critic, Vice-President Robredo to head the anti-drug task force, but she was soon dismissed after claiming that three years of Duterte's campaign had captured only 1 per cent of the shabu. Robredo was a well-liked figure but popular support for the drug killings continued despite concerns that friends and relatives, innocent or not, might be gunned down.

Apart from crude words, misogyny appeared to show through in Duterte's vindictive attitudes both to de Lima and to Maria Lourdes Sereno who, among other positions, had opposed the declaration of martial law in Mindanao. She was removed as Supreme Court Justice in 2018 via a dubiously constitutional manoeuvre known as a *quo warranto* petition brought by Duterte's solicitor general and supported by a majority of pro-Duterte judges. It invalidated her appointment which dated to 2012. This piece of legal trickery avoided having to go through the difficult process of impeachment, hitherto the only way to remove a Supreme Court justice. It made a nonsense of the separation of executive and judiciary.

Another female critic, Ombudsman and a former Supreme Court Associate Justice, Conchita Carpio-Morales survived to the 2018 end of a term which had seen indictments against various senators including Enrile, senior officials of the Arroyo and Aquino governments and Noynoy himself, for abuse of power in the Mamasapano incident. After retiring, she remained outspoken on the drug killings and the administration's failure to defend the West Philippine Sea.

The legislature and judiciary offered little check on the president. As in the past, the majority of the House of Representatives flocked to the administration to ensure their districts' access to funds. For the first half of his term, the Senate was relatively well balanced with a strong Liberal Party representation, but that changed in 2019 when all nine candidates backed by Duterte won. They included hitherto less-known figures such as Christopher 'Bong' Go, a

FIGURE 9.1 *Rodrigo Duterte with outgoing national police chief dela Rosa, 2018.*
© *Getty Images.*

close aide from Davao, dela Rosa, Marcos' daughter Imee and movie star and
former senator Bong Revilla, indicted in 2014 for plunder in the Napoles
pork-barrel scandal but acquitted in 2018 – though he had to repay some
funds. Duterte's dominance of the Senate from 2019 made it conceivable that
he would press ahead with his plan for a federal constitution. However, even
after five years not much progress had been made in formulating a detailed
blueprint. The pandemic's priorities then pushed it aside.

Many wondered if Duterte would follow the Marcos route to martial law
and dissolution of the legislature. However, while it had been an obstacle for
Marcos, it was little restraint on Duterte's power. Nor was the Supreme
Court an obstacle. It had long been noted that justices were reluctant to
challenge administration decisions in general, and naturally sided with those
who appointed them. The turnover was quite high due to a retirement age
of seventy. Duterte was especially fortunate in timing. Aquino only appointed
four in his term, so the incoming president was able to make immediate
appointments as well as inheriting several from Arroyo's time who were
generally sympathetic. All significant decisions went Duterte's way including
allowing a hero's burial for Marcos, preventing the jailing of Senator de
Lima, not standing up against EJKs, and allowing Philippine withdrawal
from the International Criminal Court.

Most astonishing of all was the majority decision to remove Chief Justice
Sereno at the demand of the administration with a *quo warranto* petition.
Even by its own modest standards, this was an extraordinary submission
effectively showing that the court was not a separate branch of government.

Sereno was superseded in quick succession by three Arroyo appointees friendly to Duterte, Teresita de Castro and Lucas Bersamin, who on retirement from the bench became head of the Government Service Insurance System, and then Diosdado Peralta. The latter had made the Sandiganbayan decision to award 20 per cent of San Miguel shares to Danding Cojuangco rather than to the coconut farmers who had paid for it. One Arroyo appointee who did not fall in line with Duterte was Antonio Carpio who three times should have been Chief Justice. The man behind bringing China to The Hague opposed, among other votes, the sacking of Sereno and the jailing of de Lima. On retirement he became a beacon for liberals and the rule of law and for the defence of the West Philippine Sea.

In his first years in office, Duterte added to his popularity by notionally attacking corruption. A Presidential Anti-Corruption Commission was set up and later the departments of Public Works and Justice set up task forces to investigate particular allegations, but the broader impression, at least as judged by the Philippines' position on the Transparency International league table was that corruption increased having fallen under his predecessor. The pandemic was to see major scandals at the Department of Health and in procuring over-priced supplies through politically-connected agents. However, the broader impression, at least as judged by the Philippines' position on the Transparency International league table was that corruption increased under Duterte having fallen under his predecessor. Indeed, the pandemic was to see huge scandals at the Department of Health and in procuring over-priced supplies through politically-connected agents.

Duterte was also partly successful in attempts to silence independent media. His majority in the House voted to deprive the largest broadcasting network ABS-CBN to lose its television licence. Efforts to silence the independent on-line news outlet Rappler saw its founder and editor Maria Ressa sentenced for criminal libel. The suit was brought by a business associate of a mainland Chinese businessmen who donated to a drug rehabilitation centre to be built within Fort Magsaysay, the nation's biggest military base.

Freedom of the press to report without being threatened with charges ranging from tax evasion to criminal libel still had strong backing among the urban middle class, but the public remained broadly supportive of Duterte, whether because of a yearning for a strong leader, or having tired of the type of democracy which followed EDSA. Duterte's network excelled at keeping up a barrage of propaganda and fake news via social media. Even though his rule did not appear to have had better results than Noynoy's years, the belief in the leader remained strong even though the majority, as reflected in social surveys, were uneasy about the extent of the killings and also wanted a much tougher line with China. There was a broad popular belief that crime had declined thanks to the fear instilled by the police. There was indeed statistical evidence for this belief, at least in Manila, if the EJK killings were left out of the crime account. Small-time criminality was apparently reduced. However, the accuracy of official data was also an issue as governors sought to impress Duterte with their work.

Duterte's attack on ABS/CBN was more the result of a personal grudge against the Lopez family than any consistent anti-oligarch project. He had to retreat from a populist confrontation with the Ayalas and the Metro-Pacific group over their water companies when it became clear that the nation's international reputation for abiding by contracts was being questioned. Like Marcos, taking down a powerful family could be useful but there was scant broader attempt to change society. Indeed, there could not be as dynasty and oligarchy were so closely connected.

In any case, attacks on oligarchs would only impede the most constructive part of Duterte's agenda, his 'Build, Build, Build'. This was a fine slogan to focus on an obvious need for massive improvement in the nation's physical infrastructure. This had not been ignored by Aquino but his social programmes competed for budget priority. Big projects take time to be realized, particularly if they involve multilateral lenders or are public-private partnerships. Implementation was often slowed by land acquisition issues and shortages of technical personnel.

Duterte saw China as a source of money and implementation capacity which could spur a dramatic increase in construction. Reality proved rather different. Of one hundred key projects announced at the start of his term, it was unlikely that more than half would be completed by 2022. Chinese promises of grants and loans were slow to materialize and, in the case of the Kaliwa Dam project in Luzon, faced strong environmental opposition. Employment of Chinese labour by Chinese contractors was another obstacle. Sensitivity to a Chinese influx was increased by the boom in Chinese immigration to run the Philippine Offshore Gaming Operators (POGOs). Duterte's tilt to China did, however, spur Japan to make its own offers, including financing a $5 billion underground railway project for Manila. Other resources went towards repairing damaged infrastructure. Other rail projects in Luzon and one in Mindanao moved ahead but slowly.

Rivalry between airport projects, including a massive new one for Manila in Bulacan, the expansion of one at Sangley Point, and the upgrading of Clark Air Base and the existing the Ninoy Aquino International Airport (NAIA) caused delays to all of them. In short, until the onset of the 2020 pandemic, Duterte's administration continued the gradual increase in infrastructure investment begun under Aquino but there was no great leap forward. Indeed, in 2017 the Asian Development Bank made a $100 million loan to provide expertise in project preparation and implementation. Even Duterte's authoritarianism could not overcome the legal and political obstacles to quick execution. Capital formation as a percentage of GDP rose from 20.5 per cent in 2010 to 24.4 by 2016 and 26.4 per cent by 2019, but much of this was housing rather than supporting infrastructure. With government revenue as a percentage of GDP rising only modestly under Duterte, and defence outlays increasing rapidly, the big infrastructure projects were heavily dependent on the private sector and foreign money. The infrastructure development of the Philippines was on a gradual upward course until the pandemic changed objectives as well as capacity. The same applied to manufacturing to the extent that it remained partly underpinned by consumer demand flowing from remittances which continued to grow through 2019 before being abruptly checked, though remaining resilient.

Despite the 'Build, Build, Build' efforts, economic and fiscal policy remained largely unchanged. Finance Secretary Carlos Dominguez III combined being a Duterte classmate from Davao with long business experience and a ministerial post under Cory Aquino. Budget director Benjamin Diokno became governor of the Central Bank when the incumbent died. Diokno had been behind earlier tax reforms and headed the programme, Tax Reform for Acceleration and Inclusion (TRAIN) enacted in 2017. This provided for lower income tax rates but significantly higher consumption taxes. It was the first of several measures planned to raise government revenue to finance infrastructure. It caused a brief upswing in inflation but had the intended impact on revenues. Central Bank policy remained cautious and the peso fairly steady. The current account of the balance of payments slipped into deficit for the first time in several years but not by enough to cause alarm. Foreign currency reserves were stable, government borrowing at around 2 per cent of GDP was also sustainable without raising costs. Overall, this conservatism reassured a business community and middle class which might have been unnerved by Duterte's other words and actions. In spite of lockdowns and the generally slow legislative process, reforms pushed by economic ministers and business and backed by Duterte were headed for passage by the end of his term. These included the liberalization of the foreign investment and retail trade allowing majority foreign investment in new areas of infrastructure and services.

Another boost to revenues came from the POGOs. Whether they paid their full tax obligations was questionable but the POGOs brought foreign currency earnings and demand for office and residential space for the operators and thousands of support staff, Chinese and local. These for a while helped absorb supply from an office and condominium building boom. Together with continued gradual growth in BPO, the growth of the metropolitan middle class and malls catering to them made some districts of the capital appear modestly prosperous. The POGOs, however, faced challenges other than the pandemic. The entry of so many Chinese became a political issue while China itself began a crackdown on offshore gambling.

Duterte's enthusiasm for China was bolstered by his ties to mainland businessmen, as well as a dislike of the US. Distancing from the US was made easier once Donald Trump was in office, abandoning the Trans-Pacific Partnership which was supposed to cement US economic relations with east Asia and the Pacific. Trump's defence commitment to Asian allies was questioned and his policy towards China's appeared erratic. The two had much in common, given to self-obsession, crude language and unpredictable pronouncements. Trump had little problem with Duterte's drug killings or attacks on the media.

However, the China dream gradually faded as the term advanced. The decision to set aside the Court of Arbitration decision in the hope both of persuading Beijing to moderate its actions and attract Chinese money did not achieve the intended results. Money promises were slow to materialize, and China did not let up on its activities in the Philippine EEZ in the South China Sea.

Trump's policy towards China evolved into a more confrontational approach just as other countries in the region became more worried about China's ambitions. The Philippine military, never happy with anti-US tirades, leaned on him to backtrack from abandoning the Visiting Forces Agreement. At the operational level, contacts between US and Philippine forces remained close. Nationalists began to shift their attention from attacking collaboration with the US military to focus on China's threats.

Threats on the home front ensured that Duterte required the backing of the military, fostering his relationship with pay rises and an increase in numbers and spending on equipment. However, he also paid more attention to the police than the military. As a percentage of GDP, military spending remained close to 1 per cent, a very low figure given the internal and external challenges. The army continued to absorb 70 per cent of the individual service budget to address sporadic conflict with the NPA and some Muslim groups.

Duterte had begun his term looking to negotiate with the Communists, claiming leftist sympathies and past contact with JoMa Sison, known for quiet accommodation with the NPA in Davao, so long as it did not cause trouble in the city. He even initially brought some leftists into his government and appointed Jesus Dureza as peace envoy to talk to the NDF, but Dureza was fired in 2018 and Duterte announced the use of 'death squads' to counter the NPA 'sparrow' units to assassinate specific individuals. On and off talks continued for four years and many abortive cease-fires later nothing permanent had been achieved.

After a disastrous 2017, the situation in the Moro region took a turn for the better. That year had seen a five-month siege of Marawi City in Lanao del Sur. A military attempt to capture a leader of the Abu Sayyaf group, which had aligned itself with the international Islamic State (IS), led to the takeover of Marawi by Lanao's influential Maute group, a local jihadist group based around the Maute brothers. After months of ground action, bombing and artillery fire the rebels were killed or escaped but the centre of the city with its great mosque and university campus lay in ruins and its inhabitants made refugees.

The rebuilding of the city was to be a very slow process, but the Marawi tragedy probably speeded up implementation of the Comprehensive Agreement on Bangsamoro reached by the Aquino administration in 2014 but held up in Congress. Further delay seemed likely as Duterte toyed with

FIGURE 9.2 *Marawi City after the battle, 2017.* © *Getty Images.*

federalist issues. However, after Marawi, the Bangsamoro Organic Law (BOL), giving a significant degree of autonomy to the region, was passed in 2018, despite reservations about its constitutionality. The new Bangsamoro entity replacing the Autonomous Region of Muslim Mindanao (ARRM) came into being in February 2019. It was a messy construct as decisions on whether or not to join were made locally. Thus, Basilan opted in, except for its major city, Isabela. Cotabato province opted out, except for some barangays. The region thus comprises the provinces of Lanao del Sur, Maguindanao, Cotabato City, Sulu, Tawi-Tawi, Basilan (except Isabela City) and sixty-three barangays in six municipalities of Cotabato province. Small militant and/or kidnap groups continued to operate in some areas and security still rests with the national military and police. It was possible the Bangsamoro Autonomous Region in Muslim Mindanao (BARMM) might establish its own military but like many aspects of its organization and powers much remained to be seen. Overall, the situation by late 2021 was more peaceful than it had been for many years but many obstacles to development remained.

The last two years of Duterte's presidency were dominated by the pandemic. Although blame for what, at least by the standards of its Asian neighbours, was a disastrous outcome did not fall on Duterte in particular, but it did show up the weakness of the Philippine state and the low quality of many of Duterte's political appointees to important ministries and operational departments – not least a chaotic and overburdened Department of Health. Duterte's own inclinations added to the problems of the pandemic.

His instinct was for controls and lockdowns over testing and tracing. The country was very late in acquiring vaccines – and Duterte's seeming preference for China's Sinovac rather than Western ones. The severity of lockdowns in 2020 caused the economy to shrink 7 per cent, far higher than elsewhere in southeast Asia, and brought particular hardship to the millions in the informal sector. The lockdowns were no more successful in curbing the virus than less stringent ones in Indonesia. The Philippines also kept its schools closed for longer than almost any country. There was, however, only a small fall in remittances in 2020 and a substantial rise in 2021, further underlining dependence on labour export.

The disastrous GDP performance in 2020 was followed by recovery of only about 5 per cent in 2021 due to renewed lockdowns. Meanwhile, the government debt burden was expected to rise 11.6 trillion pesos in July 2021 from 9.6 trillion a year earlier, despite the efforts of a conservative fiscal policy team to restrain spending. Given the low debt level in 2019, the rise was not especially alarming, particularly as only one-third was in foreign currency. However, the speed of the rise showed the compounding cost of lockdowns.

Duterte took his style of government from Davao to Manila, but the nation was a more complicated place and he had little time for details or issues other than a few such as the drug war. On those details he expected immediate obedience. Cabinet meetings were largely irrelevant and ministerial access to the president was difficult. Competent ministers could get on with their jobs but incompetents often stayed in place if they were unquestionably loyal. Appointments were weighted towards associates from Davao, and to retired generals, men accustomed to following orders.[3] In Philippine politics, as elsewhere, friends and benefactors were rewarded with positions and deals, but Duterte raised this to a level well above that of his predecessor. He behaved as one seeing himself as above the law, ruling from a bully pulpit.

However, even he could hit limits. The pandemic saw the Commission on Audit questioning the spending of billions of pesos allocated for Covid protection given to a newly established company linked to a mainland Chinese friend, Michael Yang. The funds bypassed the Department of Health and were administered by an office in the Department of Management and Budget run by an individual with links to the president. Duterte railed against the Commission but some senators previously protective of Duterte wanted an investigation. Whatever the truth of the matter, the senators' reaction suggested that Duterte's personal power was finally waning as the end of his term neared and politicians and businessmen began to place bets on the succession.

As the 2022 election loomed, Duterte saw a need to protect himself from prosecution should the opposition win. Initially he chose to run for vice-president while various presidential hopefuls came into the frame: Sara Duterte, Leni Robredo, Ferdinand (Bongbong) Marcos Jr., perennial candidate Panfilo Lacson, Manila mayor Francisco Domagoso, better known as Isko Moreno, a media figure before entering Manila local politics, and the one grass roots candidate, champion boxer Manny Pacquiao. Duterte himself proposed his long time faithful aide, Bong Go. But in a bewildering series of shifts and feints Duterte opted for a senate seat, and then decided not to run at all. Meanwhile in a surprise move Sara Duterte agreed to opt for the vice-presidential race supporting Marcos for president. Go quietly left the contest. Quite who choreographed this dance was not clear as Duterte had been publicly dismissive of Bongbong's abilities and character but this team suits him well, with former disgraced presidents Estrada and Arroyo also supporting the alliance. It was a huge challenge for leading opposition candidate Robredo and her running mate Liberal party senator Francis Pangilinan. The weight of money and on-line propaganda appeared to favour Marcos who appeared successful in re-writing the history of his father's rule among a population mostly too young to remember the reality and more attuned to social media than to established news providers.

Much appeared to depend on whether Lacson, Pacquiao and Domagoso stayed in the race splitting the anti-Marcos/Duterte vote – though Pacquiao could take votes away from the alliance in his native Mindanao. All three had once been, to varying degrees, supportive of Duterte. In the face of this, much also depended on whether Robredo's reputation for a cool head, liberal ideas and sympathetic personality could galvanize mass support as Cory Aquino had done but without the same level of the name recognition which counts so much in Philippines elections. But the nation has a record of sudden shifts in sentiment, and of other election-time surprises.

Notes

1 Statista, 2020.
2 Synthetic Drugs in Southeast Asia: UN Office on Drugs and Crime, 2021.
3 Sui Generis, Marites Vitug in Rappler, 30 August 2021.

Region I
(Ilocos Region)

**Ilocos
Norte**

★ *Laoag*

• *Batac*

Vigan ★

**Ilocos
Sur**

• *Candon*

La Union

★
San Fernando

Alaminos

• *Dagupan*

Lingayen ★

• *Urdaneta*

• *San Carlos*

Pangasinan

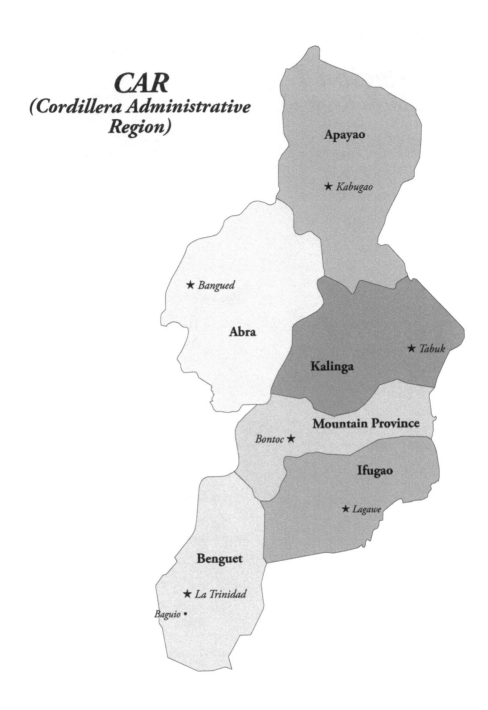

CAR
(Cordillera Administrative Region)

Apayao

★ *Kabugao*

★ *Bangued*

Abra

★ *Tabuk*

Kalinga

Mountain Province

Bontoc ★

Ifugao

★ *Lagawe*

Benguet

★ *La Trinidad*

Baguio •

Region II
(Cagayan Valley)

Batanes

Basco ★

Cagayan

★ *Tuguegarao*

Isabela

★ *Ilagan*

• *Cauayan*

• *Santiago*

Bayombong
★

★ *Cabarroguis*

Nueva Vizcaya

Quirino

Region III
(Central Luzon)

Aurora

San Jose •

Muñoz •

★ Baler

Tarlac

Nueva Ecija

Tarlac City ★

★ Palayan

•
Cabanatuan

Iba ★

• Gapan

Zambales

• Mabalacat

Angeles •

Bulacan

★ San Fernando

Olongapo City

Pampanga

★ Malolos

• San Jose
del Monte

Meycauayan •

★ Balanga

Bataan

NCR
(National Capital Region)

Caloocan
North

Navotas

Valenzuela

Malabon

Quezon City

Caloocan

Marikina

★ Manila

San Juan

Mandaluyong

Pasig

Manila

Pateros

Pasay

Taguig

Parañaque

Las Piñas

Muntinlupa

Region IV-A
(CALABARZON)

Rizal
★ Antipolo

Cavite City
• Bacoor
★ Imus
General Trias•
Dasmariñas •
Trece Martires•
• San Pedro
• Biñan
• Santa Rosa
• Cabuyao
• Calamba

• Lipa

Santa Cruz
★

Laguna

Cavite

Tagaytay

Santo Tomas •
• San Pablo
• Tayabas

Lipa •
★ Lucena

Batangas

★ Batanga City

Quezon

Region V
(Bicol Region)

Camarines Norte

Daet ★

Camarines Sur

Catanduanes

Naga •
Pili ★

Virac ★

• *Iriga*

• *Tabacco*

Ligao • **Albay**

Legazpi City ★

Sorsogon City ★

Sorsogon

Masbate City ★

Masbate

MIMAROPA

Mamburao ★   Calapan ★   Boac ★ Marinduque

Occidental Mindoro   **Oriental Mindoro**   Romblon ★

Romblon

Palawan

★ Puerto Prinsesa

Region VI
(Western Visayas)

Aklan

★ *Kalibo*

★
Roxas

Capiz

Passi •

Antique

Iloilo

Victorias • *Cadiz* • • *Sagay*

Silay •

Escalante •

Kalibo ★

• *Talisay*

Iloilo City ★

★ *Bacolod*

Jordan ★

Bago •

Guimaras

• *San Carlos*

• *La Carlota*

**Negros
Occidental**

Himamaylan •

Kabankalan •

Sipalay •

Region VII
(Central Visayas)

• Bogo

• Danao

Cebu City ★

Toledo •   • Mandaue

Canlaon •   Talisay •   • Lapu-Lapu
            • Naga

• Guihulngan   • Carcar

Cebu

Bohol

**Negros
Oriental**

★ Tagbilaran

• Bais

Bayawan •   • Tanjay

Dumaguete ★

Siquijor
★
Siquijor

Region VIII
(Eastern Visayas)

Catarman ★

Northern Samar

Calbayog •

Eastern
Samar

Samar

★ Catbalogan

Biliran
★ Naval

★ Borongan

Tacloban ★

Ormoc•

Leyte

Baybay •

Southern
Leyte

Maasin ★

10

'Imperial' Manila's weak grip

Governance in the Philippines pivots around the question of whether the centre has too much or too little power. Is the Manila-based bureaucracy and control over most revenues distorting the economy and leading to the dominance of the National Capital Region and its immediately surrounding provinces resulting in neglect of development in far flung Mindanao, Samar, Cagayan Valley etc? Or are problems more related to a devolved political system with often small provinces under the control of local dynasts and other vested interests able to override weak Manila-based ministries? At present, the country has a unitary administrative system but weak implementation, as it lacks a strong centralized civil service. Budget allocations are distorted by the politics and the pork barrelling of the legislators, diverting funds to political campaigns and wasteful projects.

President Duterte came to power with rhetoric about ending the dominance of 'imperial Manila' and promising a shift to a federal system of government, but five years later little progress was apparent in either political or administrative de-centralization. Federalism has also sometimes been caught up in the issue of whether the country should shift from a presidential to a parliamentary political system. There is also debate on what sort of federal system would be best. Should it have four major easily identified components, Luzon, the Visayas, Mindanao and BARMM? Or should components be smaller, similar to the seventeen regions used by the centre for administrative purposes but currently – (except for BARMM) – lacking a political base or revenue raising powers.

Debate on how best to manage a geographically fragmented country goes back a long way. Jose Rizal himself once wrote:

When they once shake off the yoke, the tendency of countries which have been tyrannized over ... by a law of reaction the Islands will probably declare themselves a federal republic.[1]

That text has often been taken to show that national hero Rizal himself favoured a federal system though his wish to develop Tagalog as the national language implied centralism. Nonetheless, the federalist idea has been in the wings ever since the birth of nationalism, in part encouraged by the examples of the US and others. It was revived most recently by President Duterte, but acting on it was another matter. A promise of a plebiscite by 2018 went unfulfilled but it will not go away as the struggle continues between those wanting to accommodate diversity and those who fear it would weaken the national identity and the role of the national language.

Manila's dominance lies not so much in its position as capital but in its history, its port, its location in Central Luzon, the most densely populated part of the nation. It is less dominant than Bangkok is in Thailand. Nor has it been growing faster than some other port cities including Cebu and also the much newer Davao and Cagayan de Oro, where higher value-added service industries have begun to supplement their trading roles. The revolutionaries against Spain favoured a centralist and presidential system. However, the actual system which emerged from the US conquest and was carried on through the Commonwealth era to independence and again in the post-Marcos era was a curious hybrid. On the one hand, the governor, then president, wielded wide executive power and the centre controlled almost all taxing and spending. On the other hand, political power was significantly de-centralized. Early on, the Americans had sought to be seen to be ruling through a form of representative government, however narrow the franchise. This, as we have seen (in Chapter 3) assured the local power of major landowners and their economic interests. These same interests went to capture most of the seats in the House of Representatives as the franchise was enlarged while districts were quite small.

Following their own de-centralized system and reliance on local initiatives, the Americans did not create a strong, elite institutionalized civil service as the British did in places as different as India and Hong Kong. In Thailand in the late nineteenth century, King Chulalongkorn used an elite of civil servants and army to centralize a once loose-knit kingdom. Even under democratic regimes, provincial governors and districts were appointees of the central bureaucracy – the Ministry of the Interior. Nor did the Philippines have the equivalent of Indonesia's military under President Suharto. He used the prestige the army had acquired in the war for independence to project central power, one language and the supremacy of nation over regions and religions.

With martial law, President Marcos might have sought to follow the example of Suharto. Indeed, he did make an initial effort to reduce the power of local dynasts and disarm their militias, but Marcos was a lawyer not a military man, the army lacked status and was too pre-occupied with Moro and NPA rebels to run the civil administration. His 1973 martial law era constitution did, however, further centralize power not merely by expanding that of the president but by moving to a single chamber legislature, the Batasang Pambansa, with six-year terms for both president and legislature. This legislature was to be primarily elected on a regional basis rather than by district or province. It began with the prime minister as chief executive, no vice-president and an element of a parliamentary system appointed by and answerable to the Batasang. This was subsequently changed back to a system where the president was chief executive and the position of vice-president was restored. The system was created by Marcos for his own purposes and abandoned after his fall, but elements of it continued to have appeal. Its replacement, the 1987 Constitution, was similar to the pre-1973 one except for replacing two four-year terms for the presidency with a single six-year one. The House and the Senate were much the same as before.

The 1987 Constitution was intended to promote 'maximum decentralization short of federalization'. It was imprecise about decentralization of public finances, merely referring to 'just shares' and allowing local taxation subject to rules made by Congress. It also provided for significant devolution of functions and to enable this a 1991 law saw allocation of 40 per cent of the Bureau of Internal Revenue collection go to local government units (LGUs). This was further allocated by a complex formula to 23 per cent for provinces and cities, 34 per cent for municipalities and 20 per cent for barangays. The law also set rules for taxes on property, mining and other local economic activity.

However, these allocations were generally inadequate to fulfil the de-centralized obligations thrust on LGUs. This was especially so for smaller units resulting in a rapid increase in the number of cities. Creation of new provinces in response to local interests further complicated the delivery of services. Increases in local taxes to bolster health and education spending was possible, notably from property and mining, but this was not popular with the wealthier classes who would mainly have to pay them. As it was, government spending in the Philippines was not only already more de-centralized than in Thailand but even federal Malaysia and Australia.

In the Philippines, the decision-making power of the executive was centralized, the administrative sinews needed for implementation were weak. So, too, was the justice system, a mix of Spanish and US influences. In principle, it was centralized with all judges, including those at the lowest level, the Municipal Trial Courts, chosen by Manila. In practice, however, local politics played a role in the choice of judges. The reputation of the court system for corruption and delay was a further obstacle to administrative efficacy.

Discussion of federalism has long been impeded by the assumption that it requires a change in the constitution. That in turn raises fears of presidents trying to perpetuate themselves by changing to a parliamentary system or allowing two terms. The existing constitution allows for autonomous zones in Muslim regions – the ARRM predates 1987 – and the Cordillera, home to various indigenous groups in northern Luzon. However, Cordillera autonomy has never happened thanks to a lack of unity. It remains possible within the constitution for Congress to grant more administrative and fiscal power to all regions or provinces. However, even if desirable in principle there are fears that perpetuate, even strengthen, dynastic dominance. Would it spread national wealth better, or simply increase divisions between the city hubs and the resource rich areas on the one hand and the rest of the country on the other?

There was an argument that the Philippines needed more centralization, not less. The gap between policy made in Manila and its implementation was partly due to the inadequacies of central ministries but also to the small size, politicization and frequent corruption of local government units. Regional councils could collect data, advise and make plans which cover provinces and cities, but they have no decision-making or implementing authority. Whilst there has, naturally, been a desire by the members of the House to see an increase in LGU funding by Manila, there have been differing views on whether local spending power is more or less productive.

The existing regions have been a starting point for discussing the federal system, but are seventeen regions (including the BARMM and Cordillera) too many? Or too few – Sulu for example wanted its own, separate from the BARMM? Or was division by geography not in keeping with any real sense of identity? The existing regions are also imbalanced with the contiguous National Capital Region, Central Luzon and Calabarzon (Southern Tagalog) all far more populous than others. As of 2015 Calabarzon, had a population of 14 million, Caraga 3 million.

Little of the discussion on federalism has got to grips with the issues of indigenous peoples (IPs) or *lumads* as they are known in Mindanao. The need for protection of their land and language rights has long been accepted in principle but in practice remains subject to erosion and conflict. They are too numerous to be ignored but too disparate to make into coherent units as the failure to establish autonomy for the Cordillera has shown. Despite the fact that, with the exception of the pre-Austronesian groups, they are no more or less indigenous than the average rice farmer from Tarlac. Yet the IPs are often treated as inferior citizens, lacking the 'civilization' of those more impacted by the centuries of colonial rule. In effect, they are subject to abuse with their schools 'red-tagged', communal lands seized by settlers and plantation owners, and their leaders accused of supporting the NPA. Alternatively, they may be subject to well-meaning paternalism by earnest NGOs which emphasizes their differences not their similarities to the wider population. The use of English in education and official documents also diminishes the role of the national language and hence the identity of regional languages whether widespread like Cebuano or confined to small IP communities.

The basic argument for federalism is that the Philippines' fragmented geography made centralization costly and inefficient. It was unresponsive to differing local needs and was a dampener on local initiatives and was unable to harness regional pride in a country where a sense of regional identity was strong – as senate elections also showed. It limited competition between regions and held up resource development.

Against that, others have argued:

- There is insufficient administrative capacity to make a success of regional rule.
- Unless accompanied by a parliamentary system, regions could be taken over by existing dynasties expanding their power bases from province to region. Dynasticism would be an even bigger problem than today.
- Even with an equalization system to benefit poor regions, federalism would increase income disparities.
- The progress of the national language would be delayed if most of Mindanao and the Visayas adopted Cebuano.

At the very least these arguments suggest that if there is to be federalism, a smaller number of entities would be preferable, but very large entities – for example, all Visayas or all Mindanao minus the BARMM – would raise fears of separatism.

The most detailed and coherent arguments for a federal system were put forward early this century by Jose Abueva, political scientist and former president of the University of the Philippines. He coupled federalism with a change to a parliamentary system which, he argued, would force the development of a party system and enable government based on a balance of interests rather than electing celebrities or being unable to remove corrupt or incompetent leaders other than via People Power. Others noted that in parliamentary systems, authoritarian figures could emerge, such as Lee Kuan Yew in Singapore or Thaksin Shinawatra in Thailand, but they built parties first rather than relying on celebrity or family name to get elected, as has been the case with directly elected presidents in the Philippines. Abueva's federal model drew from those of Australia, India and Germany, all parliamentary systems.

He envisaged the creation of eleven states which would have power over agriculture, the environment, police and justice, public works and social welfare, but statehood would not be automatic, each state having first to show a capacity for administration. The states would have unicameral parliaments which would elect a governor and vice-governor. A career civil service structure would be created at both federal and state levels to ensure professionalism and continuity in administration.[2]

In recent times, the first specific federalist proposal from a leading politician was made in 2008 by the then Senator Aquilino Pimentel for eleven states plus Bangsamoro, the Cordillera and two Federal Administrative regions, one for Manila, the other for a Sulu (Bangsa Sug) plus the Sabah claim. Some government functions would be moved from Manila to state capitals. The proposal by Pimentel, himself from Cagayan de Oro, got some support, although he did not suggest a parliamentary system. The Senate would be enlarged to eighty-seven members with six per state and for

Manila, and nine for overseas Filipinos. National revenues would be split 80 per cent to the states and 20 per cent to the national government.

Once elected, Duterte's first step towards federalism came with an executive order for a panel to study amendments to the 1987 constitution relating to the powers of the various levels of government. Meanwhile, a different formula was proposed by others in addition to Pimentel. The proposal of the Constitutional Committee which reported in 2018 was far reaching. The core of it was to divide the nation into eighteen regions – similar to today – which would include the existing Bangsamoro and one for the Cordillera encompassing seven provinces plus Baguio City. The Bangsamoro Organic Law would become part of the constitution. Each would be entitled to 50 per cent of national revenue from income, value-added and excise taxes, and be able to levy its own taxes on property, vehicles etc. and retain not less than 60 per cent of the revenue from local mineral resources. Each would have a hierarchy of courts but final decisions would rest with federal ones. Each region would elect two senators but only 60 per cent of a 400-member House of Representatives would be elected by districts, the remainder by Party Lists. Members of both houses would serve four-year terms but be re-electable only once. Likewise, president and vice-president were permitted two four-year terms but needed to be on a single ticket. Other proposals were for including the West Philippine Sea and the Philippine Rise as well as Sabah in the patrimony. It proposed removing some constitutional restrictions on foreign investment giving Congress greater freedom to enact laws for specific sectors. However, there was little popular enthusiasm for change, the Senate being disinclined to take it up and Duterte appeared to lose enthusiasm for it.

Yet debate over the presidential system will not go away. A parliamentary system may yet have appeal in the event of reaction against strongman presidents such as Duterte and Marcos. It was only narrowly defeated in the decisions of the 1986 Constitutional Commission which led to the 1987 constitution. Promoters claim it would make parties stronger and limit the abuse of patronage as illustrated by the Liberal Party's loss of eighty of the 130 seats won in the 2016 election as members switched parties in return for largesse. To attract local politicians, parties need patronage. Otherwise, the elected will coalesce around the supporters of the president. Being elected to the House is already of apparently diminishing value as indicated by the declining number of candidates. The cost is too high relative to the rewards, even allowing for distribution of pork. Many dynasts have deserted district elections in favour of a party list seat – where they occupied forty-nine out of sixty-one seats after the 2019 election.[3] The domination of dynasts at every government level remains a roadblock to modernization of the economy. Yet only the dynasts can pass the laws they are supposed, under the constitution, to enact to end this system of family competition for the spoils of office.

Agreeing a formula for federalism is formidable enough, even more so when linked to other moves, whether to a parliamentary system or changes in term limits. The interests of 340 members of the locally-elected Representatives differ from those of the twenty-four nationally-elected Senators. Arguments will go on, backed by differing theories and interest groups but meanwhile they can seem irrelevant to the social and economic problems facing the country which have long been identified but for which remedies have been slow to arrive. Democracy flourishes but within the limits defined by an outdated social structure.

Notes

1 Jose Rizal, *Filipinos dentro cien anos,* Barcelona: La Solidaridad, 1889.
2 Jose V. Abueva, *Towards a Federal Republic of the Philippines with a Parliamentary Government*, Marikina: Centre for Social Policy and Governance, Kalayaan College, 2005.
3 Manuel L. Quezon III, 'An Epidemic of Clans', *Philippine Inquirer*, 9 June 2021.

11

Lost advantage

Governing systems are a means to an end. On that basis, the Philippines must wonder about its system and about responsibility for its relative decline in human development relative to most of its neighbours. By the standards of most of south and southeast Asia, the Philippines, under US tutelage, had an early start in mass primary education. By 2019 it reportedly had the highest literacy rate in southeast Asia, with females aged between fifteen and twenty-four at the top with 98.9 per cent and overall literacy at 98.1, according to UN data.

However, that achievement hides less flattering data on the standards of education. A survey by the Programme for International Student Assessment in 2018 found that the Philippines ranked last in reading among seventy-nine countries assessed and second last in maths and science.[1] The survey found that at Grade 4 only 19 per cent of children reached even the 'low intermediate' benchmark.[2] It follows that the average level for subsequent grades remains low. This reflects underlying problems with both the quantity and quality of education. A 2018 Asian Development Bank (ADB) report related the overall education system quality slightly above that of Thailand but below Indonesia. It was below Thailand, Indonesia and Pakistan in the quality of its science and research institutions, weak in university/industry collaboration and in overall creative output. In global assessments, 80 per cent fell below minimum proficiency levels for their grade, and 72 per cent of fifteen-year-olds were low achievers in reading, maths and science.[3]

At least as indicated by government spending, education has relatively low national priority, accounting in 2020 for about 16 per cent of government spending. Total national spending on primary and secondary education was at no more than 3 per cent of GDP, less than other countries in the region including Indonesia and well behind Malaysia, China, Thailand and Vietnam although the Philippines has a larger population percentage of school age.[4] Government spending did rise quite fast from a low point in 2005, with more classrooms and books. The year 2017 finally saw the increase in the number of years of secondary education from four to six. One year in kindergarten before five years of primary school also became compulsory. However, the implementation of the system is weak and the quality of education is variable. Despite the need for more and better teachers, employment growth in education over the decade to 2020 was lower than in any sector except agriculture. The Covid pandemic also revealed the lack of facilities for on-line learning. There was no face-to-face schooling at all for much of 2020 and 2021, and distance learning materials then provided were hard to follow. Schools remained closed much longer than in most Asian countries. The World Bank estimated that Learning Adjusted Years of Schooling (a measure of actual learning not just years in school) would fall from an already modest 7.5 years to between 5.7 and 6.1 years.

There are several reasons for poor performance even before the pandemic but they start not in the classroom but with malnutrition. About 30 per cent of children under five are stunted,[5] and others thin for their height, while others are overweight. The early cease of breast feeding, inadequate intake of vegetables, protein, iodine and vitamins are all involved. Some progress was made in the years immediately before the Covid pandemic but low incomes and poor eating habits continue to undermine nutrition.[6]

The conditional cash transfer programme (see Chapter 8) has endeavoured to address both education and health issues by rewarding those who keep their children in school, getting them vaccinated and giving them mineral supplements, but although very popular with both politicians and international agencies these have had mixed results. Addressing widespread malnutrition, stunting, high maternal mortality rates and low educational attainment requires more than selective interventions.

Although six years of primary school has long been compulsory, it starts later than in many countries and many do not fully complete it due to factors including poverty and remote location. Rural Mindanao and Eastern Visayas have especially high drop-out rates. Private primary schools usually start a year earlier and have a seven-year system which subsequently puts pupils at a significant advantage. Overall in 2018, 87 per cent completed primary education but only 39 per cent in the ARMM. Some children start primary school late or finish early due to the need to look after younger siblings. Men from poor households are more likely to drop out of school than women.

Deep divisions in school achievement reflect the social and income inequalities reflected in the different standards between public and private schools and the minimal amount of support for tertiary education for poorer families. Many on the left see low budget support for education by the government as quite deliberate on the part of the elite-dominated political system. Education has also failed to keep up with a changing world with many tertiary graduates finding themselves ill-equipped for the skilled labour market. Links between business and the school system are weak.

Some see overall low standards of education reflected in politics being more about personalities and dynastic jousts than policies, now exacerbated by the near universal penetration of social media. Readership of newspapers has always been low and though there is considerable creative writing in both English and Filipino (and a little in other local languages) sales of books other than textbooks are modest. Rizal had urged that liberty was conditional on the education of the people but, noted one modern commentator: 'Rizal's misfortune is that he left great volumes of literary works and letters to a nation that does not read. Because Filipinos do not read, our country does not progress as a reflective society'.[7]

Language is also an issue at both primary and secondary school levels and for reading in general. For the first two years at government schools, instruction is in the relevant local language, Filipino and English are also taught. Then it switches to a mix of Filipino and English. Although most pupils have a basic understanding of both languages, for many, fluency in reading and writing is inadequate for good exam performance and discourages further learning.

Overall, about 70 per cent of youth attend secondary schools but many do not complete even a four-year course, and fewer the six years. Some schools are focused on technical, job-oriented training; a few, science-oriented, have entry exams. Private schools, which mostly have entrance exams, account for about 20 per cent of secondary pupils, their schools and class sizes are mostly smaller. The student-teacher ratio in government schools is high at about 40:1 in primary and 30:1 in secondary. Teachers are poorly paid and are called upon to do other government duties. Expansion of education has not been matched by an improvement in quality due to inadequate teaching standards caused by poor teacher-training. According to the World Bank, 12.8 years of schooling in the country is equal to just 8.4 years in schools with high standards. Showing its unwillingness to admit the depth of problems, the government leaned on the Asian Development Bank Institute to remove mild criticisms in a research paper which made it clear that raising educational standards should be a 'matter of national priority' and that the system 'has much room for quality improvement'.[8]

There has been progress in gender parity. Already in 2016, the ratio of girls to boys in secondary was 1.2 and in tertiary 1.3. However, the benefits of gender equality are eroded by the much lower female labour force participation rate – 47 to 48 per cent in recent years – as well as migration by many. Women are very well represented in the professions and government jobs, but less so in private business. They account for about 30 per cent of members of Congress, relatively high by regional standards. Comparatively, too, women are less likely to face violence in the home and are generally less subject to gender bias than women in most developing countries.

In principle, the move to six years secondary school education should be improving the standard of tertiary education. There is a remarkable number of post-secondary institutions – more than 1,600 – and 112 chartered universities. Some universities and colleges are state-financed, the biggest being the University of the Philippines at Diliman in Manila. Leading state universities include Mindanao State University, whose main campus in in Marawi, and the Polytechnic University of the Philippines in Manila. There are also a large number of other state and local government institutions mostly focused on specific subjects and vocational training, but despite its size and importance, this group of public colleges have a budget only about 10 per cent of that of the Department of Education which is responsible for state primary and secondary schools. As a result, public universities and colleges charge significant tuition fees and provide little support for living expenses.

Much tertiary education is privately operated, some being non-profit, others profit-driven. Several leading universities have their roots in Catholic religious orders, the well-known Ateneo de Manila being Jesuit in origin, the oldest, Santo Tomas, established by Dominicans in 1611, and de la Salle. In Dumaguete, Silliman University was originally Protestant but is now non-denominational. Others include the University of the East and Far Eastern University. All universities are more or less selective depending both on reputation and location, taking students on a number of factors in addition to academic performance. In general terms, even the best Philippine universities rank only in the middle of international league tables even though such tables tend to be biased towards English-language institutions. In a 2020 ranking, only the University of the Philippines and Ateneo appeared in the top 500 globally.

Medical education is of a high standard but many doctors and nurses migrate. Nurses' training has seen a boom and bust, with 37,000 passing the exam in 2009 but only 12,000 in 2019 as the market became saturated. Likewise, although there were about 130,000 registered doctors in 2020 only about 43,000 were in practice in the Philippines.[9] Money to recruit more nurses is scarce. At 12.5 nurses and midwives per 10,000 population the Philippines lags behind Indonesia and is far behind Thailand. Doctors are very scarce – 3.9 per 10,000 people overall, ranging from 10.6 in the National Capital Region (NCR) to 2.1 in Caraga and 0.9 in the then ARMM (2017 data quoted in The Philippine Health System Review, WHO, 2018).

The system has generated enough information technology and literacy skills to enable the BPO industry to keep growing but this is concentrated in a few urban locations and does not reflect the general level of skills or their application to industry and agriculture. A 2021 report by the Asian Development Bank noted that although there was awareness of the need for more and better technical and vocational training to improve productivity and keep up with changes in technology, much needed to be done. In particular, it needed to build on the increase in schooling years to twelve. The government's Technical Education and Skills Development Authority (TESDA) regulates training courses but its role and resources were limited and its collaboration with the Department of Education and the Commission on Higher Education was weak. Investment in technical and vocational training – and particularly in teachers of it – was an economically viable alternative to more spending on higher education.[10] The lack of priority for education was illustrated by the diversion in 2021 of TESDA funds to Duterte's anti-insurgency fund.

The numbers taking technical courses was increasing, said the ADB, but too many courses no longer led to employment or skills taught were out of date. There was an actual decline in communications skills. The study noted that though BPO- and IT-related employment had risen fast, employing 1.8 million in 2018, lower-end jobs in these fields were vulnerable to technological change. There has been progress. The percentage of employment in industry classified as low-tech has fallen to 60 per cent from 66 per cent in 2000 but higher skills are going mostly into service industry supported directly or indirectly by remittances and BPO.

Lack of skills, combined with the poor employment growth in the manufacturing sector, has meant that in 2018, 52 per cent of the total workforce was in informal (and mostly very low income) employment. Although an improvement on 57 per cent in 2010, it is still a number which reflects the relationship of poverty to educational opportunity. Although joblessness is a problem, a much bigger one is the minimal incomes earned by so many from a full day's work. It also explains why years of apparently strong GDP growth have made little if any dent in the poverty levels. The better educated move to get better jobs and have fewer children, and so the cycle continues. A gradual decline in the fertility rate will help reduce inequalities over time but education needs a much bigger share of the budget than it currently receives.

It is much the same story with health where shortage and unequal distribution of funds lies behind the continued prevalence of diseases such as tuberculosis, and inadequate response to dengue and HIV.[11] Maternal

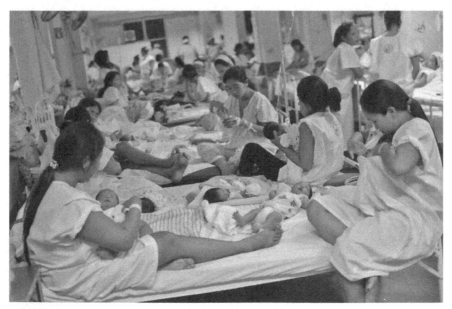

FIGURE 11.1 *The pressures of maternity on hospitals.* © *Getty Images.*

and neonatal mortality rates remain a cause for concern as is stunting among children. Although 90 per cent have access to safe drinking water and 70 per cent to modern sanitation, disease incidence is high among the rural poor who also have the most children and vaccination rates (pre-Covid) well short of targets. Suspicion of vaccines is a problem to which politicians have contributed but the bottom line is that LGU are underfunded and often too small to implement programmes effectively. Failure to vaccinate all has meant that measles and diphtheria cases still occur and while steady progress has been made in reducing maternal and neonatal deaths and communicable diseases including TB have fallen, there has been a steady rise in diabetes, heart, lung and vascular diseases caused by poor diet, obesity and smoking.

Although the percentage of government spending on health has been rising, the administrative arm, PhilHealth, has been wracked by several scandals including payments for operations which never took place. There is also said to be an unhealthy relationship – as in some other countries – between doctors and the pharmaceutical industry, with branded products being substituted for cheap generics by pharmacies. Recent years have seen some effort to improve the health infrastructure with more hospitals and clinics. There are now about as many public as private hospital beds but heavily skewed to the more developed regions. The NCR has three times the number of beds per million as the rest of the nation. Almost all middle- and upper-income women deliver their babies at health facilities but only 57 per cent of the poorest do so.

Total health spending is around 4.7 per cent of GDP but 65 per cent of this is in the private sector, beyond the reach of many. Health represents only 8 per cent of government spending and health infrastructure in rural areas is often quite inadequate to deliver basic care. The net result is that the overall health outcome in the country is now at the same level as Indonesia, which was once far behind. The two now have the same overall life expectancy – seventy-one years – and the same position (107) on the 2020 Human Development Index. The proportion of government spending on health is little over half that of Thailand. The best health care is as good as in most developed countries, but the average is poor, albeit slowly improving. The gap between top and bottom is exceptionally wide with what the World Bank called a 'silent pandemic' of undernutrition leading to the Philippines' low score of 0.52 on the Human Capital Index, indicating that the future productivity of today's children is barely half its potential with proper nutrition and education. Undernutrition among children has barely improved in thirty years.[12] Meanwhile, those overweight and obese have climbed to 37 per cent of adults according to a 2020 report of the Nutrition Research Institute due to calorie-rich but nutrient-poor diets. Most of the Millennium Development goals saw improvement in health, child and maternal mortality, years of schooling, incidence of HIV, malaria and tuberculosis, but the rate of improvement was weak by Asia-wide comparison.

Decades of failure to address the issue of population growth is part of the reason behind the failures in education and health. Blame is normally laid at the door of the Catholic Church opposition to birth control, but also to blame were the elites who used such methods themselves but mostly made little effort to enable lower income groups to access contraceptives. Too many young mouths to feed is only part of the story of enduring poverty and inequality. The fertility rate has been steadily declining and the years from 2015 to 2020 saw a particularly sharp drop from 3.0 per women of fertile age to 2.4, partly in response to the Reproductive Health legislation, but it is expected to remain above 2.0 until at least 2040. So, while the long-term future for a stabilizing but not elderly population is bright, the medium term shows the population, 112 million in 2021 and still growing at over 1 per cent a year, is expected to reach 142 million by 2040. The median age in 2020 was only twenty-six. Given such a youthful population, the problems of education and health could well be considered many times more important than those of drugs and insurgency.

Notes

1   Organization for Economic Cooperation and Development, Programme for Interntional Student Assessment, Report for 2008.

2   *Philippine Daily Inquirer*, 27 December 2020.

3   Basic Education in the Philippines, World Bank, 1 July 2021.

4   United Nations, Human Development Report, 2020.

5   United Nations Children's Fund (UNICEF), Situation Analysis for Children in the Philippines, 2018.

6   Undernutrition in the Philippines, World Bank, 15 June 2021.

7   Rado Gatchalian, 'For a More Enlightened Nation, Let's Read Rizal', *Philippine Daily Inquirer*, 24 June 2021.

8   Pacifico Veremundo in *Philippine Daily Inquirer*, 3 September 2021.

9   Department of Health, Philippines.

10   *Technical and Vocational Education and Training in the Philippines in the Age of Industry 4.0,* ADB March 2021.

11   WHO/Asiapacific Observatory on Health System, *The Philippine Health System Review*, 2018.

12   'Undernutrition in the Philippines', World Bank, 15 June 2012.

12

The root of poverty

For two decades the country's quite impressive GDP growth has been propped up by two factors which have everything to do with labour and very little with capital: remittances from workers overseas and the business process outsourcing and related internet-based activities. Both have thrived on individual and small firm initiative and the zeal of companies overseas to take advantage of the supply of cheap English speakers with basic on-line skills.

Meanwhile, the weakest part of the Philippine economy is the most fundamental: agriculture. Absorbing 22 per cent of the workforce it now accounts for only 8 per cent of the economy, displaced more by services than industry. The problem lies in its very modest growth of productivity and the high cost of much of its output. This in turn is a burden on the farmers, all food consumers, and on the government. In 2019, 34 per cent of farmers and fishermen were deemed poor, compared with 22 per cent for the population overall.

Rural poverty is most prevalent among corn and coconut farmers but is widespread in a seemingly self-perpetuating cycle of large families, small incomes, low educational levels and poor health. Over the twenty years to 2019 productivity rose only 32 per cent compared with 73 per cent in Vietnam and 50 per cent in Indonesia.[1] Or to it put another way, productivity has barely kept pace with population growth in a country with little potential to expand its agricultural land. Between 2016 and 2019, annual output increase fell to 1.3 per cent. There has been a slow drift from the land to the city and to overseas employment so manpower productivity has improved, but land productivity is far below its potential while food prices are mostly higher than in neighbouring countries. Reasons for this include protectionism, the dwindling size of farms, a lack of investment, wrongly targeted government programmes, poor transport and the high cost of fertilizers and seeds. Despite talk of improving food security, the 2021 budget for the Department of Agriculture was just 1.5 per cent of the total government budget.

Rice has suffered from most of these ills. There has long been a belief that the country should be self-sufficient in rice, although in reality it has been imported for most of the past 120 years. Policies focused on keeping out cheaper foreign rice with quantitative restrictions and throwing much of the Department of Agriculture's budget at input subsidies and irrigation for rice production. Rice gets almost half the budget though it is only 18 per cent of production by value yet consumers pay almost twice what Vietnamese pay for it.

Partial reform came in 2019 with the Rice Tariffication Act which replaced restrictions with tariffs – 35 per cent for rice from ASEAN countries and 50 per cent from elsewhere. Yet the tariff illustrates the degree of protection required to give even those with irrigated land a reasonable living. Rain-fed rice farmers are even worse off. The replacement of quantitative restrictions with tariffs saw a small reduction in acreage but the underlying trend remained with production around 12 million tons and imports of 2 million tons. The high local price of rice flows through to the whole economy and particularly hurts the urban poor who spend most of their meagre incomes on food. Undernutrition is prevalent because so many households cannot afford sufficient foods in addition to rice. A 2021 World Bank report noted that a healthy diet cost sixty-eight pesos a day compared with actual spending of only forty-eight pesos.

Another big issue is the small size of farms, due to land reform combined with population growth. There has been limited progress in increasing farm size via cooperatives and leasing arrangements. Land ownership and the demand for land reform have been a major political and social issue since independence. Combining policies which promote consolidation while pushing on with implementation of the Comprehensive Agrarian Reform Programme (CARP) has been problematic. CARP has been difficult enough to implement for many reasons, including landowner opposition, local politics, disputes on land pricing and between potential beneficiaries. Its goals of social justice, reducing poverty and increasing productivity have not always been mutually compatible. Another issue is a peasant preference for security over productivity, attachment to the family farm and the subsistence ethic. Many who have become part of the urban proletariat maintain an interest in a small piece of family land as security, however tiny. This understandable attitude holds up farm consolidation and investment in replanting or new crops. Another obstacle to consolidation is complicated kinship links.

Corn, the nation's second most important crop, has been politically less sensitive than rice because now – though not in the past – it is mainly for animal feed. Grown mainly in Mindanao and the Cagayan Valley, production nearly doubled from 4.4 million tons in 2002 to 8.2 million tons in 2020 by use of improved seed. Even so, although it receives the same high tariff protection as rice, production is insufficient to meet all domestic demand of about 9 million tons. Total grain imports have been rising steadily with population growth and increased feed needs for poultry and pigs, and consumer demand for wheat products. The principal import is wheat, over

5 million tons, costing around $1.7 billion with approximately half being used for milling and half for feed.

Coconuts tell another dismal story. Although coconut oil, copra and related products have long been the largest agricultural export by value, output at around 14 million tons was almost static in the decade to 2020 and export values were variable, particularly when facing competition from palm oil from Indonesia and Malaysia. Coconuts have some advantages over palm for growers. They are easily inter-planted with other crops, have a long life and good resistance to typhoon winds. A high percentage of Philippine trees, however, are old with an average yield of only forty-three nuts per tree. The cost of replanting with new varieties, with yields four or five times greater and increases in production, could readily be absorbed by increasing biodiesel requirements and supplanting palm oil imports. Of an estimated 3.5 million hectares planted to coconuts, only 2 million is of higher yielding varieties. The industry was ravaged in the Marcos years by the coconut levy (see Chapter 6) which was supposed to help development but actually was a source of cash for politicians. In 2021, recovered funds of 70 billion pesos became subject to the Coconut Farmers and Industry Trust Act with wide powers over its disposal, though there were fears that it would become either another pork barrel or swallowed up in the national budget. A fragmented industry which provides livelihoods for 4 million often very poor farmers mainly in Zamboanga, Bicol and Eastern Visayas regions is not easily modernized without much more government help. Conversion of some of the land to oil palm may also benefit small holders as is the case for Thailand.

A better story has been provided by less traditional exports, notably fruit. Bananas are the second largest export crop. Production in 2019 was at 9.2 million tons of which almost one third, valued at $1.9 billion, was exported. Mindanao accounts for about 90 per cent of output and the Davao region alone for some 60 per cent. The industry is highly organized with a few large plantation companies such as Dole and Del Monte, and numerous smaller growers linked to them by contracts. However, there is a taste gap between the higher-yield, large Cavendish bananas, which are the bulk of exports, and other types preferred by the local market. In most years, the Philippines has been the world's second largest exporter with Japan, China and Korea the major markets. The industry has been criticized as an environmentally-damaging monoculture but it is expected to continue expanding its acreage in Mindanao and, according to the UN's Food and Agriculture Organization FAO, output is set to rise by an average 1.5 per cent a year.

Pineapple has been another steady growth story. The nation is the world's largest grower, again focused on Mindanao, with output headed to the 3 million ton mark and the second largest exporter with sales close to $200 million, mostly to Japan, Korea and China, but tropical fruit exporting is highly competitive so staying at the top is not easy.

Philippine mangoes have long been noted for their flavour and exports boomed in the 1990s but in recent years both production and exports have levelled off, productivity and the market has become more competitive. Links between growing, packing and exporting can be problematic as this is a delicate fruit with short shelf life and needs to meet high phylo-sanitary standards, especially in Japan. The Philippine market share has been in decline as Thailand and India have become the leading Asian exporters, and Indonesia also became a player in this market. Philippine annual exports have struggled to reach the $100 million mark.

The Davao region produces excellent durian but only in around 2019 did growers start looking to export into a fast growing market, particularly in China. So far the Philippines is a tiny player compared to Thailand and Malaysia but offers bright prospects for those who can wait for new trees to bear fruit and have a supply chain to get the fruit to market quickly.

Sugar, once the lead Philippine export, has for some years seen an annual deficit with output in 2019 at 2.1 million tons and net imports of about 300,000 tons. This is despite a sugar price far above the world price. Imports would be higher still but for a tax discriminating against high fructose corn syrup. The industry itself, particularly in its Negros heartland, has a long history of conflict between *hacenderos* and their seasonal workers and tenants. There are some 65,000 farms of which 80 per cent are less than five hectares in size. The industry as a whole directly employs about 700,000 people. Overall yields are low but especially so for the small farms where they average only five tons per hectare compared with 7.3 tons for those over 100 hectares.[2] Many farms are too small or hilly or closely planted to enable mechanization, even if the owners had capital to invest in machines. Poor rates of recovery of sugar from cane during milling are another problem.

Coffee, too, is a product which was once an export but is now mostly imported. Local production accounts for only about a quarter of annual demand of 170,000 tons and growing. Similar failures have been seen with other tree crops. The Philippines imports around $1 billion a year of palm oil, itself producing only about 100,000 tons or less than 10 per cent of demand. Output has been static for ten years partly due to opposition from *lumad* communities and NGOs protecting what is left of the forests. Areas of forest which had earlier been cut down for logging were not replanted to oil palm. Nor has there been any development similar to Thailand where there has been a huge increase in palm oil production with smallholders replacing old coconut and rubber trees with oil palms. In the Philippines, rubber too has stagnated with production averaging about 425,000 tons over the past decade.

Less noticed as consumer staples other than rice, corn and sugar are the root crops, principally cassava, sweet potatoes and taro. They are lowly regarded but a lifeline for millions, particularly farmers with poor soils and in hilly country. They need relatively little attention and are resistant to drought. Cassava is grown almost everywhere, whether as a diet staple or for the market. About one third of the annual output of around 2.6 million tons is for human consumption, one third for animal feed and one third for industrial use. Despite a high calorific content, little effort has been put into encouraging growth and use, so production has been almost static for several years while Thailand has developed a large industry which links small farms in its dry northeast region to production and export of chips or cattle feed and starch powder. Sweet potatoes are also widely grown in the Philippines and are a part of ordinary diets as well as animal feed but at around 500,000 tons a year production is modest compared with Vietnam and Indonesia.

With seas all around and several freshwater lakes totalling about 200,000 hectares, the Philippines has long been a fish-eating and exporting nation, but fish has been declining as a proportion of the national diet as the population expands and the sea becomes over-exploited. Fishing still provides a direct livelihood for an estimated 1.5 million people but they have the highest rate of poverty. The sector contributes just 1.2 per cent to the GDP and only 16 per cent of the agriculture, fishery and forestry sector. In 2019, marine caught fish accounted for less than 50 per cent of total aquatic production of 4.4 million tons. With aquaculture expanding by an average of 2 per cent in recent years, the sea catch has been at best static. More than half the aquaculture tonnage is accounted for by seaweed not fish and represents only 10 per cent of the output value.[3] The principal farmed fish are tilapia and milkfish (bangus).

Commercial vessels whose biggest single catch is skipjack tuna, have seen a decline while coastal fishing by small boats has been nearly static. Although exports were still $472 million in 2018,[4] they have fallen and overfishing threatens future catches. Indonesia has also been a keen competitor, particularly in the Sulawesi Sea. The Philippines' access to its EEZ in the South China Sea has been limited by China. The brightest part of the sector has been seaweed exported in dried form or processed into carrageenin. Exports of it were worth in $207 million in 2018, making it the second largest export from the aquatic sector after tuna.

The country was once a major exporter of prawns but disease and management issues caused it to lose its position to Vietnam and other southeast Asian producers, although there was still export of $43 million. Other seafood exports in 2018 added another $200 million but that year the Philippines also imported fish (including prawn feed) of $672 million so that without the seaweed, net fish exports would be small. The future of fisheries thus lies mainly in the development of farmed fish, perhaps including tuna. However, more investment and improved technology have been seen as essential given that most aquaculture is currently a small scale family activity. Thus, it provides employment but returns are low given the levels of productivity and the cost of feed.

All told, farming and fishing fall far short, not only of their potential but of the productivity of their neighbours. This in turn results in high prices which reduce demand for non-food products and makes Philippine labour much less competitive and the country less able to attract the manufacturing investment which has gone to Vietnam, Thailand and elsewhere. This then increases national reliance on the export of labour and on remittances. The weakness of the sector is the root of many of the nation's economic and social problems. Fragmented geography and the shortage of flat land are particular obstacles but they do not explain lower productivity and are only a partial cause of poor commercialization of crops. Inadequate infrastructure has been a problem for all industries, not just agriculture, so big increases in infrastructure spending in recent years will bring rewards, but the problems of the sector are more complex than money.

The problems lie in political and social issues many of which cannot readily be addressed by the government in Manila. At the local level, politically connected groups protect private interests at the expense of wider ones while NGOs representing environmental and indigenous land rights also inhibit changes, good and bad. Costs of power and things such as fertilizer add to costs both of production and processing. Land ownership is often seen through a socio-political rather than economic lens. Nonetheless, much more could be done to raise productivity with education, the extension of services and if budget resources were directed away from rice to crops for which the country has a comparative advantage.

Some of the same issues affecting agriculture also impact the development of mineral resources. Back in the 1970s, mining stocks were the largest sector of the stock exchange. Atlas Mining's Toledo mine in Cebu was the largest copper mine in east Asia; other big names included Lepanto, Philex, Marcopper and Benguet. By 2019, mining's contribution was just 0.7 per cent of the GDP and 6 per cent of exports, primarily gold and nickel. By value, gold accounted for 41 per cent, nickel sulphides for 21 per cent, nickel ore for 18 per cent and copper for 19 per cent. The mining industry has itself to blame for bad management and a record of environmental disasters. Atlas suspended production in 1994 as a result of low prices and flooding issues before resuming on a diminished scale in 2008. The collapse of Marcopper's tailings dam on Marinduque Island in 1996 contaminated rivers and fields with toxic waste and forced many people to move. Philex Mining's long-established copper and gold operation at in Benguet had an even bigger tailings dam failure in 2012, though it was not toxic. There have been several other lesser episodes and numerous cases of illegal mining being accompanied by pollution and de-forestation. With only three localities – Surigao, Palawan and Benguet – having significant mining activity there has been scant political support for an industry with such a poor reputation. Mines are also depleting assets which will sooner or later be closed and already have weak linkages to local economies.

Despite such obstacles, output of nickel increased seven fold between 2008 and 2015, and has continued to at a high if fluctuating level. The government became more supportive, pushing new projects held up by environmental issues and made a plan to sell off to the private sector closed mines which it had earlier acquired via defaults on loans by government-owned banks. These included a huge nickel deposit at Surigao on Nonoc Island. Surigao is also the location of another huge nickel deposit, at Siangan, but so far, its owner, Philex Mining, needs to raise a billion dollars to develop it. Another big project awaiting approval and in need of upwards of $1 billion investment is the Kingking gold orebody in Davao de Oro, a project of the Villar group.

Typical of the problems of new mine development was the Tampakan deposit in South Cotabato. This 2.9 billion ton ore resource of 0.5 per cent copper and 0.19 per cent gold has been the subject of detailed development proposals involving local investors and major international miners since 1994. The expectation that it would finally get underway in 2020 was dashed when, noting the surge in gold prices, the local Tampakan government deemed its agreement with the developer, Sagittarius Mines, unfair. Not all projects suffer this fate as procedures now enable indigenous group involvement. The Balabag gold and silver project in Zamboanga del Sur, backed by the Villar group and the Canadian mining company TVI, has an agreement with the Subanon people.

Less likely to expand is coal. In 2017, the Department of Energy published a blueprint for coal production to rise from around 15 million tons a year to 52 million by 2022 and 282 million by 2040.[5] This was fanciful nonsense. Although there was a theoretical resource potential of 2.3 billion tons,[6] mineable reserves were currently only 450 million, almost half on Semirara, a small island between Panay and Mindoro. Semirara mining accounts for almost all current production. Other exploitable deposits are in Cotabato and the Cagayan Valley. There seemed a strong case for coal development as coal imports rose steadily reaching 28 million tons in 2019 because of the reliance on coal-fired power, accounting for about 52 per cent of output. However, dependence on coal came under increasing attack from environmental interests, and any new mines were seen as unlikely to be competitive with Indonesian ones. The government has made a commitment to gradually phase out coal-fired power stations.

Looking at mining as a whole, land disputes, environmental objections, NPA activities and the presence of many small illegal miners were also obstacles that projects regularly faced. There was a reaction against mine operators who long got away with abysmal standards. Aquino imposed a moratorium on new mining permits and Duterte banned new open pit mines. Mining became more closely scrutinized by the Department of Environment and Natural Resources after Regina Lopez, acting minister early in President Duterte's administration, sent shock waves through the industry by closing many mines. Most were reopened but Lopez left a new benchmark for environmental concerns.

Although the country has many mining companies, none of them are large by international standards and their technical resources and limited. Nickel Asia is the biggest with mines in Surigao and Palawan but there are small producers including illegal outfits protected by local interests and shipping ore direct to China. Principal shareholders in the bigger companies mostly have diverse interests in sectors such as property development and retailing so they limit their financial commitments to the long-term commitment needed in mining. Thus, the industry's mix of fragmentation, local and national political rivalries, social conflicts, weak government oversight, corruption, tax evasion and interminable legal disputes are a microcosm of national problems.

Hydrocarbons have been a different story. Although oil deposits have been known in Cebu since the 1890s there was no production until the Alegria oil field went into production in 2018. However, it is a modest operation at no more than 200 barrels a day. There has been little onshore drilling because of the complexity of the geology. Offshore held more promise and the discovery of the El Nido and Matinloc gas fields on the shelf west of Palawan raised hope for further offshore riches. These two fields produced some 40 million barrels over forty years but were exhausted by 2019 and closed. Meanwhile, high expectations for the Recto (Reed) Bank further west have been stymied by Chinese claims and interference with exploration

The only offshore production remaining was gas from the Malampaya deposit northwest of Palawan. Discovered and operated by Shell, it is in 820 metres of water and its reservoir 2,300 metres below the seabed. Producing some 12 million cubic metres a day, delivered by a 500-kilometre pipe to power plants in Batangas it fuelled approximately 20 per cent of the national power supply for several years. However, it was being rapidly depleted so that soon after 2022 the country would need to be importing LNG.

Projects in wind and solar energy began to take off by 2020 as new coal projects were shelved in the face of environmental concerns, falling prices of renewables and opportunities for pump storage facilities. Eventually, the nation may be able to bring down energy costs closer to those of its neighbours but geographical fragmentation will remain an obstacle and base load power will remain hydrocarbon dependent for the foreseeable future. Meanwhile power prices continue to contribute to the weak state of the industrial economy.

Notes

1 *Transforming Philippine Agriculture*, World Bank, June 2020.
2 US Department of Agriculture, Philippine Sugar Annual Report, April 2020.
3 *Fisheries Statistics of the Philippines 2016–2018,* Philippine Statistics Authority, 2019.
4 *Philippine Fisheries Profile 2018*, Philippine Department of Agriculture, 2019.
5 Road Map for Coal, 2017–2040, Department of Energy, Philippines, 2017.
6 Philippine Department of Energy, December 2019.

13

An unempowered economy

A second marker of unbalanced economic growth is low power consumption, both effect and cause of other problems. It reflects the modest level both of industrialization and of household uses of power-consuming durable goods. A contributory factor is the relatively high price of power which has regularly been higher than almost everywhere else in Asia apart from Japan, and notably higher than in Thailand, Vietnam, Taiwan and Korea. It has also fluctuated significantly in accordance with imported coal prices and of Malampaya gas, whose price is linked to oil.

Power production and distribution is a three-tier system consisting of private generating companies which to some degree compete on price and feed into the National Grid, a government owned but privately operated network with separate grids for Luzon, Visayas and Mindanao. The operator is owned by local tycoons Henry Sy and Robert Coyiuto and the State Grid Corporation of China with a 40 per cent share.

End user distribution is by private franchise holders, the largest of which is Meralco for Manila and most of the adjacent provinces. In many areas, distribution is by local cooperatives. In addition, there are various areas outside the grid which have local power stations some owned by the State such as the National Power Corporation (NPC). The NPC is also the industry regulator and runs geothermal and hydro plants.

Power is expensive partly because most fuel is imported and faces import duties, value added tax at 12 per cent, plus other government charges such as the Missionary Electrification Charge to subsidize off-grid generation in remote areas. There are also still some costs associated with high-cost deals to rush new capacity after a supply crisis in the 1990s and take-or-pay contracts. Malampaya gas is especially expensive and used for much base load production in Luzon. While wholesale power prices fluctuate, overall prices are largely set by cost-plus arrangements between suppliers and distributors. Competition exists but is limited despite rules which restrict any one supplier to 30 per cent of one grid and 25 per cent of the whole grid supply.

Over the two decades to 2019 capacity grew at double digit rates so that from a shortage in the 1990s, supply reached a modest level of excess over reserve capacity. Gas from the Malampaya field was an initial driver but growth thereafter was mainly provided by new coal-fired stations. However, given the relatively high contribution of service industries, demand growth from 2018 to 2040 was forecast by the Department of Energy at 5 per cent a year, or less than GDP. Indeed, the department may have significantly understated growth in demand as 2021 saw rolling brownouts (voltage cuts and load reduction) in Luzon even while the economy was weak because of the pandemic.

With fading hopes to find new offshore gas fields without compromising sovereignty, security of supply required the building of LNG terminals to import gas as Malampaya phased out and projects were in the pipeline in 2020. The other crucial issue was whether, in the face of climate change acknowledged as a threat to the nation, effort would be put into renewables not coal. The country had a good record in developing geothermal resources and hydropower but these were necessarily small projects. Wind farms and solar power both had great potential and attractive feed-in-tariffs encouraged small-scale investments. Gradually lowering costs were expected to make them become truly competitive and scaled up to become the supplier of most future demand, but they also needed more organization and capital than base load coal generation. The need for either gas or renewables on a large scale was underlined in 2020 with the decision not to allow any more large coal fired plants though San Miguel's Global Power Holdings had 3,000 MW of projects on the drawing board. A lead in renewable energy was taken by the Ayala group company, AC Energy. Although owning large coal plants, its future focus is on wind, solar and geothermal, also investing in wind in Indonesia and Vietnam and geothermal energy in Indonesia. A 20 billion peso capital injection from Singapore's Government Investment Corporation in 2021 gave it 17.5 per cent of AC Energy. There was on and off talk of reviving the 600 MW Bataan nuclear plant which was completed in 1986 but it never operated due to the fear generated by the Chernobyl disaster in Ukraine, along with its alleged vulnerability to earthquakes and associations with Marcos-era corruption. Although maintained, putting it to work would be costly and doubtless arouse environmental opposition.

Power consumption as a percent of GDP is expected to decline marginally. Nonetheless, the power sector has long been a major and gradually increasing contributor to the industrial sector of the economy while that sector overall has declined from 39 per cent of GDP in 1983 to 30 per cent in 2019. The power industry helped compensate for the declining role of manufacturing from a peak of 26.6 per cent in 1973 to 18.5 per cent in 2019.

That statistic alone says much about the outsize role that services have played in economic growth and the relative failure of manufacturing to follow the path of other eastern Asia developing economies. Thailand, for example, went from 21 per cent manufacturing in 1980 to 32 per cent in 2010, before declining to 25 per cent in 2019. In Korea, it went from 17 per cent in 1970 to 28 per cent in 2011 and was still at 25 per cent in 2019.

Likewise, the key components of manufacturing in the Philippines reflect its domestic orientation. In 2018, food and beverage industries accounted for 37 per cent of manufacturing, little of which was exported. The transport sector has lagged especially far behind due to the past failure of automotive industries to become competitive with its ASEAN neighbours. The Duterte administration launched a Manufacturing Resurgence Programme and Toyota and Mitsubishi Motors cooperated to focus on specific models which might be exportable, but in 2021 there was still a long way to go.

The textile and garment industries were once key exporters, but both have suffered relative decline though they still employ some 600,000 workers. Yarn and textiles have suffered from inadequate investment, rising power prices and smuggling, so the garment industry is a major importer of fabrics. The local garment industry also suffered from the import of second-hand garments while exports have not been helped by child and other labour issues. Exports were worth $906 million in 2019, a fraction of those of Vietnam and Indonesia.

Even the special skills associated with traditional fine fabrics made of pina (pineapple), ramie and jusi (abaca) fibres have not been well exploited particularly given that in the nineteenth century, garments of pina and jusi in particular were given as presents to royalty. Although garments, such as the Barong Tagalog are often worn at formal occasions, the fabric has made little headway internationally. Indeed, in the Philippines, barongs are now made of ramie, polyester, cotton or mixes with silk. The pineapple was introduced to the country by the Spanish who brought it from South America but the indigenous skills for making jusi were adapted for the pineapple, with its finer though less durable fibre.

The Philippines remains the premier producer of abaca, the toughest of natural fibres. Although heavy-duty abaca ropes have mostly been replaced by synthetics, abaca is still a significant export but most demand is for pulp used in specialized paper making and heavy-duty textiles. Production increased only slightly, to 72,000 tons worth about $100 million, in the decade to 2019 though now with the environmental reaction against plastics, abaca has renewed potential.

Electronics remains important in gross export terms and employment, but the import content is very high and the value added locally quite low and linkages to other parts of the economy are weak. Internationally, competitive manufacturing has not been helped by wages in the formal sector which have long been out of proportion compared to the informal sector, elevated by the high price of rice and electricity. Labour is more organized than among competitors and technical skills are more variable. These issues add to the geographical disadvantage that even Central Luzon faces relative to, for example, the Eastern seaboard of Thailand or Saigon.

However, one industry which once carried high hopes and where geography is more an asset than a liability is shipbuilding. The country has many small shipyards doing repair work and building small craft. The arrival of foreign investors with shipbuilding projects in Cebu, Batangas and Subic Bay suggested a great future for a labour-intensive industry. In 2018, the Philippines became the fourth largest ship exporters by gross tonnage. However, disaster struck with the closure of its biggest yard, at Subic, just a year after the launch of three 20,000 TEU container ships, as well as oil tankers. (TEU is twenty foot equivalent units, a standard measurement for containers.) The yard was owned by Hanjin of Korea and inaugurated in 2007. It employed about 20,000 and had been delivering about twelve ships a year but it collapsed under the weight of debt of about $1.3 billion, despite tax breaks and cheap power provided by the government. Other reasons for the collapse of the company included labour management and issues for a company used to dealing with Korean levels of discipline and skills. The huge foreclosed yard was expected to find some new uses but broader hopes for shipbuilding were dashed by what was the nation's largest bankruptcy and industrial failure. Shipbuilding output collapsed from an average of 1.5 million gross tons in 2014–18 to just 400,000 in 2019.

Some ship exporting industries survived and prospered. Tsuneishi Heavy Industries of Japan employed directly or indirectly some 10,000 at Balamban in western Cebu, building and repairing bulk carriers. Also at Balamban, Austal, an Australian company, built smaller, higher value, specialized craft such as ferries and patrol boats. Neither company has experienced the labour issues faced in Subic. The Singapore-based Keppel group has a yard in Batangas which has been in operation since the 1970s, building supply ships, rigs, dredges and other specialized craft as well as carrying out repair work.

Although inter-island shipping is big business and Filipino sailors on foreign ships are a major source of remittances, the industry has failed to develop its potential. Trained skilled and semi-skilled seamen are abundant thanks to local training programmes but a relatively small proportion of the total become masters or chief engineers. One reason is that local shipping companies with international routes or ownership are almost non-existent while some ship-owning countries required a percentage of their own nationals in the senior positions. Philippine shipping companies remained almost entirely focused on inter-island and coastal trade.

Cement output has been rising steadily but not by enough to meet even faster rising housing and infrastructure projects so in 2019, 15 per cent of demand was met by imports. Local production is dominated by Holcim Philippines, a unit of foreign giants LafargeHolcim, Cemex of Mexico and the San Miguel group through Eagle Cement. A planned purchase of Holcim by San Miguel was stopped by the Philippine Competition Commission in 2020.

The star of Philippine manufacturing appears, at first glance, to be semi-conductors and electronic equipment. With steady growth over thirty years, by 2019 exports reached $30 billion and the industry employed, directly and indirectly, more than 3 million people.[1] It has thus been of critical importance in both foreign trade and employment. The largest segment is semiconductor assembly but there are also many international firms in computer, consumer and automotive electronics and telecoms businesses, including familiar names such as Toshiba and Samsung.

However, though local skills have been more than adequate for printed circuit packaging and device assembly there has been only a small amount of local entrepreneurship in product design and innovation. The industry's attempts to go up-market and up-stream largely stalled so that component imports were about 80 per cent of output, leaving net value-added in the country at around $8 billion. Thus, despite its importance, the industry also reflects deeper problems such as food costs, infrastructure development, bureaucracy and lack of commitment of big local capital to enter new and internationally competitive industries. The industry's concentration in the provinces around Manila also further strengthened Central Luzon's economic dominance.

Better spread geographically is the nation's largest manufacturing sector, food and beverage. For many years up to 2019 it grew at a slightly higher rate than the economy and became an ever-larger portion of the manufacturing sector, with gross output of about $36 billion in 2019, and accounting for about 40 per cent of manufacturing's contribution to GDP. It is characterized by a few giant companies and a large number of small operations. Growth has been driven not only by population and urbanization but also a shift to prepared and packaged foods among all income groups. There is relatively little export other than of beverages, notably rum, and a significant reliance on imports of wheat, meat, milk products and soybeans, with the US the largest source.

The industry's major players include the San Miguel group which in addition to a dominant position in beer brewing, includes Magnolia, the largest dairy product and fresh meat company, PureFoods, which dominates processed meats and San Miguel Milling in flour. JG Summit's Universal Robina has a vast range of packaged foods and beverages as well as producing chickens, hogs and animal feedstuffs. Foreign brand names are also to the fore, including Nestle, Nissin, Dole, Coca-Cola and Lotte Chilsung.

Likewise, food retailing is divided between myriad small shops (sari-sari stores) and wet markets as well as a few giants, principally the SM Group, Robinsons, Puregold and 7-Eleven convenience stores. Fast food chains are ubiquitous, but the names are more diversified than their ownership. They are headed by the home-grown giant Jollibee which also owns two other locally originated brands, Chowking and Greenwich Pizza. There are many McDonald's, Kentucky Fried Chicken and Shakey's and other foreign brands but mostly controlled by big franchisees. In the big cities at least, independent family restaurants are less evident than in neighbouring countries.

All developing economies cannot follow the same industrialization path. The Philippines has some geographical problems that its neighbours lack in terms of export manufacturing, but it failed to achieve scale in industries ones such as textiles and garments where it had a head start. Then there's the forty years of false starts in the auto sector despite the opportunities for scale production of components provided by ASEAN agreements. Policy, institutional and corporate failures all played a role. In turn this weakness slowed the growth of wage-earning in the urban areas and hence to reliance on low-income informal jobs.

Over the past two decades, the BPO sector has to a large extent compensated for this in major urban areas, while the remittance flows from overseas Filipinos have relieved poverty more broadly. However, the weakness of the industrial infrastructure will be more apparent if those two sources falter. Reasons for the weakness can be found partly in government policies varying from high protection to incompetent state intervention to free markets, though with exclusions for foreigners. Business has often been focused on investments with shorter returns or on securing oligopoly and keeping out foreign competition. While socialist Vietnam and China opened themselves to foreign capital, the Philippines dragged its feet. Meanwhile, the service and retail sectors benefitting from the remittance boom dominated the capitalist economy more than ever before.

Unorganized labour has been exploited and organized labour sometimes proved awkward and relatively costly. The BPO and remittances made for a strong exchange rate which has penalized manufacturing, which was also hurt by large-scale smuggling enabled by corrupt officials and politicians. The weak agricultural sector kept rural incomes and hence demand for manufactures low. Poor physical infrastructure raised costs.

On the brighter side, the BPO and the related software industry can continue to grow provided it can continue to raise its skills levels. Tourism, post the pandemic, still has much potential even if shorn of the offshore gambling industry which provided a huge boost to the Manila office and apartment rental industry in 2017–19 until reined in by China. For a few pre-Covid years (2015–19) formal employment was rising at 4.6 per cent a year, albeit it from a low base. If it can regain momentum at a time when workforce growth is beginning to slow, the post-Covid decade could see a resumption of formal job creation and a reversal of the trend of the past so that the nation can become less reliant on the export of labour for economic growth. Given the poor state of education, that means industries which can provide regular employment for low- and medium-skilled workers in manufacturing and construction, not just higher skill service jobs. Otherwise, the nation will have to continue to see salvation from those with most initiative – the ones who leave.

Note

1 EETASIA.com, 2019.

14

Beyond the Bayan

Economic and social failures combine with demography to create the issue for which Filipino people are world-renowned – migration. Of all the populous nations of the world which rely heavily on migrant remittances – Bangladesh, Egypt, Mexico, etc. – none equals the Philippines either in its contribution to GDP (9 per cent) or in the diversity of its migrants or the range of the locations where they make their livings. Even the range of their occupations may come as a surprise to those overseas who may tend to identify them with specific occupations such as domestic helper or seafarer.

There are indeed plenty – 20–25 per cent each – in both of those categories but at least until the pandemic, the world had witnessed nearly five decades of steady expansion in both numbers and locations. By 2019, the total employed overseas and on ships had reached about 2 million. In addition, there has been a steady stream of permanent migrants, mostly to the US and Canada but also to Australia, and, more recently, Japan, the United Kingdom, Italy and other European countries. The US community has been growing steadily for decades and now totals some 4.1 million, roughly half migrants and half locally born. There are about 1.6 million in California though at 13 per cent, Hawaii has the highest percentage of the state population, partly reflecting the migration of agricultural workers in the 1930s (see Chapter 3). The established communities of settled migrants in high income countries have been as important a source of remittances as those of the OFWs on contracts. Permanent migrants also on average have higher qualifications than OFWs. Although their links to the motherland may gradually weaken, higher incomes ensure continuing large scale financial support.

In 2019, there were approximately 2.2 million OFWs according to official estimates[1] – and probably also at least 100,000 undocumented ones. However, these are only a minority among a Filipino diaspora now totalling about 10 million, reflecting a surge in permanent migration since 1980, mostly to developed Western countries. The OFWs come from all over the country but primarily from relatively well-off regions such as Calabarzon, Central Luzon and Ilocos in Luzon, from Western Visayas more than poor Eastern Visayas, and in Mindanao from Davao and Soccsksargen not Caraga or Zamboanga. A partial exception to the low contribution of poor regions to the OFW tally has been the BARMM because of Islamic State's links to Saudi Arabia and the Gulf. Regions providing most OFWs tend to have better education and higher awareness of opportunities, with some localities having traditions of migration dating to the 1970s and 1980s.

Women accounted for 56 per cent of the total and were younger on average than the men, but men predominated among those over forty. There were even bigger gaps between the types of employment with 62 per cent of women in elementary occupations (mostly household) compared with 10 per cent for men, mainly in skilled and semi-skilled work. The proportion of professionals (mostly nursing) was higher for women at 9.8 per cent compared to men at 8.5 per cent. Sales and services accounted for 7 per cent of both sexes.

The pandemic led to redundancy for hundreds of thousands of migrant workers. Low oil prices and travel restrictions cut into employment opportunities. These were likely to be temporary but there were indications of demand reaching a peak in Singapore, Hong Kong and the Middle East, though quite likely offset by demand from other countries in east Asia. However, despite challenges in 2020, remittances were sustained almost at the 2019 level and rose in 2021, a tribute to the efforts of overseas Filipinos to sustain help for their families back home.

Average remittances per worker (as reported by a survey not by the Central Bank) in 2020 were 106,000 pesos (approx. $2,200) mostly remitted through banks or money transfer agencies, plus cash brought home and transfers in kind of goods such as electronic equipment. Amounts per person were roughly similar from the Middle East and East and Southeast Asia but 40–100 per cent higher from America, Europe and Australia reflecting the higher qualifications generally required. However, although remittances through formal channels were roughly stable there was a fall-off in cash and remittances in kind due to travel restrictions.

The benefits to the local economy of these injections of foreign exchange and contribution to household incomes have been clear enough. Millions of families now and over the past few decades have been kept above the poverty level by remittances, and in many cases enabled building of houses, the acquisition of consumer durables and paying for schooling and medical bills. However, the pattern of migration in terms of geography and educational level also suggests that income gaps have increased with the poorest classes and regions benefiting least.

The overall social impact has been hard to measure and to some extent controversial. Families are split up as one parent moves abroad. In many cases children are left to be looked after by grandparents, aunts etc. The benefits of money for better schooling may be lost by emotional deprivation. Separation of parents may lead one or both to new liaisons. Flow of remittances may make those who stay behind reluctant to work hard themselves. There is no lack of tales of men using remittance money for beer rather than school books or medicines.

However, Philippine society being child-friendly and with extensive kinship relationships reaching to both maternal and paternal sides has shown itself able to adjust well to one or both parents being away. Nor is there much shame in finding new relationships when old ones fade or partners are separated by circumstance. As for children left behind while mothers work overseas, the breadth of networks of relatives usually ensures they grow up in a family. Mothers become heroes to their offspring as they work so hard overseas to support and educate them.

For the future, the Philippines will continue to have a surplus of labour, particularly semi-skilled and technical workers at a time when developed countries in both Asia and the West have ageing populations. Japan's population is already shrinking and others such as Korea and Taiwan will follow soon. The Philippines has several characteristics which seem to ensure that demand for workers will be strong. For east Asia there is the appeal of proximity and that physical, racial differences are less pronounced than migrants from south Asia or further afield.

The numbers of Filipinos in Japan have already surpassed those of any country in Europe, being estimated at 325,000 in 2020. However, it has not been a steady rise. Women have remained roughly two-thirds of the migrant stock. Earlier they had arrived as singers and entertainers, Filipino bands establishing themselves on the national stage as well as in local bars and nightclubs. Not only were they known as fine musicians but they could sing in Spanish as well as English and being from a nation of many languages they were favoured by the Japanese. As entertainers they were sometimes viewed as substitutes for Americans. Some male migrants became known for their boxing and other sporting prowess

There was a surge of female migrants in the 1990s, after a relaxation of visa requirements for skilled workers was reversed in 1989 over allegations of trafficking, as many women went into the sex industry. Numbers began to rise again due to demand the for care givers and household workers, and both sexes have found work in technical fields, especially if they have had the opportunity of studying in Japan or being brought in by Japanese companies to learn particular skills.

There was also a significant number of marriages to Japanese men, with Filipinos second only to Chinese as a source of brides for Japanese men. At first these marriages were mainly to entertainers working in Japan but a marriage of convenience industry also developed using intermediaries and mail-order. At one point there were more marriages between Japanese and Filipinas than Americans and Filipinas, the total exceeding 8,000 in 2004. Divorce was common and there were many reports of marital abuse enhanced by clashes of culture. Divorce without consent left many Filipinas without either rights or the means of supporting children. Numbers of such marriages fell sharply following the introduction of stricter rules, including visas for entertainers. By 2016, numbers were down to 3,371 or 22 per cent of all marriages between Japanese men and foreign women. Nonetheless, thousands of Filipinas continued to marry Japanese, making stable unions, having children and even adapting to life in rural Japan.

Taiwan has also witnessed marriages of local men with Filipinas. However, the number is small – cumulative about 7,000 – relative to the mostly unskilled workers who constitute the 157,000 (2020 official figure) of Filipinos on the island. They were the third largest group among the 700,000 foreign workers. In addition, there are an unknown number of Filipino-Chinese professional and business people who have family and business links there and in Fujian who have taken citizenship, an impossibility for ordinary workers who face limits on their stay in Taiwan.

The Filipino presence in South Korea is significantly lower than in Taiwan with a total in 2019 of only 62,500, slightly under half being women. Filipinos in Korea also have a slightly higher than average educational level and age for foreigners. Nonetheless, they are mostly in low wage and undesirable occupations. They were then only 2.5 per cent of the foreign population. In 2015, marriage visas constituted 52 per cent of the Filipina total, or about 10,500. The number has almost certainly risen since, due to the large Korean community in the Philippines. In 2020, there was an estimated 100,000 Koreans resident in the Philippines, some retired but many with Philippine companions and children. There are also known to be several thousand children (known as Kopinos) whose Koreans fathers have returned to Korea leaving the mothers behind. Given the proximity of the Philippines, its warm climate and low cost of living, the number of retirees is expected to keep growing.

In the West, Filipino familiarity not just with the English language but with Western, or at least American, popular culture and even legal traditions has been seen to make them easily more accepted. Christianity has also been a bridge to the West. Generally, they have acquired a reputation for hard work and adaptability, even of good humour. These hard-to-measure characteristics, real or imagined, have played a role and will continue to do so.

Countries in Europe without historical links to the Philippines now have significant numbers – approaching 200,000 in Italy, the Catholic Church being an informal link. A count in 2016 showed 167,000. Although many are domestic helpers on limited contracts, more than half have acquired long-term residence. The UK is estimated to have a Filipino population of about 200,000 and had become by 2018 the largest group, after Indians, of foreign employees of the country's National Health Service. The UK's exit from the European Union was likely to increase demand for them. In addition, in 2018, the UK was equal third with Korea (6.5 per cent) and after the US (25 per cent) and Japan (25 per cent) in the percentage of the 1,365 Filipinas marrying foreigners in the Philippines.

Although worker numbers in Europe were relatively small compared with the Middle East, their incomes were higher and their prospects of, eventually, acquiring permanent residence and then citizenship very much higher, with citizenship offering the prospect of bringing in a spouse or finding a job for a relative, seeding the growth of the community at large.

North America, however, has received by far the most permanent settlers, averaging 50,000–60,000 in recent years. More than 50 per cent were women but this number fell to 36 per cent, excluding those who migrated as housewives rather than in their own right.

Until 2020, remittance figures overall were quite high but steady growth from $18.7 billion in 2010 to $25.6 billion in 2015 and $30.1 billion in 2019 reflect not only an increase in numbers of OFWs deployed but the growing size of communities more permanently settled. Seafarer remittances also grew slightly faster overall, from $3.8 billion to $6.5 billion. Non-cash remittances added another $3 billion to a total remittance tally of $33.5 billion.

Those from North America were top but grew more slowly – from $9.9 billion in 2010 to $12.7 in 2019, while from the Middle East they rose from $2.9 billion to $5.9 billion. However, there may be a need for caution in individual country totals because of the methods used by remittance centres and banks and in currency denomination of remittance. For instance, remittances from the UK were consistently double those from Italy though worker numbers were similar, while those in Canada fluctuated very widely.[2] US numbers were probably inflated by correspondent bank relationships.

From Asia, the top source in 2019 was Singapore at $1.9 billion, more than double 2010, followed by Japan at $1.8 billion, Hong Kong at $801 million, Korea $683 million, Taiwan at $597 million and Malaysia at $466 million. The last rose especially sharply over the decade.

Migrant workers came from all parts of the Philippines but were far from evenly distributed. There was a natural tendency for clusters to emerge in particular barangays with relatives and friends following pioneers to particular places. Nor were they from particularly poor barangays and tended to have higher than average educational levels. One study of all households in a barangay, Camachile in Bataan,[3] found that 31 per cent of people over eighteen were current or former migrants of whom 62 per cent were men. Experience of migration dated back to the 1970s and the average period spent overseas was eight years. The longer workers stayed away the more they earned. In choosing a location overseas, income level was the main determinant for 50 per cent, followed by knowing other people in that location.

Camachile was far from being a very poor barangay even without remittances. It was close enough to the Bataan industrial zone and refinery to provide some technical as well as labouring jobs. All households had electricity, 40 per cent had flush toilets and most had fridges and other appliances. Those with low incomes and no remitting relatives were truly poor.

Of the migrant workers, 33 per cent were in trades such as masonry and carpentry, 18 per cent in unskilled construction or domestic work, 14 per cent in retail and similar services, 6 per cent each as technicians, plant operatives, clerks and supervisory workers and 8 per cent as professionals such as teachers and nurses. Educational levels were higher than average for the barangay and there were indications that on-the-job training enabled some to get promotion to higher grades. Aspirations to migrate were still only for a minority but kinship links were important in easing the process with help and advice and introductions to recruiters.

The hard-labouring army of OFWs is a tribute to the sacrifices that individuals will make to support their families, but at least as important from a monetary point of view are the remittances of those who have succeeded in migrating permanently to much richer countries. The most significant of these is, unsurprisingly, the USA where in 2018 there were about 2 million Philippine-born residents, a number which had increased fourfold since 1980. Filipinos have for several years been the fourth largest migrant source after Mexico, China and India. In 2018, newcomers totalled 47,300. Including the locally born, the community now number over four million, with the largest concentration in California, notably the San Francisco Bay area and San Jose where they are 3.5 per cent of the population. The highest in percentage terms is in Honolulu where 8 per cent is Filipino, a legacy of the agricultural workers who came in the 1930s (see Chapter 3).

The Filipino migrant community enjoyed significantly higher household income ($93,000 in 2018) than the national average, but they rated poorly compared with the other main Asian communities in California in terms of academic achievement and among the professional and Silicon Valley elites but above Hispanics, Blacks and other immigrants. The Filipino community has had little visibility relative to its size. Filipinos were often not regarded as Asian even by themselves, let alone by Chinese and Koreans or the wider community.[4] Spanish-derived names make it hard to distinguish them from Hispanics to whom they may also relate through the Catholic Church and other facets of culture shared with former Spanish colonies. They felt little identity with the Asians of 'chopstick societies' who in turn saw them as not fully Asian. Their browner skin could also be an issue for pale-skin conscious northeast Asian societies. Filipinos were more likely to live in mixed race districts and far more likely to marry outside their ethnic group. In time, links to the Philippines, and hence the willingness to remit, was likely to fade. However, so long as the community continued to receive large annual migrant increments, the US community would remain the largest source of remittances.

Second in permanent migrant destinations in recent years has been Canada where, from a late start, the Filipino community grew to about 1 million by 2019. Thanks to changes in immigration policy, annual arrivals surged from 11,000 in 2002 to 50,000 in 2015 making them the leading source of migrants. Numbers settled back to 35,999 in 2018 and 27,000 in 2019, surpassed only by India and China. Philippine migrant stock in 2019 was 588,000 or 7.8 per cent of the Canadian total. At 294,000 in 2019, the

Philippines was fifth after the UK, China, India and New Zealand of foreign-born residents. Over the decade to 2019 annual migrant numbers averaged 11,000 of which 61 per cent were women, the highest percentage of all source countries.

Add a few thousand acquiring permanent residence in European countries, Japan and Korea and the annual total in the decade to 2019 was in the region of 100,000. This is still a small part of a nation growing by about 1.3 million a year. In many ways they, like their OFW compatriots give the Philippines an international identity not similarly accorded to, for example, their Malay neighbours in Indonesia for whom permanent migration has never been a goal for more than a small number. However, it raises two initial questions. Is it due largely to the failure of successive governments to provide opportunities at home? Or is it the natural response of free individuals to move to richer lands, just as Europeans once flocked to America?

Many who have achieved distinction in professional fields, in academia and in media who never intended to migrate end up by doing so after being lured to an overseas post to find that there are insufficient opportunities and salaries to lure them back home. The country is losing many of its best and brightest partly because of a familiarity with English and Western culture but also because of slow economic growth at home and social barriers in a country where family and patronage play such an important role in job opportunities. These may be as great as any faced by new immigrants to other lands.

Nor have any returnees established themselves as leading political figures able to drive new ideas and inspire a shift from dynasties. Overseas Filipinos have been able to vote since 2003 but although Manila has encouraged registration in 2016 only 31 per cent of 1.38 million registered actually voted. In 2019, registration had increased to 1.82 million but only a minority voted. In 2016, they voted for Duterte and for Marcos rather than Robredo for vice-president. Direct representation of OFWs in congress is effectively non-existent. The Party List should have enabled them to be a force there, but for several elections there were too many competing groups for any to succeed. Then their names were usurped by the rich and powerful with no connection to OFWs. In 2019, The Seafarers won two seats, one filled by an executive of a construction company and the other by one from Udenna Corporation, a favourite of President Duterte. The OFW Family Club won a seat for boxer Manny Pacqiao's brother, and Diwa, supposedly a workers' rights group one for the clan of Manny Villar, the nation's richest person.

The nation boasts several layers of bureaucracy supposed to promote employment overseas while protecting Filipinos from abuse and trafficking. The results of the various bodies have been mixed. The Philippine Overseas Employment Administration (POEA) is responsible for licencing employment agencies to ensure that they are honest and do not overcharge. It also provides information on job opportunities and links to major recruiters such as health ministries in the Middle East. It has wide and sometimes controversial power to stop OFWs going to countries on its blacklist, supposedly a means of protecting workers but which limits their freedom of choice

However, employment bans have been shown sometimes to bring improvements in treatment. In 2018, outrage at the rape and murder of a domestic helper spurred Duterte to ban new contracts to Kuwait. This was only lifted after the Kuwait authorities agreed to permit workers to keep their passports, use their mobile phones and not be forced to change their employer. The Philippines has about forty labour attachés in overseas posts. Their reputations have been varied and too much zeal can upset recruitment agencies which have the ear of POEA officials.

Controls on nationals leaving the Philippines of their own accord have been a source of corruption as well as contrary to the freedoms that Filipinos are supposed to enjoy. Agency fees are often higher than permitted as a result of collusion between those in the Philippines and those in recruiting countries so payments may require OFWs to borrow from money lenders at their destinations. OFWs naturally find it difficult to organize themselves. Laws, as well as conditions of employment, short-term contracts and lack of gathering places are all hurdles. That said, as Filipinos sometimes have articulate spokespersons and have, at least according to studies in Hong Kong, been less abused than other nationals. Home media is alert to abuses which keep labour attachés under pressure.

Given the numbers of employment agencies involved, the POEA has had a constant battle to identify abuses. In the first half of 2019, for example, twenty-one foreign and nineteen local agencies were blacklisted. However, the POEA has also had corruption issues in its own ranks, unsurprising given that OFWs cannot move without an Overseas Employment Certificate issued by it. Longer term and diaspora issues are dealt with by the Commission on Filipinos Overseas. It registers migrants and aims to keep the young generation of overseas Filipinos in touch with their language and culture and cooperate with Filipino schools overseas which follow the domestic syllabus but mostly Filipinos rely on themselves not government support.

As for permanent migrants, the relative ease with which they have melded into their new nation works against developing strong community organizations. They are for example far less visible than Chinese in California, though their numbers are only a little less. The organizations that they create among themselves are mostly based on province or other local identity not on the notion of Filipino. Further complicating their self-identity is the reluctance of many to be identified as Asian, which many, at least in the US, associate with being Chinese, Korean or Japanese. Culturally, many feel closer to Latinos or South Pacific Islanders because of Church and language links. That most permanent migrants have gone to English-speaking countries has had an impact back home. It helps sustain some of the links and cultural affinities created by 350 years of Spanish and American rule. Awareness of common linguistic and cultural bonds to Malay neighbours, Indonesia and Malaysia, is weak despite the legacy of Rizal and of Macapagal's Maphilindo proposal.

In short, the global impact of Filipino labour and migration is yet to be reflected in any fundamental changes in the Philippines itself, other than many of the most talented and ambitious. Indeed, middle class Filipinos who stay at home may resent their own dependence on remittances and see those who leave as ungrateful for their education at public expense. Yet the push and pull of demographics, local and overseas, ensures that the age of Filipino migration is far from over. What remains to be seen is whether the existence of this vast community will eventually have a significant impact on the evolution of society and politics back home.

Notes

1 *2019 Survey on Overseas Filipinos*, Philippine Statistics Authority.

2 http://www.bsp.gov.ph/statistics/keystat/ofw2.htm

3 Aubrey D. Tabuga, *A Probe into Filipino Migration Culture*, Quezon City: Philippine Institute for Development Studies, 2018.

4 Anthony Christian Ocampo, *The Latinos of Asia. How Filipino Americans Break the Rules on Race,* Palo Alto, CA: Stanford University Press, 2016.

15

Of 'free trade' and the short arm of the law

The general problems of governance and the specific ones of Mindanao come together in an issue which affects the whole country in a variety of ways, petty and serious, local and central: smuggling and similar illicit economic activities. In addition, there are large parts of the informal economy which operate in a grey area of legitimate trading of petty contraband goods

It is no surprise that smuggling is such a big issue. A country of sailors, traders and many islands provides a natural environment for this informal type of 'free trade'. Mundane items such as untaxed cigarettes and pornographic videos, cheap fakes of famous fashion and electronic brand names have huge markets and engage tens of thousands of small traders in their distribution. The sheer number of people with a stake, however small, in the illicit trade adds to the difficulty of stamping it out. Politicians generally set such a poor example that appeals to national or civic interests cut little ice and neither the police nor the judicial system inspire much confidence among the masses who must fend for themselves in the informal employment offered by these nominally illegal or extra-legal activities.

The proximity of coasts under other jurisdictions and with different pricing systems offer plentiful opportunities for all kinds of items to be shipped to and around the Philippines whether from other countries such as Indonesia and Malaysia with similarly porous coastlines. Not only is Sulu a short hop from Sabah but Davao and General Santos City not far from northern Sulawesi. Language differences are no barrier as Filipinos, like their neighbours, are naturally multilingual, growing up listening to various local languages plus English and maybe Malay, Hokkien and even Arabic. Likewise, it is not so far from Vigan and Laoag to the China coast, and Taiwan is even nearer. China offers low-cost manufacturing of everything from shabu to toothbrushes, cars to underwear, and has demand for untaxed mineral exports. Kinship links to Filipino Chinese businessmen, mostly of Fujian family origin, provides the trade infrastructure. Thanks to high local prices even bulk items such as rice, petroleum products and cement are subject to inward smuggling from places such as Vietnam and Taiwan.

Illicit enterprise not only causes social damage (in the case of drugs) but deprives the government of badly needed revenues. It also funds local dynasts, sustaining their families' grip on power and helping clans become 'fatter' by installing their kin in multiple government positions. The problems of Muslim Mindanao/Sulu are fuelled and underpinned by the power of several local dynasts and by an especially long history of smuggling. Particularly the Sulu area of Bangsamoro, there has been a focus on a few high-profile kidnap for ransom cases, perhaps because the contraband trade in commodities such as cigarettes became saturated. A bigger and continuing industry is the smuggling and distribution of drugs, mostly the methamphetamine known locally as *shabu*. It not only finances some jihadists but adds to rivalries between Muslim groups and funds the private armies of local bosses.

Duterte's focus on the drug trade was politically popular but the evidence that it greatly reduced drug use is limited. Small-time street-level vendors were an easy target but few of those higher up the chain were targeted. A few local politicians alleged to be in the business were killed but these were widely assumed to be a fraction of local power brokers, including police chiefs, involved. An even bigger income generator for governors and mayors has been *jueteng*, a numbers lottery game which is illegal but widespread. It provides a dream of instant riches for the poor, employment in selling tickets and a good profit from which political bosses can finance their campaigns or personal wealth. President Estrada was undone by former friend, the governor of Ilocos Luis 'Chavit' Singson, who had admitted giving him millions in *jueteng* profits (see Chapter 7). Instead of being punished for his role, Singson was promoted. Although now partly replaced by other forms of gambling, a national *jueteng* is still a source of revenue for some provincial and town political bosses, and the local police.

Local officials and police are almost always involved in cases of illegal mining and forestry, though there is scant virgin forest left in most provinces. Attempts to oppose these by environmental activists and local interest groups have on several occasions proved fatal to them. Yet these illicit local income streams are spread around the country and may provide employment. There are many very rich, but not in the billionaire class, who thrive at provincial level from land, property, and local and regional commerce. They are more connected to local than national politics. The leverage that being a major city mayor, provincial governor or member of the House of Representatives makes it easy to profit from illegal activities.

However, money generated by control of local politics tends not to accumulate. It is a 'money comes quick, goes quick' situation as staying in power is expensive. To sustain networks of mutual obligations requires the ability to provide jobs and money-making opportunities. There are approximately 150 dynasties whose names recur as dominant or rival political families in the nation's eighty-one provinces and thirty-three major cities. Very few are in both the top wealth and political leagues. The newer

Chinese fortunes in particular tend to avoid politics as far as possible as they lack provincial bases and fear being on the wrong side when regimes change. Democratic politics is expensive and parties, in practice, non-existent, so deep pockets are usually needed to compete and winners are expected to defray the cost with kickbacks on deals. The cost of democracy partly explains why dynasts flourish while recent elections have shown that the competition for office has become less intense than before. Costs have risen and the risk/reward ratio has shifted.

If provincial level illicit money is at least spread around, the same cannot be said for the smuggling which goes through major ports and official channels due to the extent of corruption in the Bureau of Customs at major as well as minor ports. As much as one-third of goods traded goes un-reported, according to estimates made by comparing Philippine trade data with that of its foreign partners. Attempts have been made to clean up the Bureau of Customs but though some improvements have resulted, the rot goes deep and example from the top is weak to non-existent. Fuel smuggling through the Subic Freeport Zone and other ports is estimated, according to the legal fuel distributors, to account for as much as 50 per cent of petrol and diesel sales through unbranded 'white' filling stations. A price difference of maybe 15 pesos on fuel which has evaded excise and other taxes is attractive to users while providing a healthy profit for sharing among organizers, politicians and officials.

To the revenue and local production, losses caused by smuggled imports are added to those from exports, for example of nickel ore, which are unrecorded and escape royalties and profits taxes. These largely benefit local politicians as well as the businessmen involved. Large companies may mostly follow the rules but there are many small mines which enjoy the protection of politicians who get a cut of the proceeds, and deal with no-questions-asked buyers from China. Generally, the traditional strong links between the Filipino-Chinese community and traders from Fujian has enabled all kinds of trade which have undercut local producers or deprived the government of the revenue needed to build infrastructure and improve a weak educational system. In non-Muslim Mindanao, the NPA extorts protection money from mines and plantations, and dynasts profit from illegal nickel and gold mines or take their cut from illegal logging.

At the same time, there is some technically illegal trade which is actually socially very useful. A notable example is trade in second-hand clothes which is conducted both on a significant scale by women with wide supply networks but also on an individual or family scale by overseas workers, notably in Hong Kong, supplying relatives back home with clothes for sale as well as for their own use. Such trade also involves handbags, accessories and electrical and electronic appliances. Here at least, rich country tendencies to follow fashion and discard the slightly outdated can be put to productive use as both tradeable items and consumer goods. Extensive family networks can provide significant markets for such items. Some trade operates outside the law but not against it. For example, an un-licenced street vendor may pay a tax to a local government to be able to operate or come to a deal with a shop-owner where one attracts trade to the other by offering complementary items.

Tracking the unrecorded part of the economy is difficult. Nonetheless, one series of estimates puts the average between 1960 and 2011 at 34.8 per cent, while trade-only data for later years suggests a similar pattern.[1] In terms of balance of payments, there has been a large and continuing capital outflow. Even official records show a surplus on current accounts of the balance of payments for most years since 2000 not fully reflected in the build up of reserves. To this must be added the main ways of exporting money outside recorded channels – over-invoicing of imports and under-invoicing of exports, or complete evasion of trade documentation, i.e. smuggling. Given that there have been no significant exchange controls for several decades, the reason for such improper invoicing is mainly to avoid taxes, in the process accumulating money for investment offshore. Imposing exchange controls would probably make scant difference to the unrecorded outflow, at least so long as the peso remains fairly stable. It has been so ever since the 2008 global crisis, so tax avoidance rather than fear of currency decline appears to be the major reason behind unrecorded outflows.

Inward smuggling of goods has been financed by the inflow of service economy receipts from BPO, remittances and tourism, thus contributing to the erosion of manufacturing's role in the economy. This was also reflected in the way that big business came to be dominated by a few giant service-oriented conglomerates – banking, retail, telecoms and real estate – mostly lacking in the skills or interest to invest in capital intensive manufacturing. The lop-sided nature of the economy has been self-reinforcing.

Inward smuggling of people has also been a significant industry, especially in the first years of the administration of President Duterte when Manila, in particular, became the locus for the offshore gambling industry aimed at the China market. In addition to thousands of Chinese allowed in to operate these businesses and related services, significant additional numbers were able to come in through sweet deals with immigration officials. Such flows also facilitated the development of networks for smuggling other goods, including drugs, rice, textile and petroleum products, and the development of small illegal mines, notably nickel.

The rot in the system begins at the top. Whilst there was some pick-up in tax revenues during the Aquino and Duterte eras, the penalties for criminal tax avoidance are weak and seldom applied. As can be seen above, Lucio Tan's near-monopoly on tobacco simply repaid the government losses (or some of them) for forging tax stamps. Wrote economics professor and former Economic Planning Secretary Solita Monsod: 'Lucio Tan is a role model for the worst kind of conduct as far as our national objectives are concerned. He signals that you can evade taxes and get away with it, pay the courts and get the judges to decide in your favor, get good lawyers and delay your cases. The messages that are given by the kind of treatment that he gets from the government are the antithesis of what we need for sustainable development: an even playing field and government intervention of the right kind.'[2]

Tan, whose original empire was created by Marcos, continued not only to prosper and expand his empire (Chapter 16) but showed his loyalty to Chinese President Xi Jinping, hosting him in Manila and attending the president's military parade in Tiananmen Square at a time when China's forces were moving in on the West Philippine Sea. The wheels of justice against large-scale corruption also move at glacial speed. In June 2021, the Supreme Court finally ruled against Marcos crony, Herminio Disini, for kickbacks of about $80 million received from Westinghouse over the Bataan nuclear plant (see Chapter 7) construction of which began in 1976 but was scrapped in 1986 after more than $2 billion had been spent. By then, Disini had been dead for seven years. The same court also confirmed a 2012 Sandiganbayan judgement which found Disini liable but exonerated the Marcos couple despite evidence that they collected 95 per cent of the 5 per cent commission that Disini received from Westinghouse.

The sense of entitlement and invulnerability for many at the top makes breaking the law as much a necessity as merely normal to those below. Resulting losses of revenue for the government and funds for investment in employment-generating business perpetuates poor education and health, and hence other ills of society. The interaction of history, geography and the political and administrative systems suggest that reducing tax losses, regularizing trade and cleaning up the system to build a more modern, urban society will be a long process. Willingness to avoid illicit commerce and tax avoidance requires public trust that the funds will be used fairly and efficiently. Some things have improved partly thanks to the oversight efforts of NGOs but so long as crimes are exposed but not effectively prosecuted, trust is unlikely to improve, and people accept that pork barrels are the norm in business, public administration and politics. The interests of dynasts and oligopolies in the smuggling systems also partly explain opposition to foreign investment. Multinational operators are more likely to follow the rules and keep a paper trail which is genuine, not created to fool the Customs or Internal Revenue departments.

These failings are also common elsewhere, and corruption can oil the wheels of trade by speeding decisions or eliminating bureaucracy. The Philippines suffers not just because illegal actions distort and delay. Wrong policy priorities stemming from political and sectional interests are equally to blame. As the World Bank noted in a 2021 report, 'Economic competition has been restricted by policies that favour existing conglomerates'. The natural response of ambitious businessmen and petty traders trying to survive has been to find paths to profits by circumventing rules in general – following the examples set by their peers in business and politics.

Notes

1 Kar and LeBlanc (2014) quoted in Patricio N. Abinales 'The Problem with a National(ist) Method', in Mark R. Thompson and Eric Vincent C. Batalla (eds), *Routledge Handbook of Contemporary Philippines,* Abingdon: Routledge, 2018.

2 Asiasentinel, 20 November 2015.

16

Happy families of conglomerate capitalism

Many not only see a connection between modest socio-economic performance and the extent of illicit commerce. They see it equally in the narrow group of conglomerates which dominate much of the retail, manufacturing and utilities base of the economy. In turn, these conglomerates are mostly closely held by the families of their founders. Dilution takes place over time as families expand, but it is a slow process.

The Philippine conglomerates with their cross holdings and ownership of a spectrum of businesses from retail to real estate, banking, telecoms, ports and power in part owe their very rapid expansion in recent decades to the growth of the remittance and services economy. They are thus intermediaries as worker remittances create demand for banking, telecoms and retail services, and BPO businesses and gaming centres need office buildings, power and telecoms. With neither government nor foreigners owning much thanks to privatization and protectionism, a few big groups dominate to a degree greater than anywhere in a region where such conglomerates are not unusual.

The narrow base of big capital is well illustrated by the stock market which has a market turnover less even than that of the relatively new Vietnamese market and a market capitalization which, despite double-counting due to cross holdings, is similar relative to the size of the economy. Turnover has in recent years been running at about 11 per cent of capitalization, half that of Indonesia, one-third that of Malaysian and Vietnam, one-seventh that of Thailand and a global average of around 40 per cent. This is despite the exchange being older than any in southeast Asia apart from Singapore/Malaysia. Foreign participation helps liquidity but the Philippines' share of regional and global funds has fallen steadily.

The stock market mostly supplies family members with the ability to raise cash and diversify their assets away from the family business. The years 2020–1 saw some hopes of change due to high global liquidity in response to the Covid pandemic. Manila saw five big new listings totalling more than 750 billion pesos but of these only Converge ICT raised new money to finance an expanded fibre network. Started by Dennis Anthony Uy in 2007, Converge is the nation's most successful technology start-up. The biggest new listing was Monde Nissin, a food company headed by Betty Ang who married into the Kweefanus family of Indonesia, which controls the Nissin and Khong Guan food businesses there as well as Monde Nissin. The Ayala group also set a trend listing some of its properties as a Real Estate Investment Trust (REIT), A-REIT. This was followed by two more REITs enabling property developers to raise capital for their group interests without losing control.

Despite this progress in listings, turnover and public participation remain low. A contributing factor is that much household savings is dominated by two giant, government-run groups, the Government Service Insurance System for public employees and, for the private sector, the Social Security System. These both combine short-term social security provisions with retirement schemes. However, their investment policies are opaque and focused mainly on government bonds, other debt instruments, including loans to members, and real estate. Equity investments are small by comparison. Household savings otherwise are mostly in bank deposits where real yields are minimal thanks to generous margins in banking.

Private life insurance companies have long existed and provide equity-linked investment schemes but the total number of policy owners is still small compared with the government ones. Total savings for the nation is around 15 per cent of GDP and household savings in particular lags regional peers.

Businesses large and small find it hard to avoid engagement with politicians who look for financial support in return for favours. This is particularly the case at local level where contests are often between dynasties, but it can also be the case with the conglomerates, some of which are from time to time subject to populist polemics aimed at 'oligarchs'. As seen earlier (Chapter 6), President Marcos sought to bring down some of these and build up new ones beholden to him. President Duterte also promised anti-oligarch moves but his only significant move was against the Lopez group, denying it a television broadcast licence for once-dominant ABS/CBN. Not by chance, this was a huge boost to the profits of its rival, the GMA Network.

The concentration of wealth in a few conglomerate and family hands does not, however, mean that there is no movement. Indeed, as the descendants of the earlier founders of great wealth multiply, so their holdings become more dispersed, enough to support many multi-millionaires but not so many in the billionaire category.

The very rich groups divide roughly into three time periods. The first is the Spanish and old *mestizo* group dating to the nineteenth century or before. Pre-eminent is the Zobel de Ayala family which controls the broad-based Ayala Group and the Bank of the Philippine Islands, the nation's oldest and second largest. Ayala has a range of property and utility investments including ownership of large parts of Makati financial district, which it developed, and the vast Ayala Alabang luxury housing estate in the southern suburbs of the metropolis. The related Soriano family also used to control food and beverage giant San Miguel but its flagship Anscor (A. Soriano Corporation) now has a mixed bag of interests. The Ayala group has a reputation for conservative management and an aloofness which has so far served it well.

Today, the only other billionaire in the top ten with old Spanish roots is Enrique Razon, a low key individual who has made his family's business into the only local company with major overseas interests. Port operator International Container Terminal Services Inc. is controlled by Razon with 62 per cent of the shares. Razon is the third generation of a family in the port business which is the most internationalized of all Filipino firms with container berths stretching from Makassar and Jakarta to the Congo, Croatia, Brazil and Mexico. A few other companies have made money overseas but, like Jollibee, based on demand from expatriate Filipinos. Razon also controls stock market-listed Bloomberry Resorts which owns Solaire Resorts which has a casino hotel in Manila and is planning more. According to the *Forbes* magazine 2021 Philippines, Razon was the third-richest Filipino with assets of about 300 billion pesos.

Still important old Spanish *mestizo* families include the Lopez group. Its once sugar-based wealth now extends to the Manila Electric Company (MERALCO) and the ABS-CBN media group. Through the First Philippine Holdings, the Lopez group has diverse power and property interests including the listed geothermal producer Energy Development Corporation.

The Cebu-based Aboitiz group's Spanish origins date to the 1880s and is a major player in power generation and construction. The group controls the listed Republic Cement, the second largest cement producer, and owns mid-sized Union Bank, also listed. The Araneta group, originally from Negros and a political player since 1898, has vast Manila property holdings, mostly in Quezon City, where it owns the Araneta Coliseum, once the world's largest single dome arena, and various fast-food franchises. Both these groups now have various family members in different parts of the business. The Aranetas were active in government in the US era and one, lawyer and politician Salvador Araneta, founded two universities and, with Jose Concepcion, the Republic Flour Mills, now diversified, and the listed food manufacturer RFM Corporation.

Next in terms of business longevity are Chinese names with roots which go back to the late Spanish or the early American periods. The leading example is the Gokongwei family, originally a Cebu-based retailer which moved into food manufacture in the 1950s and now has food, retailing, telecom and other interests under listed JG Summit and Universal Robina which also owns Robinson's department stores and Cebu Pacific Airlines.

Most of the very big Chinese names emerged after 1945. The most successful of all was Amoy-born Henry Sy who started a shoe shop in 1948 and built what became Shoe Mart and then the SM Group with two interrelated listed companies, SM Investments and SM Prime. The group is now by far the nation's largest mall owner. It is also a property developer and bank owner with holdings in Banco de Oro and China Bank, plus stakes in numerous other enterprises including hotels and gambling. Sy's family is now the richest by far with his six offspring estimated to be worth about $16 billion between them.[1]

A more recent billionaire Chinese retail innovator is Tony Tan Caktiong, son of Fujian immigrants, who started Jollibee fast food shops back in the 1970s. It now has more than 1,000 outlets and a brand name established in most countries where there are many Filipinos. It also owns other fast food brand franchises including a joint venture in Vietnam. It has stuck to its original field rather than attempting to become a conglomerate.

As elsewhere in southeast Asia, property development has been the quickest of all routes to wealth. Thus, Fujian-born, Hong Kong-raised Andrew Tan has built a multi-billion dollar business of which the public faces are the Alliance Global Group and Megaworld Corporation. Condominium development is its forte, but Tan also owns the McDonald's fast-food franchise and Emperador, a hugely successful brandy which he started from nothing but is now popular in many countries, including Spain. Emperador and Tan's resort development Travellers International Hotels are separately listed on the stock exchange.

The post-1945 generation of Chinese tycoons has mostly tended to steer clear of politics. Payoffs to local power brokers were always necessary but lower profiles were preferred than would be needed to enter politics directly. Suspicions of Chinese, and especially Fujianese, clannishness made the richest and newest fortunes wary of a return of the anti-Chinese sentiments which had surfaced in the post-1945 period.

A key part of corporate development from the 1960s onwards was the accounting firm SyCip Gorres Velayo (SGV) founded by Washington ('Wash') SyCip in the 1950s. It quickly became the largest in the country. For decades SGV's public face, SyCip played a key role in relations between business groups and government. SGV showed a high degree of professionalism in accounting, auditing and advisory roles but SyCip tempered this by the acceptance of changing political realities and was especially influential in the Marcos era. He also established overseas links and was particularly important in relations with the World Bank and IMF in the 1970s. Alumni included Cesar Virata who ran its management consultancy before becoming Finance Minister and later Prime Minister under Marcos, and Roberto Ongpin appointed Trade and Industry Secretary in 1979.

The only one of the current billionaire elite who has neither Chinese nor Spanish ancestry also owes his career to SGV and his riches to property development: Emmanuel (Manny) Villar, now number two in the Forbes rich list. He also used wealth to move into politics, or, according to some accounts, used politics to help his business and has now established a new political dynasty. Villar rose via SGV to head the World Bank-backed Private Development Corporation of the Philippines from which he borrowed to start his own business. He was elected to the House of Representatives and by 1998 he was Speaker of the House. In 2001, he was elected to the Senate. In 2010, he stood for the presidency, coming third to Aquino and Estrada. In 2013, Villar was succeeded in the Senate by his wife Cynthia while their son Mark took over from his mother as Representative for Las Pinas House seat and was appointed by Duterte Secretary of Public Works.

Many of those who had been elevated by Marcos in return for a flow of funds to buy off actual or potential enemies eventually failed, though despite losing Philippines' assets mostly had many millions stashed away offshore, much in real estate in the US. However, there were also survivors among those who became mega-rich under Marcos. Top of the survivor list was Fujian-born Lucio Tan whose Fortune Tobacco group had a virtual monopoly of cigarette production and also started a brewery to compete with San Miguel. It was a vast cash generator for Marcos and enabled Tan to get into other industries, including banking – the Allied Bank Corporation. Following the fall of Marcos, Tan's companies were sequestered by the Presidential Commission on Good Government. However, he and the tobacco monopoly continued to thrive. He was cash-rich and in the 1990s acquired control of Philippine Airlines, the national carrier, and a large stake in the Philippine National Bank which he merged with his Allied Bank in 2013. He was a prominent financier of Estrada and remained close to the Marcos clan. In 2006, the Sandiganbayan anti-graft court nullified the sequestration, an outstanding example of the failure to prosecute ill-gotten wealth.

Nor did Tan's ability to milk his adoptive country result in patriotism towards it. In 2015 he, as a 'famed patriot', and Xi Jinping attended a military parade in Beijing just at the time China was driving Philippine fishermen from their waters and the government was arguing its case against China at the Permanent Court of Arbitration. In 2019, Tan brought state-owned China Communications Construction Corporation to the doorstep of the capital with a joint venture project to develop Sangley Point airstrip on the edge of Manila Bay, into a new airport. The survival of Tan's empire says a lot about the underdevelopment of the corporate sector, the venality of politicians and judges, and the latent resentment of ordinary Filipinos at the conglomerates. Tan family assets are now held through the Tangent Corporation which has a controlling stake in listed LT Group which holds a combination of tobacco, brewing, property and banking interests. Tan's son and heir died suddenly in 2019 so the future now rests with a grandson born in 1992, Stanford-educated electronics engineer, Lucio Tan III. The group suffered grievously from the pandemic due to ownership of Philippine Airlines.

Another survivor from Marcos-era looting was Eduardo 'Danding' Cojuangco, from a branch of the prominent Tarlac landowning family and cousin of Cory Aquino. He had long been aligned with Marcos who used him to challenge Ninoy Aquino's power in Tarlac. Added benefits were that

FIGURE 16.1 *Power and poverty in Manila. Pasay slums with Makati business district in background.* © *Getty Images.*

his wife, Gretchen Oppen, part German daughter of a major Negros landowning family, was much appreciated in Malacanang during the Marcos years for her beauty and wit.

Danding, who died in 2020, was the major beneficiary of a levy on coconut production introduced by Marcos, which was supposed to upgrade coconut production under the direction of the Philippine Coconut Authority headed by Defence Minister Juan Ponce Enrile. It also created United Coconut Planters Bank (UCPB). Much of its income flowed not to helping the mostly impoverished growers but to cronies and their companies, notably Cojuangco who merged his own small bank with UCPB. In 1983, coconut cash enabled him to acquire 20 per cent of San Miguel from the Zobel family which had fallen out with their cousins the Sorianos. He became chairman of San Miguel until he fled with Marcos to Hawaii in 1986.

That was only the beginning of a thirty-year saga of court cases over the 51 per cent seized by the PCGG. Suffice to say that Cojuangco got back 20 per cent and management control and later sold some of his stake to his protégé Ramon Ang who had been running it – and engaging in multiple deals to diversify from food and beverage production into power and toll roads. The largest shareholder now is Inigo Zobel through his holding company Top Frontier Investments. Inigo is a cousin of Jaime and Fernando Zobel, respectively chief executive and chief operating officer of Ayala Corporation. San Miguel's other interests now include listed Petron, the largest oil refiner and marketer in the country.

Another who survived the clean-up which was supposed to follow the fall of Marcos is Roberto Ongpin. An accountant from the SyCip Gorres Velayo (SGV) stable – he was related to the founding Velayo – Ongpin was tapped by Marcos in 1979 to join his team of technocrats as Trade and Industry Minister. That portfolio did not prosper as economic problems piled up but Ongpin had a lucky break. He became the unofficial liaison between the government and what was called the 'Binondo Central Bank', a group of Chinese dealers who operated the currency black market and could help stabilize the gap between official and black market dollar rates. The leading dealer was one Benito Tan Guat who, after the fall of Marcos, financed his son, Willie Ocier, to partner with the well-connected Ongpin in a real estate venture. Ongpin never looked back, building a property and resort empire that was listed as Belle Corp. He later moved into offshore gambling with PhilWeb Corp., a company which started life in 1979 as a mineral explorer but changed its focus in 2000.

Ongpin was claimed by Duterte to be an oligarch and lost a gambling licence, but that was restored when the business was sold to the Araneta group – now allied with the Marcos family through marriage to Irene, daughter of the former president. (The Aranetas are also related to 2016 presidential candidate Manuel Roxas and President Arroyo's husband Miguel Arroyo.)

Another beneficiary of Marcos' favours who was also cleared by the Sandiganbayan in 2019, thirty-three years after the Marcos fall, was Bienvenido Tantoco. The Tantocos had founded the upmarket Rustan's department store group and under Marcos obtained a duty-free store licence concession on luxury imports. Bienvenido's wife, Gliceria, frequently accompanied Imelda Marcos on her many travels and acted on her behalf in multi-million dollar purchases of buildings in New York, paintings and antique furniture. Her husband was appointed ambassador to the Vatican.

Another whose riches mostly survived the Marcos era was Antonio Floirendo, who built a huge banana plantation business in Davao through relationships with politicians. He too accompanied Imelda on some of her travels, acted for her in asset purchases and provided the house in Hawaii where they lived in exile. He was never charged by the PCGG. The Floirendo family now has connections through marriage to the Lopez and Danding Cojuangco clans.

In addition to these very big names, there are a few dozen lesser but familiar ones which repeatedly recur on shareholder lists and boards and in glossy magazines, including Elizalde, Zamora, Concepcion, del Rosario, SyCip, etc. in some cases inter-marrying with each other and with political families. The mainstream represented by the Makati Business Club may want to be apolitical but that can be difficult as some big names including Ayala have found during the Duterte era.

Other prominent Chinese families include that of Robert Coyiuto Jr whose Fujian immigrant father established Prudential Guarantee, one of the largest non-life insurance businesses in the country. It remains privately held. He also controls Oriental Petroleum, a small oil producer and explorer. The Coyiutos are also close to the Gokongweis, and linked by marriage to Fujian-born Tan Yu, whose Asiaworld Group made him among the richest Filipinos till his death in 2002. Tan Yu had moved from copra trading into textile manufacture, and real estate in Taiwan and Manila.

Others high up in the wealth stakes include the heirs of Hong Kong-born George Ty, boss of Metrobank until his death in 2018. The company also owns the Toyota assembly plant and franchise which it revived after the collapse of Marcos crony Silverio's Delta Corporation. Another Chinese banker, Frederick Dy, took control of Security Bank in the 1990s. The Bank of Tokyo Mitsubishi owns 20 per cent. The bank is listed as its parent, GT Capital Holdings, the holding company for Ty interest which include 15 per cent of Metro-Pacific Investments.

Older-established Chinese families also founded and still control Rizal Commercial Banking Corporation. The Yuchengcos began as timber traders in the early twentieth century, but the business was mostly built by Alfonso Yuchengco whose daughter Helen Yuchengco-Dee is now chairman of the bank. She married into the Dee family of China Bank. The Yuchengcos are also linked to the SyCips. David SyCip, younger brother of Washington SyCip, formerly ran the Rizal Commercial Banking Corporation; Taiwan's Cathay Financial Group now has a 23 per cent stake. The Gotianun family, related to the Gokongwei family, controls the listed Filinvest Development Corporation whose subsidiaries include developer Filinvest Land and East-West Bank and also has hotel investments. It was founded by Fujian-born Andrew Gotianun, 1926–2016, and is now controlled by his sons.

One outstanding fortune rests, unusually for the Philippines, neither on commerce nor finance. DMCI, David M. Consunji Investments, is a company formed by a young civil engineer in 1954, and has constructed some of Manila's best-known buildings as well as bridges, highways and dams. David Consunji served Marcos as Minister of Transport 1970–5 but thereafter re-focused on his business which is now controlled by his sons. Listed DMCI Holdings owns 56 per cent of Semirara Mining, the Philippines' only major coal mining operation and which also owns a power producer.

Newer entries to the very rich lists are scarce, one exception being Puregold, a supermarket and dry goods chain only founded in 1998 by Lucio and Susan Co which now has some 350 outlets plus some non-retail interests in hotels and gambling, and China-born Dennis Anthony Uy of fibre optic innovator Converge which only started in 2009 but was early backed by Warburg Pincus the US-based private equity group. Of similar vintage is engineering industry success, Megawide Construction Corporation, founded in 1997 by two graduates, Edgar Saavedra and Michael Cosiquien. Listed on the stock exchange since 2011, it has since won several major projects from under the noses of bigger groups, including new terminal buildings at Cebu and Clark airports, and numerous apartment complexes.

However, the company has not yet accumulated a property asset base to put it into the top wealth league. Saavedra is now boss alone.

President Duterte's contribution to the wealth list so far is an ethnic Chinese businessman from Davao, Dennis Uy. He expanded from oil terminals and marketing to buying, together with China-ASEAN Investment Cooperation Fund, Negros Navigation, an old-established shipping company previously owned by the Aboitiz Group and renamed 2GO Group. After Duterte's election, Uy acquired rights for a casino in Cebu and development rights at the Clark Global Freeport Zone, adjacent to Clark airport. He had massive plans for hotels, offices, casino and a university and acquired a national telecom licence. He partnered state-owned China Telecom which has 40 per cent of the company, named Dito, challenging the current duopoly of the Philippine Long Distance Telephone Company (PLDT) and Globe. Uy's holding company, Udenna, also had hotel, fast food franchises and other interests, a remarkable record of growth in less than two decades, latterly with help from Duterte including a dubious and disputed deal to acquire the Malampaya gasfield.

Another Duterte business associate to blossom was Michael Yang (Yang Hong Ming) whose relationship with Duterte began in Davao and has blossomed to the point of being appointed a presidential economic advisor, even though he is a Chinese citizen from Xiamen. Yang has been a key figure in bringing in Chinese investors through the mainland's Friends of the Philippines Foundation and was close to the former Chinese ambassador in Manila, Zhao Jianhua. In 2021, Yang's shadowy network became embroiled in a scandal over apparent massive over-pricing of Covid-related medical supplies through an upstart company Pharmally Pharmaceutical.[7]

There are also unlisted family-owned retailers whose wealth is hard to estimate, most significant is the Que family which owns what for many years was and may still be the largest retail pharmacy, Mercury Drug. Started by Chinese petty trader, Mariano Que, in 1945, it now has more than 1,000 outlets, though it now faces competition from South Star Drug, part of Gokongwei's Robinsons Group. Still enjoying overwhelming dominance in its much smaller sector is the National Book Store started in the 1940s by husband and wife team, Jose and Socorro Ramos. It is now the prime seller of books, stationery, school supplies in the country it is a private company.

Due to foreign investment restrictions, local subsidiaries of multinationals are conspicuous by their absence on the stock exchange. One exception, however, is Metro Pacific run by prominent Filipino Manny Pangilinan but ultimately controlled by the family of the late Indonesian tycoon, Lim Sioe Leong, now headed by his son Anthony Salim. Lim was the favoured capitalist of former Indonesian President Suharto. Through a web of companies headed by Metro-Pacific the Salim group controls two of the nation's largest utilities, Meralco which supplies power for the whole of metropolitan Manila, and the PLDT, once a government owned monopoly privatized in the 1990s. Gokongwei's JG Summit and the Lopez Group also have stakes in PLDT.

In addition to those families whose wealth can be partly traced via listed companies, there are less visible mega-rich ones which owe much of their fortune to the expansion of cities, notably metropolitan Manila where they had long owned land. The Ortigas family owned the land of what is now the Ortigas business district. The ADB became one the first to move its headquarters there in 1991.

The Tuason family owned Diliman hacienda which is now the location of the vast University of the Philippines campus, and part of Quezon City itself by far the largest component of metropolitan Manila. Madrigal is another old-money family which is part of the metropolitan elite whose assets are somewhat dispersed but the name still has clout as do Montelibano, Jalandoni, Javellana, Romualdez, Prieto, Delgado, Lichauco and a dozen or two more who are not dominant in any industry but have diverse interests in land, property, commerce and finance.

The tight family control that all the above exercise over their groups help sustain a situation where wealth is largely in the hands of two groups – several Chinese, a few Spanish and various *mestizo* mixes. As in several Latin American countries there is a link between class and ethnicity, particularly at the level of national prominence. It also carries through into politics, particularly at the provincial level. The names above mostly have national or at least metropolitan wealth origins and presence.

In time, specifically Chinese identity tends to fade as links to the mainland, including language, are forgotten and the Philippines is ever more home. However, China's push into the region with arms as well as money has complicated the picture. So, whilst Duterte may embrace Beijing for a series of reasons, future populists might take a very different line to the point where anti-China sentiment becomes directed at local Chinese or at least those perceived as least integrated. The Chinese preference for white skin is also reflected in attitudes to the browner skin of national norm. The links between ethnicity and wealth are potentially troublesome given the disparities which exist and the apparent inability of the political and justice systems to level the playing fields.

Notes

1 *Forbes* Magazine, September 2019.
2 *Forbes* Magazine, September 2021.

17

Mindanao: beckoning frontier

The island of Mindanao is the most misunderstood part of the nation. Decades of on and off conflict in its Muslim region has long stolen the headlines. Under President Duterte, this provided an excuse for declaring martial law over the whole island. The reality is that for decades the island proved a land of opportunity for hundreds of thousands who moved from over-populated islands, mostly the Visayas, to the relatively underpopulated Mindanao. Even now, after years of in-migration its population is only about 40 per cent that of Luzon, though Luzon is only slightly larger in area. The total, including the Sulu Archipelago and other adjacent islands, is about 25 million of which the Bangsamoro Autonomous Region of Muslim Mindanao (BARMM) is about 4.2 million.

In earlier times, Muslim rulers loosely controlled about half the island's territory but today only about 24 per cent of the population is Muslim, of whom about 70 per cent live in the BARMM. Of these, some 2.6 million are on the mainland and 1.4 million in the archipelago. Widely scattered so-called indigenous people (IP) also known as *lumads* (a Cebuanao word for indigenous) are another 4–5 per cent with both sets of minorities in spasmodic conflict with the settler-descended majority, or with each other.

Movement from the Visayas to Mindanao long pre-dates the Spanish, at least according to Mandaya and Kalangan, the languages of Agusan and Surigao, the provinces which constitute most of today's Caraga region (Region 13). Migration was not an entirely one-way, north to south process, particularly in recent years of urbanization. Manila itself has been a magnet, but overall, and especially in the 1950s to the 1970s, Mindanao received most of the settlers.

In-migration over almost 100 years combined with high natural population growth naturally caused conflict, not just between the people of the Muslim polities of western Mindanao but between the indigenous groups and the newcomers elsewhere. The *lumad* groups speak separate but related languages and often have concepts of land ownership which differ from those of the state. Official and NGO efforts to protect ancestral domain claims find it hard to compete with local power interests. Some claims are no longer realistic given the proportion of *lumads* to the population. *Lumads* themselves also have conflicting claims.

According to a 1903 census, the total population was just 706,000, about half designated as 'civilized' and half as 'wild'.[1] The former were concentrated in Misamis and the latter in Cotabato. Things began to change rapidly under the Americans, better organized and more focused on creating wealth than their colonial predecessors. Americans had recognized the potential of Mindanao in a way the Spanish, not commercially-minded and focused on conflict with the Moros, had never done. From the earliest days of American rule, Davao was a base point for investment in mining and plantations in the little populated areas of central and southern Mindanao. Moro and indigenous groups shared an abundance of land but their loose claims were vulnerable to the Public Land Law which was supposed to formalize ownership but in effect opened the way for US entrepreneurs to establish rubber, abaca and other plantations. On the north coast, Iligan and Cagayan de Oro offered entry points for opening land in Misamis and Lanao and Butuan for Agusan and Surigao and on the south coast Davao for southern Cotabato and the Compostela Valley.

American entrepreneurs arrived to exploit forests, look for minerals and plant abaca in Davao and rubber in Basilan. Formal internal colonization also began, mostly in Cotabato, where settlers were awarded blocs of land based around new townships. Muslim and indigenous leaders might object but at least in Mindanao, though not the Sulu archipelago, there was initially plenty of land. Nor was settlement initially on a large scale. Between 1918 and 1936, the government assisted only about 6,000 families make the move[2] – though there was also informal migration which became self-reinforcing, mainly to Misamis, Cotabato and Davao. The Japanese, meanwhile, took over the Davao abaca plantations and spurred the city's wider commercial development.

The big boost to settlement came with the Commonwealth government, President Quezon recognizing the agricultural and forestry potential of the region as a way to underpin the national economy and raise the Christian population to counterbalance the Moros. Specifically, he invested in roads and other infrastructure which enabled independent settlers to have access, to stake claims, to plant crops. Settlers, mostly from the Visayas, squatted, planted and created new realities. The most spectacular development was led by General Paulino Santos who persuaded Quezon to declare the fertile but little populated Koronadal Valley in south Cotabato as a reservation for settlers. Existing peoples were, in theory, able to register their own land, but soon the valley had 10,000 newcomers speaking Cebuano and Ilongo (the language of western Visayas) laying the foundation of today's city named after the General and working the rich lands nearby.

The Davao region, meanwhile, had attracted large numbers of Japanese to develop timber and plantation industries and Davao city was on its way to becoming the largest in Mindanao, with far more Japanese than Americans. Japanese ran shops, restaurants, fish canneries and export enterprises, often with sleeping Filipino partners to get around alien laws.

The 1930s Japanese-led developments were key to making Davao the premier city of the island that it soon became. Although many Japanese left in 1945, their lands and enterprises were quickly taken over by immigrants from the Visayas and Luzon.

The next big waves of immigrants came with President Magsaysay, hoping to reduce the pressure on land in Central Luzon and hence the appeal of the Huk rebels. He arranged for thousands more migrants to be provided with homesteads in Mindanao which had the added benefit of increasing the size of the non-Moro population. Others followed in their wake looking for new land and opportunities in every part of the island except those where Moro populations were sufficiently numerous to keep them at a distance. As well as Davao and General Santos, Northern Mindanao saw large scale immigration evident today in its plantation crops and the prosperity of Cagayan de Oro.

The settlers greatly expanded the planted areas but were responsible for massive destruction of forests, some for logging, others to plant crops. Between 1948 and 1960 alone, Mindanao received 1.2 million migrants with Cotabato and Davao accounting for two-thirds of the total.[3] Massive destruction of forests was one consequence, whether for logs for sale or to clear land for crops. Between 1950 and 1987, 45 per cent[4] of forests were lost, with consequent erosion and flood problems.

Davao is an immigrant city, par excellence. President Duterte represented both the rise of Mindanao and its colonization by Visayans. From being the political boss of the Cebu city of Danao, Duterte's father Vicente moved to Mindanao in 1959 becoming governor of the then undivided province of Davao in Mindanao and later a Nacionalista member of Marcos' first term government. The Dutertes were thus in on the ground floor of Davao city's rise from relative insignificance to the third most populous in the nation (after Manila and Cebu). It had only been established as a town in 1848 and became a city in 1936. From the 1950s to the 1990s, Davao city's population rose by 3–4 per cent a year and then continued to grow by at least 2 per cent. Reflecting these immigrant waves, the predominant language, indeed the lingua franca of the island, is Cebuano. Ilonggo is also widely spoken. Both now eclipse the indigenous local languages such as Manobo, and those of the Muslim peoples from Lanao and Maguindanao. Less than 100 years after Visayan migration began, Cebuano and to a lesser extent Ilonggo, have become the dominant languages, while 70 per cent of the population is Christian. The languages of Maguindanao, Maranao and Tausug (of Sulu) dominate in their areas, and *lumad* groups speak their own languages among themselves. Creole Spanish known as Chavacano is also still spoken in Zamboanga, but overall, the settlers have come to dominate the region as a whole as surely as immigrant groups dominate Canada and New Zealand.

The *lumads*, too, are now mostly Christian and their relative position has been eroded by intermarriage, but enough keep their identity and sense of ownership to resist the pressure for their land and resources. Although their ancestral lands are supposed to be protected by law, the reality has been different. The *lumads* have always been on the defensive with their leaders singled out for assassination. *Lumad* resistance has long been a recruiting ground for the NPA which sometimes enabled it to force plantation and mine owners to pay protection money. The NPA recruited *lumads*, landless farmers and poor tenants, while the mining, plantation and established settler interests looked to the military. The military was, in effect, an agent of immigrant and corporate interests as well as the State. Duterte, the Cebuano immigrant, favoured opening ancestral lands to companies to generate wealth. *Lumad* leaders were targets for assassination in the same way as the organizers of poor sugar workers in Negros and coconut farmers in Bicol had been.

Duterte, the populist politician in a settler society, was able to exploit two Mindanao themes simultaneously. Firstly, as iterated in many speeches, that the interests of other regions had been sacrificed to 'imperial Manila'. Secondly, if only by implication, he appealed to the linguistic identification of Cebuano, now the main language of Mindanao against *lumad* identity. The total number of *lumads* in Mindanao is unclear as many became absorbed in the immigrant communities or became Christians, but about 4–5 per cent of the population of Mindanao identify with one group or another. The main groups are the Manobo, mostly in central Mindanao but widely spread, the Subanon of the northwest, the Teduray of Cotabato/Maguindanao and the Mandaya of Agusan and Surigao. The survival of their traditions and beliefs after 600 years of Muslim then Christian dominance has been remarkable even though many have converted to Christianity and been partly absorbed in the mainstream with which they share the same original Austronesian culture.

The scale of the internal colonization after 1935 was only partly a result of colonial rule or the Quezon initiatives. The underlying demographic driver was that because of improved government in the late Spanish period, and the impact of the US on public health, the population in the Visayas and Luzon in particular grew exceptionally fast. The people of Mindanao had far more land than they were able to occupy and cultivate. They also lacked the political power to halt settlement. The Commonwealth and then independence saw a government with even less interest in protecting Moro and *lumad* land rights than the foreign rulers. In 2019, the BARMM had the nation's highest fertility rate but it was not enough to reverse its relative decline given the continued, if now slow migration of other Filipinos into non BARMM regions.

Mindanao's development has not been helped by political divisions inspired by the ambitions of local leaders to be province governors. For instance, one of the smaller ones Sarangani was created out of South Cotabato and is itself in two halves separated by South Cotabato and General Santos City. Camiguin, with a population of only about 100,000, was separated from Misamis Oriental, Davao Occidental carved out of Davao del Sur, Davao de Oro (formerly Compostela Valley) out of Davao del Norte, Zamboanga Sibugay carved out of Zamboanga del Sur and Dinagat Islands out of Surigao del Norte. From a national administrative point of view, the division into regions made more sense: Zamboanga (Region 9), Northern Mindanao (Region 10), Davao (Region 11), Soccsksargen (Region 12) comprising South Cotabato, Cotabato, Sarangani, Sultan Kudarat and General Santos, Caraga (Region 13) comprising the Agusan and Surigao provinces, and the BARMM. However, apart from the BARMM, the regions have only an advisory and coordinating role.

Despite being a land of opportunity and relative prosperity, particularly in the Davao and Northern Mindanao regions, much of it remains poor. The BARMM is the poorest region but the Caraga region, comprising the two Agusan and two Surigao provinces, is not far behind. Others include the three Zamboanga provinces of the Zamboanga region. Although the conflict in the Muslim areas unquestionably contributed much to poverty, lack of development has been widespread in other provinces, including those where land is plentiful and attracted migrants. Reasons for poverty vary. Zamboanga, for example, has long coastlines but narrow coastal strips and beyond that rugged, mountainous terrain.

Caraga encapsulates many of the problems of the wider nation. In theory, it is endowed with great forests, well-watered lowlands and lakes, a variety of mineral deposits, a coastline which offers opportunities for fisheries, and beaches and scenery to lure tourists. The regional capital, Butuan, is the oldest identifiable city in the country, dating back more than 1,000 years and with trading links to Java and China. In recent times, however, Butuan has been overshadowed by the growth not only of Davao City but also Cagayan de Oro to the west. Its development has been slow despite being on the sea and at the mouth of the Agusan river which reaches 300 kilometres into the heart of Mindanao. Agusan del Sur has the rich Agusan Valley but a population of only 700,000 (2015) spread out over 10,000 square kilometres and held back by poor infrastructure.

One large mining company, Nickel Asia, operates modern mines but much mining is small- to medium-scale and uncontrolled, raising little if any revenue for the government while polluting rivers and lakes. Efforts by the Department of Environment and Natural Resources to regulate mines has been spasmodic and has met resistance from entrenched local political interests with their representatives in Congress. Some 70 per cent of the region is categorized as forest but with much having been logged over during the Marcos years, secondary forest is not productive and private owners deter potential settlers who could cultivate it. Illegal logging continues, causing soil erosion and flooding.

The lands of the Agusan Valley and the lower slopes of the surrounding hills produce a large surplus of rice, corn, coconuts, bananas etc. Agusan incomes are higher than those of Surigao, and Agusan Sur attracts settlers from poorer neighbours, but the rate of farm tenancy is high, productivity is low and poor market access inhibits faster development. The region's potential awaits the arrival of capital and improved husbandry into farming itself as well as into roads and environmental management.

Worst off have been the Surigao provinces where few benefit from mining and forest wealth. The Paper Industries Corporation of the Philippines (PICOP) once employed more than 10,000 people in and around Bislig on the coast of Surigao del Sur. At its peak it was the biggest pulp and paper operation in Asia, annually producing 150,000 tons of paper and board. With a 186,000 hectare concession and by replanting clear-cut old forests with fast-growing species it should have been an example of sustainable industrial forestry, but after forty years in existence, it finally collapsed in 2008 under the weight of debt to the government, bad management, outdated technology, poor quality product, NPA activity, strikes, ancestral domain claims on its forests, illegal logging and settlement. It also had a history of dependence on a protected domestic market.

In addition to this waste of a massive investment, there was relatively little investment in the oil palms which replaced much of the old forest in Indonesia and Malaysia. Although Caraga accounts for about 40 per cent of Philippine palm oil production, the nation has remained a huge importer despite Mindanao's favourable climate. Some of the blame for this rested with ideological opposition to private plantations supposedly in *lumad* interests. Foreign NGO denigration of palm oil also did not help.

Dynastic politics in Mindanao is at least as strong as in Luzon and the Visayas and applies to the big cities as well as the least developed provinces. The Dutertes rule not only Davao City but, indirectly, the other Davao provinces except Davao de Sur where the Cagas family has long dominated. Other names which recur as governors, mayor and members of the House of Representatives include Pimentel in Surigao de Sur, Pelaez in Misamis Oriental, Amante in Agusan del Norte, Matugas in Surigao del Norte, Zubiri in Bukidnon, Mangudadatu in Sultan Kudarat and Maguindanao, Tan in Sulu, Dimaporo in Lanao del Norte, Adiong in Lanao del Sur and Ampatuan in Maguindanao. Their rivals are also mostly dynasts. Lesser dynasts are also found at lower levels of government.

As the first president from Mindanao, Duterte not only made much of his (transplanted) roots but showed willingness to support some of its entrepreneurs, notably Dennis Uy who received a national telecoms licence and development rights at Clark Freeport Zone (see Chapter 16). He was generally supportive of plantation and mining companies though as mayor he had had to have agreements with the NPA to keep them out of the city. Despite Mindanao's known mineral wealth, mining has long been a battlefield between competing interests, on the one hand creating social strife and pollution while on the other failing to generate the revenues that local and national governments need. National policy reversals have deterred investment. Despite the promise of minerals, some big mining projects have been stalled for years, notably a huge, partly foreign-invested copper and gold project at Tampakan in South Cotabato with an estimated 2.9 billion tons of 0.6 per cent copper and 0.2 per cent gold. However, gold mining in Davao del Norte and Davao de Oro has prospered, with several small but higher-grade deposits.

Plantation agriculture also faces opposition from *lumads* trying to protect their ancestral domain and the demands of landless farmers. Mindanao accounts for a high proportion of the nation's agricultural exports and the big producers want more land. The nation is among the top three global banana exporters, with Davao, Northern Mindanao and SOCCSARGEN[5] regions predominating, plantations varying from the vast ones such as that of Dole to small family farms. Northern Mindanao and SOCCSARGEN provide most pineapple exports and Mindanao as a whole accounts for more than half of coconut production, concentrated in the Northern Mindanao, Davao and Zamboanga regions. Mindanao is also a significant producer of rubber, mainly from Zamboanga and SOCCSARGEN mostly from smallholders.

Despite occasional disease problems and fluctuating market prices, these cash crops explain a lot about the income differentials between and within regions with value added, even when productivity is low, exceeding that of the rice and corn areas such as the Agusan valley. Overall, although Mindanao remains well behind Luzon and the Visayas in economic and social development, the picture is mixed. The Davao region encompassing the four Davao provinces – Sur, Norte, de Oro, Oriental – ranks fifth out of seventeen national regions in per capita income, a reflection of its agricultural and mining wealth as well as Davao City. Meanwhile, the nation's two poorest regions are nearby – the Caraga region encompassing the Agusan and Surigao provinces, and, poorest of all, the BARMM.

Development of cities has also lagged behind. Davao City, Cagayan de Oro and General Santos were conspicuous for emerging as prosperous trading hubs on the back of nearby agricultural development. On the other hand, Cotabato City has a high level of poverty despite a long history as a trading centre because of the problems of its BARMM hinterland. The processing of agricultural, fishery and forest products and oil refining generates some manufacturing activity but the closure of major projects such as PICOP and the Iligan steel works were major setbacks to the urbanization of Mindanao as well as to the broader economy. Meanwhile, inland cities such as Valencia and Malaybalay in Bukidnon which grew dramatically in the 1960s and 1970s have lagged behind with poor communications offsetting climatic attractions which might bring industries and BPO in addition to agricultural processing.

All in all, the future of the Philippine economy, and the resolution of internal conflicts, now rests more on better harnessing the land and potential of Mindanao than on what happens in the regions around the national capital.

Notes

1 US Bureau of Census, 1905, quoted in the *Philippine Quarterly*, Vol. 25 No 12, 1997.

2 T.J.S. George, *Revolt in Mindanao The Rise of Islam in Philippine Politics*, Oxford: Oxford University Press, 1980, p. 111.

3 Patricio N. Abinales, *Orthodoxy and History in the Muslim-Mindanao Narrative*, Quezon City: Ateneo de Manila Press, 2010, p. 168.

4 Ibid., p. 169.

5 An acronym for the region in southwestern Mindanao comprising the provinces of Cotabato, South Cotabato, Sarangani and Sultan Kuderat and the city of General Santos.

Region IX
(Zamboanga Peninsula)

Dapitan •

Dipolog ★

Zamboanga
del Norte

Zamboanga
del Sur

Ipil ★   Zamboanga
Sibugay

★ Pagadian

• Zamboanga City

• Isabela City

Region X
(Northern Mindanao)

★ Mambajao
Camiguin

**Misamis
Oriental** • Gingoog

El Salvador
•

Cgayan
de Oro City ★

★ Oroquieta

**Misamis
Occidental**

Iligan ★

★ Malaybalay

• Ozamiz

Tangub •

★ Tubod

**Lanao
del Norte**

Bukidnon

• Valencia

Region XI
(Davao Region)

Davao
del Norte

★ Nabunturan

Davao
Oriental

Tagum
★

Davao
de Oro

• Davao
City

• Panabo

• Samal

Mati
★

Digos
★

Davao
del Sur

Malita
★

Davao
Occidental

Region XII
(Soccsksargen)

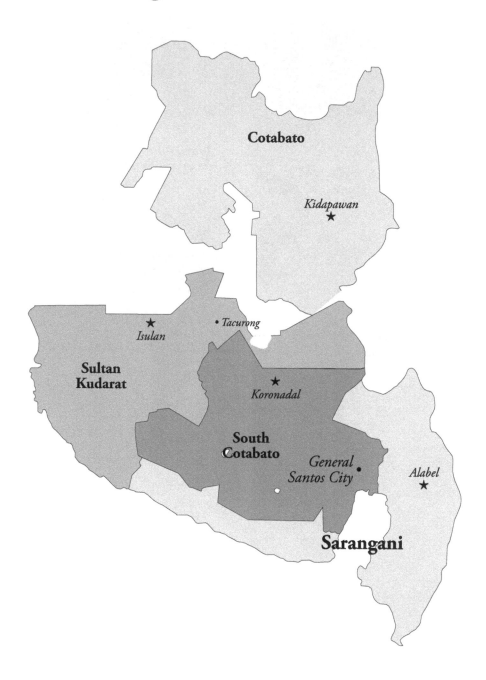

Cotabato

Kidapawan ★

★ Isulan

• Tacurong

Sultan
Kudarat

★ Koronadal

South
Cotabato

General
Santos City •

Alabel ★

Sarangani

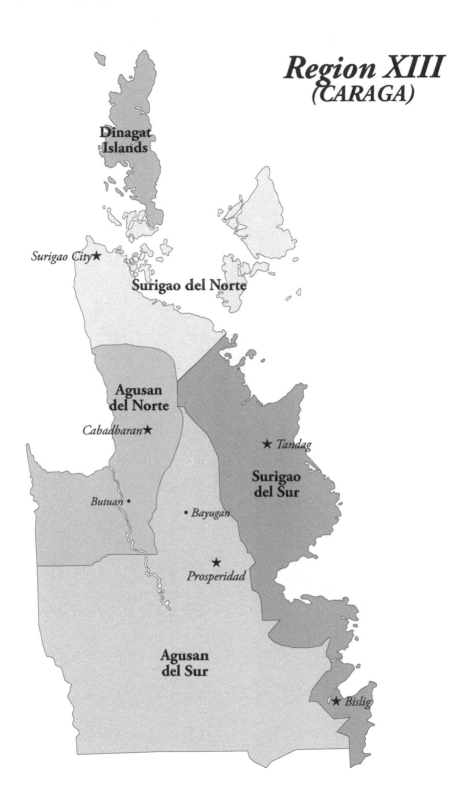

Region XIII
(CARAGA)

Dinagat
Islands

Surigao City★

Surigao del Norte

Agusan
del Norte

Cabadbaran★

★ Tandag

Surigao
del Sur

Butuan •

• Bayugan

★
Prosperidad

Agusan
del Sur

★ Bislig

18

Moros, datus, military and more

Duterte saw himself as a Mindanaoan, but the historical perspective of Muslims was always rather different. When the Spanish arrived, the Muslim sultanates ruled western and part of central Mindanao and the Sulu Archipelago. Even Islam was relatively new to the region, becoming established in the fifteenth century. Sultans came to have hegemony over roughly half of Mindanao but in many areas the majority remained non-Muslim.

In the northeast, when Magellan arrived in 1521, a non-Muslim rajah still ruled Butuan. It was subject to attacks by the sultanate of Ternate in the Malukus, but Butuan was a shadow of its former self when it had been in direct trade contact with China in the fourteenth century and a source of finely-worked gold objects dating back 500 years showing evidence of its links to Java and hence to India. In the sixteenth century and for a long while afterwards, the interior of the island was mostly the land of indigenous groups speaking related Austronesian languages and with similar but not identical beliefs and cultural practices.

In many respects, for 300 years of Spanish rule most of Mindanao went its own way. Sultans and datus ruled Muslim areas, the indigenous groups (today's *lumads*), neither Christian nor Muslim ruled themselves, the Spanish and the Church had their enclaves. Economically, Mindanao and Sulu were barely touched by the trade and plantation developments in Luzon and the western Visayas in the nineteenth century.

For most of Spain's reign, its most persistent Muslim adversaries were the Sulu sultanate and the seafarers of the Maguindanao coast. For more than 200 years, the sultanate controlled the Sulu Archipelago and the Samal and Iranun seafarers who brought slaves and booty to the Sulu markets from raids into the Visayas and Luzon. 'Sulu's power rose through the introduction of firearms into eastern Malaysia and began to decline at the introduction of steam war vessels'.[1] Seafarers from the Maguindanao coast also took part in the conflicts which did not come to a decisive end until a massive Spanish invasion and occupation of Jolo in 1876.

Even thereafter, Sulu remained the particular locus of incidents which aroused the wrath of Muslims generally and the Sulu Tausugs in particular.[2]

The Americans had perpetrated the Bud Dajo massacre in 1906 (see Chapter 3). The 1968 Jabidah massacre (see Chapter 6) of young Tausugs recruited to invade Sabah spawned the Moro National Liberation Front (MNLF) and insurrection. In 1974, the MNLF captured Jolo, leading to the destruction of the town. Sulu pride in its own identity was one issue, but the underlying cause of Moro rebellion on the Mindanao mainland was rather different. The massive influx of settlers which began under the Commonwealth and was accelerated by Magsaysay, increasingly impinged on traditionally Muslim lands, whether cultivated or not. The more who arrived from the Visayas and Luzon, the more they came to be at loggerheads with existing communities. In turn, clashes over land came to be seen in religious terms, Muslim against Christian. Non-Muslim groups were either ignored or absorbed. Local conflicts became more and more frequent, with Christian vigilante groups using violence to drive out Moros from their land for settlement by newcomers.

Moros sought common defence with the foundation of the Muslim Independence Movement in 1968. It later changed its name to Mindanao Independence Movement (MIM) but its identity was clearly Islamic and had no attraction to Christians and little to *lumads*. Indeed, it was to be one of the weaknesses of Muslim demands that they claimed a much larger area of Mindanao (and part of Palawan) than they realistically occupied. The demographic changes of the past century had reduced them so that their enclaves of western Mindanao and Sulu, now comprising the BARMM, account for only 12 per cent of the land area and 17 per cent of the Mindanao population.

Out of the MIM came the Moro National Liberation Front (MNLF) headed by Nur Misuari, a Tausug who had been politically active at the University of the Philippines in the 1960s and was a founder, along with future Communist Party leader JoMa Sison, of Kabataang Makabayan (Patriotic Youth). Its capture of Jolo in 1974 and the town's subsequent destruction by the army launched a wider war. Sulu was later also the origin and sustenance of Abu Sayyaf, a group with a Wahabist doctrine imported from Arabia and dedicated to kidnap and smuggling while attaching its banner to extremist international Muslim causes, notably al-Qaeda and Islamic State.

For the fifty years from the MNLF launch to the 2019 establishment of the BARMM Moro lands were to see intermittent fighting involving two major and several minor Muslim groups, the Philippine army and police, clans and politicians reflecting local dynastic interests and ethnic groups. An agreement to establish the ARRM was first made in 1976 between the government and the MNLF but the emergence of the more radical MILF and then of other groups led to many more years of intermittent conflict. The ARRM government was a shell with little authority.

Turbulence was assured by the power struggle between the MILF and the ever-volatile Misuari. Although the MNLF became overshadowed by the

MILF, he continued to be a source of trouble in the archipelago. In 2013, an MNLF faction aligned with Misuari proclaimed a Bangsamoro Republik and attempted to seize Zamboanga City where there was a large MNLF enclave in a mostly Christian city. Fighting lasted several days with many deaths and thousands displaced. The same year, Misuari gave verbal support for a force which invaded Lahad Datu town in Sabah on behalf of Jamalul Kiram III, one of several claimants to the Sulu sultanate.

These events, however, did not stop a 2014 agreement between the MILF and the Aquino government to create an authority with more powers and funding than the ARMM. The creation of the BARMM was long held up in Congress but the Bangsamoro Organic Law (BOL) was enacted in 2018 after the Marawi siege and deemed constitutional. The creation of the BARMM was a major step towards more lasting peace with its provisions for receiving a direct grant of 5 per cent of national government revenue, plus other financial assistance, and enabling the imposition of Shariah law for Muslims. It was not given a separate police force, as originally intended under the 2014 agreement, but it had a regional force within the Philippine National Police which provided for localization. The BOL also provided for a parliamentary form of government, a concession to the MNLF and its backers in the Sulu Archipelago who feared domination by the mainland majority. In addition to the original ARMM provinces, a plebiscite saw Cotabato City and several municipalities in North Cotabato join, while Isabela City in Basilan opted out.

Following the 2019 plebiscite, a Transition Authority was set up to last until elections in 2022. The Authority was dominated by the MILF, which improved the chances of it eroding the support for the extremist holdout of the Bangsamoro Islamic Freedom Fighters (BIFF) in Maguindanao. However, transitioning from being a secretive organization with tight-knit leadership to running a multi-component administration was a huge challenge. Yet progress under Interim Chief Minister Murad Ebrahim, long a top MILF commander, was real, as was the gradual transformation of the MILF into a political party, the United Bangsamoro Justice Party.

An interim parliament was also established as a forum for debate on policies and airing of grievances. The cohesion of the region was to be tested by elections originally planned for 2022 but now postposed to 2025. In question,, too was the commitment of the central government to put its full weight behind making the BARMM a success. Duterte had only reluctantly, and after the 2017 Marawi siege, given political support to the passage of the BOL, partly because the issue could interfere with his own plans for a federal system for the country as a whole. Re-building of Marawi also proved a very long process, the central government's paltry efforts doing nothing to earn the gratitude of the tens of thousands of citizens made homeless by the destruction. The reconstruction of Marawi became the responsibility of the Bangsamoro Transitional Authority (BTA) but the task required massive help from Manila.

Longer term, the region faced most of the same divisive forces which has spawned different and often competing rebel groups over the previous half century. Firstly, there was the most obvious three-way struggle between the Maranao, the Maguindanao and the Tausug-led people of Sulu, with their history of domination of rule over the archipelago. Although the archipelago is ethnically divided between Tausug, Yakan, Samal and others, it had an identity. Sulu and its governor, Abdusakur Tan, voted against joining the BARMM, though as a member of the existing ARRM, Sulu had little choice but to join. Tan favoured a national federal system in which Sulu would have its own identity known as Bangsa Sug: Land of the Sug. So long as federalism remains on the national agenda there would be doubts about the permanence of the BARMM in the face of Sulu's separatist desires.

Sulu itself also exemplified the role of clan links in local politics with even the venerable MNLF split into factions. Abu Sayyaf was mostly seen as a group promoting extremist Islam through terror and kidnap but its continued if fragmented existence owed as much to both local traditions of piracy, raiding and smuggling and family links, which provided protection for its activists.[3] Intermittent bombings continued as the divides between Islamists, drug runners and gang warfare were vague.

Keeping control of the archipelago remains a problem for any administration whether in Manila or, as in the case of ARRM and BARMM, Cotabato City. It stretches almost 400 kilometres from Basilan to Sibutu, just off the Borneo coast, comprising about a hundred inhabited islands and dozens of others, a population of various ethnic groups, centuries of seafaring experience and forests and rubber plantations (notably on Basilan) for hiding. Sulu is also central to the Philippine continued claim to Sabah (or at least part of it) in the name of the Sultan of Sulu. The claim is a desert mirage but continues to captivate politicians in Manila. It would have been an amusement if not for the damage it did to relations with Malaysia in particular.

Sulu was not the only significant BARMM doubter. Cotabato City, though the de facto capital, had never joined the ARRM and its mayor opposed joining the BARMM. In the event, 58 per cent voted in favour but given that the population was 70 per cent Muslim and joining was promoted by Duterte and the Catholic Church, the division was evidence that suspicions of the MILF ran deep in this mixed and commercially focused city.

While the MILF may seem to be a united force with an Islamic agenda, its heartland, Maguindanao, has a singular centrifugal feature. It exceeds all other provinces in the domination of local politics by clans and dynasties at provincial and village level. This was long a land of private militias such as those of the Ampatuan clan which perpetrated the 2009 massacre of members of the rival Mangudadatu clan and accompanying supporters and journalists. The Ampatuans had earlier been the subject of assassination attempts. These families long enjoyed immunity from Manila by delivering local votes to national candidates. Their militias sometimes played ambiguous roles in the conflict between the military and the MILF. There remains no easy way to reduce clan power while their captive votes remain important in Manila and in the future BARMM parliament.

Lanao del Sur had similar features. Families such as the Dimaporos and Alontos long held sway in official politics while the MILF enjoyed widespread support. Clan loyalties also partly explain the Maute family of Maranao's occupation of Marawi in 2017 in the name of the IS. The IS was a useful banner for other small groups such as Ansar Khalifa as well as the BIFF, a MILF breakaway which refused to accept anything less than full independence for Bangsamoro. Casualties among these militant groups were very high, but poverty as well as the appeal of jihadism facilitated recruitment.

Private militias played varying roles with or against the MILF and other Muslim groups. Separating clan interests and family feuds from Muslim ideological commitments can be difficult in a region with a long history of what is locally called 'rido' – clan conflicts. Even in 2020 there was still an estimated seventy-seven private militias in the Philippines, almost all of them in the BARMM. Traditions of violence, whether against local rivals or the state, run deep.

Elections in 2022 would test the influence of the MILF against the rival dynasts as well as the ability of those elected to rise above Maguindanao/Maranao/Tausug divisions. The BARMM parliament will have eighty members, half elected geographically, half by Party List, which should help the MILF's established United Bangsamoro Justice Party, but only with a sustained reduction in the number of weapons, and the disbanding of clan militias could lasting peace be achieved.

Support from Manila for the BARMM has been seen as lukewarm. The possibility of federalism lingered and politicians in Manila still looked to the region mainly for votes delivered by the dynasts. The Duterte government appreciated Sulu's preference to have its own region separate from the BARMM and gave face to Nur Misuari by appointing him to be Philippine representative to the Organization of Islamic Cooperation (OIC). The 2020 Covid pandemic also diverted money and attention elsewhere. It was reluctant to spend more resources and wanted the Muslims to sort of their own problems rather than seeing that the Transitional Authority and MILF could have sufficient impact to reduce the appeal of more radical groups and gangs.

Whether the latest version of a Muslim autonomous region can hold is questionable, but in its first two years it helped keep a modicum of peace, though sporadic violence, including suicide bombings continued. It has funds and power that its predecessor, the ARRM, lacked. Its ministries and mechanisms are not the empty shells they were in the ARMM, but project implementation is an even bigger problem than elsewhere, and liaison between regional and national agencies is a work in progress. Attracting investment will be a challenge until there is a sustained period of peace. Any mining or plantation projects will also have to grapple with the ancestral domain claims of *lumad* groups which in the BARMM cover lands where they have long had only a small presence. The National Commission on Indigenous Peoples may also find itself at loggerheads with the BARMM on *lumad* issues. The *lumads* within the BARMM are a minority within a minority and so doubly susceptible to seeing their identity overwhelmed and their lands appropriated.

Beyond the issues of political stability is whether the region can be hauled out of its condition of dynastic, semi-feudal power, and its low level of education and public health for which datus and religious leaders between them are partly to blame. Mass literacy was late to arrive and sometimes a focus on learning Arabic and studying the Koran ensured that it lagged even the modest standards elsewhere. Today only 37 per cent of pupils make it to sixth grade, little more than half the national average. Life expectancy is ten years less than the nationally average and almost twenty years between lowest (in Tawi-Tawi) and highest. Women's life expectancy was only about one year greater than men, compared with seven years nationally.

The region lacks a major city focus which would encourage industry and education. Even before the destruction of Marawi, there was no magnet for industry and Marawi contrasted with nearby, mostly non-Muslim Iligan. In time Cotabato, hub of government and commerce, could play that role but extended peace is a pre-requisite for large-scale investment. Today Cotabato, despite a venerable history as a commercial centre, is only the seventh largest city in Mindanao.

The BARMM lacks the economic links to more thriving cities enjoyed by two neighbouring provinces with large Muslim minorities. Sultan Kudarat has good connections to Koronadal and General Santos cities. Although only 30 per cent Muslim, it long had a Muslim governor from the Mangudadatu family. Likewise, Lanao del Norte, only 40 per cent Muslim, had a dynast governor from the Dimaporo family and has a thriving port city, Iligan, as its hub. These two provinces are illustrations of how the two main communities can cooperate when numbers of roughly evenly matched Muslims and non-Muslims can easily accept Muslim dynasts who reflect the syncretic traditions of the region rather than Arab-inspired Islamism.

In many ways the Muslim enclave on the Mindanao mainland is too small and too surrounded by non-Muslim provinces to make a coherent economic, rather than political, region. The Sulu Archipelago might see a future closer to its fellow Tausugs and Samal in Sabah but international boundaries are unlikely to change unless the adhesion of Sabah to Malaysia is in question. Provinces are also divided into municipalities created to meet dynastic needs and too small to be efficiently run.

On the mainland, improving road communication with neighbouring provinces can boost economies and eventually provide more jobs. With the BARMM due to receive 75 per cent of royalties from natural resource extraction, peace could bring investment. A drive for better education was launched by the Transition Authority and should yield results eventually, but the BARMM also needs a lower fertility rate, currently well above the national average, and a genuine interest in integrating more closely with the national economy. The dynasts and the Arab-influenced clerics have their separate reasons for preferring things as they are, so peace alone will not be enough to bring the BARRM more into line either with the rest of the Philippines, or with neighbouring Malaysia and Indonesia. Lawlessness has been endemic to an even greater degree than in other regions so the road from open conflict to assured stability is long, and the end of dynasty and datu rule even longer. The BARMM is not much different from other less developed parts of the Philippines – just more so in the way it clings to an old order of clan competition.

Notes

1   Saleeby *The History of Sulu*, p. 118.
2   The name Tausug derives from Tao, the common Austronesian word for people, and Sug, an abbreviation of Suluk, the Malay word for a sea current. In Malaysia, Tausugs are known as Suluks.
3   Zachary Abuza and Luke Lischin, *US Institute of Peace, Special Report 468*, June 2020.

Bangsamoro
(Mindanao Area)

1. Pagayawan
2. Binidayan
3. Bayang
4. Lumbaca-Unayan
5. Lumbatan
6. Lumbayanague
7. Madalum
8. Bacolod-Kalawi
9. Ditsaan-Ramain
10. Buadiposo-Buntong
11. Datu Unsay
12. Datu Hoffer Ampatuan
13. Datu Salibo
14. Shariff Aguak
15. Shariff Saydona Mustapha

Lanao del Sur

Marawi

Kapai
Tagoloan II
Saguiran
Piagapo
Bubong
Marantao
Molondo
Balindong
Maguing
Tugaya
Taraka
Madamba
Poona Bayabao
Pualas
Masiu
Ganassi
Calanogas
Lumba-Bayabao
Picong
Butig
Amai Manabilang
Tubaran
Wao
Marogong
Malabang
Sultan Dumalondong
Balabagan
Kapatagan
Barira
Matanog
Buldon
Parang
Sultan-Mastura

Maguindanao

Sultan Kudarat
Cotabato City
Northern-Kabuntalan
Datu Odin Sinsuat
Kabuntalan
Sultan Sumagka
Datu Piang
Datu Saudi Ampatuan
Datu Blah Sinsuat
Upi
Datu Anggal Midtimbang
Guindulungan
Mamasapano
Rajah Buayan
Sultan Sa Barongis
Pagalungan
South Upi
Ampatuan
Datu Abdullah Sangki
Gen S.K. Pendatun
Pandag
Buluan
Daru Piglas
Mangudadatu

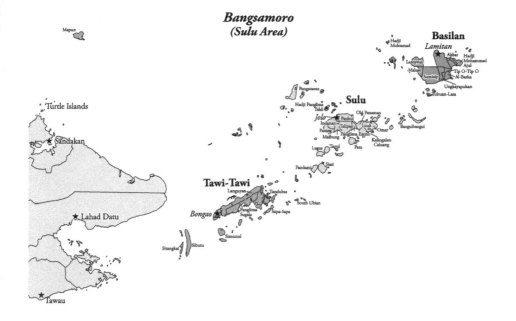

19

Religion on its sleeve

The Philippines is often assumed to be a largely (75+ per cent) Roman Catholic country and at least nominal Christians to total about 92 per cent. Symbols of religion are everywhere – crucifixes, statues, shrines, newspaper Bible quotes, radio preachers, jeepney decorations as well as churches. The Spanish friars in the late sixteenth and early seventeenth centuries had remarkable success through selflessness and good works, in laying the foundations of a belief system and a priestly hierarchy which in theory at least reached up to Rome. The friars were also adept at aligning the stories of the gospels and the saints with existing folk religion, while forbidding such practices as divorce and abortion, but outward displays such as mass attendance were not proof of inner belief or of major changes in cultural norms.

The lack of organized religion or any link between kingship and religion made 'conversion' appear relatively simple. Though the missionaries provided some protection against the ravages of the soldiers and *encomenderos*, they were still an alien group which became ever more identified as the main rulers of the islands. Today, despite the ubiquitous presence of the official Church, noted in its decades of opposition to family planning and divorce, the question remains of how far Catholicism in the country is at least as much Filipino as Roman. The friars could think that the traditional supreme being, Bathala in Tagalog, could be interpreted as the Christian God. The many spirits, *anitos*, which influenced daily life could similarly be re-interpreted as corresponding to Christian saints associated with good fortune, health and harvest.

The 'folk Catholicism' which exists today has, many argue, as many roots in a pre-Hispanic past as in official teaching and is tenuously attached to the hierarchy, especially among lower income groups. According to one argument, the friars' teachings were sometimes misunderstood from the very beginning due to mistranslations between Latin and Spanish on the one hand and Tagalog and Visayan on the other,[1] or individuals made their own interpretations to meet their circumstances.

In the eyes of the priests, the promotion of Mary as a virgin was seemingly to offset the traditions of relative sexual freedom enjoyed by women in pre-Hispanic society. Yet in the popular mind, Mary could be seen more as source of comfort, as mediator between the suffering or sinning individual and Jesus or between a sinner and the punisher threatening an eternity in hell. Nor did the church influence behaviour as much as it wanted. Early on de Morga noted 'they are not very chaste, either single or married women while their husbands, fathers and brothers are not very jealous or anxious about it'.[2]

Far from spending 'three hundred years in a convent', the Spanish priests endlessly complained about sex as 'the prince and master vice', which often trapped the friars themselves. Births out of wedlock were many and relations between women were quite common[3] according to an eighteenth century priest in Cebu who wrote of 'excessive and unbridled relations with each other' and also of 'other excesses' he could not repeat.[4]

A British visitor[5] in 1858 noted that 'chastity seems to have been unknown', a high number of births were out of wedlock. 'Violation of vows' was common. So today, 54 per cent of births remain out of wedlock and despite the ban on divorce, change of partners is very common.

The strongest evidence for the contribution of local traditions to the hold of Catholicism is its strength, despite official hierarchy's association with colonialism. The early friars may have helped to protect people against agents of the state but the orders soon evolved into rich landowners, demanding rents as well as attendance at Mass, and generally acting as a colonial authority through decades of minor risings. Official and ecclesiastical rule seldom went beyond the lowlands, whose representatives were the subject of constant interaction with un-Christianized people from the hills.

In the nineteenth century, the fissure between the dominant Spanish priests and the few local ones sowed the seeds of nationalism. The Cofradia de San Jose set up by Apolinario de la Cruz, better known by as Hermano Pule, began as a specifically Filipino religious group in opposition to the racially discriminating Spanish Church. He was executed in 1841. A generation later, the European liberal ideas of Rizal and the *ilustrados* coalesced with both popular resentment of the friars and the religious nationalism of the local priests, Burgos, Gomez and Zamora in 1872. Rather than setting the people against the religion, the latter may have inspired insurrection, at least among the peasantry. In his much-read *Pasyon and Revolution*, the influential writer Reynaldo Ileto saw a direct link between the sufferings of Christ to free the people and the suffering required to liberate Filipinos from landlord and state oppression.

The revolution against Spain also led to the establishment of a breakaway church, the Iglesia Filipina Independiente, often known as Aglipayan after its founder Gregorio Aglipay, a former Catholic priest who was close to the Katipunan leaders. Originally unitarian, it allowed priests to marry and conducted services in Tagalog. In theory, the official Catholic Church should have been at a disadvantage under the rule of a secular America which separated Church and State and allowed free rein to other Christian

FIGURE 19.1 *Built to last. Seventeenth century Paranaque Cathedral, Metro Manila. Ramon F. Velasquez, 2013, Wikimedia Commons.*

denominations. Many local priests had defected to the Aglipayans, the friars sent away, their lands seized, and some churches destroyed. The US focus on education promoted public non-denominational schools. However, the church, despite its losses of land and clergy, still had a structure and premises to continue to educate the elite, and ran the then only universities, Santo Tomas and Ateneo de Manila, until the University of the Philippines was set up in 1908. American bishops replaced Spanish ones and the first Filipino was elevated to bishop in 1905. Global Catholicism also launched a counter-attack with Jesuit priests and bishops from the US, and priests from Ireland,

Netherlands and Spain. Seminaries began to flourish again. Although Protestant groups entered, the main challenge to the Catholics was local.

Some Aglipayan priests returned to the Catholic fold but 1914 saw the founding of another new church, the Iglesia ni Cristo by Felix Y. Manalo. A fine orator, Manolo was inspired by nationalist and grass roots sentiments reflected in its use of Tagalog. It was dubbed the 'church of the poor' but its physical presence grew rapidly as a tithe required of members enabled the construction of many its distinctive churches. A ban on members marrying outside the group also helped ensure solidarity and continuity. Its liturgy was close enough to the Catholic to be familiar but priests were allowed to marry.

The American era saw the Catholic Church slowly regain much of the role it had had among all classes. Among the elite, the anti-clericalism and attachment to Free Masonry of the revolutionary era faded though in some cases it was replaced by socialist anti-imperialist ideas. Although politically conservative and dominated by foreign priests, the social role of the Church and its rites and institutions remained strong. Rome and popular religion co-existed.

For conservative and official Catholicism, the American era was one of stability and influence. The Church could work with the state while not being part of it. That remained very much the situation in the early decades of Philippine independence. Whatever its priests' sympathies for the poor, the Church was seen as a bastion against Communism and the Huks. Although seminaries were turning out many local priests, foreign ones with the umbilical links to Rome remained by far the majority. In the first two post-1945 decades there were 1,500 foreign priests – the great majority.[6] Only the Jesuits had a local majority and, from 1963, a Philippine superior.

Things changed rapidly in the 1970s in response to local and international developments. The ordination of many local priests coincided with the renewal of the Church driven by the Second Vatican Council including the replacement of Latin with vernacular languages and the beginning of more focus on non-European congregations. One local response was to form the Catholic Bishops Conference of the Philippines (CBCP) with a secretariat and plenary meetings twice a year to coordinate actions and issue guidance.

At home came the challenge of President Marcos' seizure of power in 1972. At first the church as a whole remained neutral, aware of the problem of addressing it as a political more than moral issue. However, it was gradually drawn into a deeply divisive situation. The natural conservatism of much of the hierarchy was increasingly challenged by mainstream anti-Marcos middle class, particularly as evidence of corruption and State violence proliferated. At the same time, a growing number of young, local priests came to sympathize with the lot of the poor, represented by the renewed vigour of the NPA. Some drew inspiration from 'liberation theology', the mix of Christian and Marxist ideas which saw a role for the church in freeing the poor from landowners and political oppression. A few were active supporters of the NPA. The hierarchy found that silence was sometimes impossible and made efforts to sympathize with anti-government movements while acting as a bridge. In Mindanao, bishops Rosales and Claver of Bukidnon were involved in *lumad* land rights negotiations and action against illegal logging, in Negros, Bishop Fortich helped create peace zones during the fierce NPA/government warfare and in Palawan Bishop Arigo was prominent in the anti-mining movement.

At the national level the political lead was taken by the Archbishop of Manila, Cardinal Sin, who through his personality, the support of the Bishops' Conference and via its media outlets such as Radio Veritas played a key role in the Edsa revolution. However, thereafter it primarily focused on an issue which many regarded as a retrograde step – opposition to family planning and in particular to the Reproductive Health Act. Traditional Catholic opposition had been reinforced by Pope Paul VI's 1968 encyclical Humanae Vitae which was followed more rigorously in the Philippines than in most Catholic countries. This was in the face of decades of evidence that the Philippines' persistently high fertility rate, much of it out of wedlock, was a direct cause of high poverty levels. There was also a gap between the lower income groups who had more children, whether out of choice, lack of means of contraception, and higher income groups. The Church was thus seen by critics as adding to income gaps while allying with politicians to oppose use of government funds for family planning. Church political influence, enhanced by its role in the ousting of Marcos' was key in thwarting family planning programmes during two female presidencies. Meanwhile, the women's movement was splintered and too closely associated with the extreme left for broader acceptance.

However, the new millennium also saw the Church hit by a series of sex and money scandals which were perhaps not surprising in such a large organization with eighty bishops and hundreds of priests.[7] However, it was now less easy to cover them up, and congregations, or at least the media, less tolerant of offences against the chastity demanded of priests. For long it was regarded as not unusual for priests to have a girlfriend, and to occasionally sire children. Parishioners would view it as a natural condition and the Church sometimes made provision for the upkeep of children. Priests might be reprimanded by their bishops but sins were forgiven. Cardinal Sin was later revealed as especially forgiving. However, two major scandals in 2002 involving prominent young bishops and many covered-up cases of sexual and financial misdoings pushed the CBCP to tighten up. This coincided with major revelations in other countries of priestly child abuse forcing the Vatican into abject apologies.

Scandals lowered the prestige of the Church and led to a fall in priestly vocations. All this occurred at a time when charismatic Christianity and the celebrity preachers on television, radio and the internet were a growing phenomenon, eating away at the authority of the hierarchy and the need for formal rituals.

The Church also found itself at odds with popular opinion over President Duterte's actions. It could brush off insults hurled by the foul-mouthed president about the Pope and ride out his boasts of behaviour condemned by the Church, but it could not keep silent over the mass killings of supposed drug dealers. Going against the populist tide may have benefited the charismatics and celebrity preachers who were more sympathetic to Dutertism. At a social level, the Church also lost influence to NGOs with a more secular, mostly urban background. These flourished after the fall of Marcos. Many were close to Akbayan, the moderate leftist party which consistently won seats with the 1998 introduction of the Party List members to the House of Representatives but whose influence on policy was mostly marginal.

The INC remained important. According to official 2015 data, 2.6 per cent of the population are INC adherents with churches overseas catering to local Filipino communities. Now headed by Manolo's grandson, it was also seen in scandals over money and allegations of coercion but it remains politically influential as its adherents tend to follow the voting preferences of the leader. It is in a sense a religious version of a major dynasty but with near national reach. The Aglipayans on the other hand gradually faded as a political force. Following the death of Aglipay, they abandoned unitarian belief in favour of the Trinity and joined the community of national episcopalian churches. There are still about 1 million adherents and it maintains a liberal view of social issues. Differences with the Catholics narrowed to the point that in 2021 the two agreed on the mutual acceptance of baptisms, of and reconciliation with other churches founded in the Aglipayan tradition.

Despite the predominance of the Catholics, and the long existence of national alternatives, the Aglipayans and INC adherents, there is a bewildering variety of other Christian options. In addition to groups under the evangelical banner, there are about twenty others, some international groups such as Baptists, Seventh Day Adventists, Jehovah's Witnesses and Mormons, and some very local such as the Negros-based Universalist Unitarian Church, inspired by Aglipay but with a largely rural membership and tending to support peasant grievances.

Recent decades have also seen a boom in new churches established by individual preachers using radio, television and the internet to promote themselves. The Jesus is Lord Church established in 1978 by Eddie Villanueva, 'Bro Eddie' as he is known, successfully fused evangelism with politics and money-making on behalf of his church which owns radio and TV stations and a college in his home town in Bulacan. From his days as an atheist radical imprisoned under Marcos he moved far to the right, became a politician who stood for president twice and became a Party List member of the House of Representatives. He had ambitions for the presidency and was elected Deputy Speaker of the House in 2019. His children mostly followed him into politics with one, Emmanuel, becoming a Senator in 2016 with the second highest vote. The Jesus is Lord Church was the quintessence of the singularly Philippines' fusion of religion, media celebrity and politics and, via the Villanuevas, added to popular support for Duterte.

Other popular evangelists have straddled official Catholicism and 'charismatic' preaching, notably Mike Velarde whose group, known as El Shaddai, was a presence on the airwaves for decades offering health and prosperity to those who faithfully attended gatherings – and contributed to the movement. As well as providing funds for his real estate business, the faithful could be healed of distress and poverty. Charismatic Christians, Catholic or not, focus on prayer meetings without the usual liturgy of Mass and sacraments but including personal declarations of faith. They thus incorporated the use of mass media with the appeal of individual leaders and the focus on personal faith more than ritual or the hierarchy. Politically, they tended to political and social conservatism. Velarde alone was estimated to have had 7 million followers, and similar, lesser-known preachers had millions more between them.

Duterte has an evangelist associate from Davao, Apollo Quiboloy, who founded the Kingdom of Jesus Church in 1985. It claims 4 million adherents nationally and another 2 million overseas. With money from devotees, it established a television and radio station and Quiboloy's private plane was used by Duterte in his 2016 campaign. In November 2021, Quiboloy was indicted in Los Angeles for running a sex trafficking operation.

The official Church is wary of the charismatics, whether or not they still say they are Catholics, but given their popularity there was nothing to be gained in criticizing them even though some may seem mainly concerned with money-making. They are not unique to the Philippines, though probably now more prominent there than in other predominantly Catholic countries. With them, the pre-Hispanic tradition of chanting and impromptu songs could find a voice in mass participation in group gatherings where individuals could proclaim their own commitments to God. The Church, however, had organization and tradition that was unmatchable. Millions of Catholics combine church attendance with adherence to charismatic preachers. The dividing lines are inexact and the Catholic hierarchy has to accept this, uncomfortable though that may be at times.

The Catholic network today divides the nation into seventy-two dioceses and fourteen provinces. The total number of priests is about 7,000 and there are also several thousand women in various orders active in teaching, social and health roles. As of 2020, there were four Philippine cardinals but two of them were over retiring age (eighty) and ineligible to vote in papal elections. Despite recent challenges, including slipping church attendance and rising public support for family planning, divorce and abortion, the Church continues to play multiple roles appealing to different inclinations and classes. Popular participation often focuses on pious acts and the intercession of saints. Most noted is veneration for Mary, mother of Christ, where specific churches are devoted to different aspects of Mary, for example the Mother of Perpetual Help Church in Baclaran, Metro-Manila, which regularly attracts huge crowds of devotees. These are found across the nation and attract many millions of the devout seeking help and solace. More newsworthy but much rarer are dramatic re-enactments of Christ's passion such as seen annually in San Fernando, Pampanga where penitents are tied to crosses as Christ between two thieves.

Mainstream and middle class Catholic commitments focus on church attendance, teaching and good works. The latter may include not only help for the sick and poor but overt support for the downtrodden in places such as Negros and non-Muslim Mindanao where it has been accused of giving succour to NDF-affiliated labour groups. The more liberal views on social and sex issues expressed by Pope Francis after 2013 also make the Philippine Church appear better able to respond to realities.

It is in fact striking that while the original breakaway nationalist churches were reformist as well as nationalist, none of the non-Catholic Christian groups has specially espoused leftist causes. Indeed, most have been politically conservative some seeking to enhance their influence by support for specific traditional politicians rather than seeking to define themselves through commitment to radical social change. That has mostly been left to non-believers.

Notes

1 Vicente L. Rafael, *Contracting Colonialism: Translation and Christian Conversion in Tagalog Society*, Quezon City: Ateneo de Manila University Press, 1988.

2 Morga, *Sucesos de la Islas Filipinas*.

3 Francisco Alcina, *History of the Bisayan People*, Vol. 3, trans. Cantius Kobak and Lucio Gutierrez, Manila: University of Santo Tomas, 2002, p. 281.

4 Ibid.

5 Bowring, *A Visit to the Philippine Islands*, p. 125.

6 Filomeno V. Aguilar Jr and Nicholas Sy, *Horacio de la Costa, Foreign Missionaries and the Quest for Filipinization*, Quezon City: Ateneo de Manila University Press, 2017.

7 Aries C. Rufo, *Altar of Secrets: Politics and Money in the Philippine Catholic Church*, Pasig: Journalism for Nation Building Foundation, 2013, Ch. 11.

20

Left field lies fallow

The continued success of the church in terms of popular participation and political influence contrasts with the failure of the left, whether Marxist-Leninist, liberal secular or local populist, to bring about significant social change. Failure of the left partly accounts for the fact that the Philippines has fallen far behind most of its regional peers whether in terms of per capita income growth, social stability or educational advance.

The 'ancien régime' sense generated by the persistence of dynastic politics, the widening of wealth and education gaps and the linguistic group frictions have all contributed to the survival of the region's Communist insurgency in pockets in scattered locations around the archipelago, from the highlands of Luzon, to Bicol, Negros and southern Mindanao. These reflect decades of misgovernment, poverty and violence on both sides creating seemingly interminable low scale insurgency which itself impedes development.

Other countries, such as Thailand, have ethno-religious conflicts, but none has had one as long as that with the New People's Army (Bagong Hukbong Bayan). The annual death toll is not easily assessed, but in addition to the official casualties of the military and its opponents in direct confrontations, there have been continuous murders of land rights and labour activists suspected by the military, the police or local power holders of being associated with the NDF, or for just being thorns in the side of business or landlord interests. While the NPA remains committed to armed struggle, the NDF includes a wide leftist spectrum but members face harassment and sometimes death regardless of their actual activities.

At the same time, thirty-five years of democracy since the fall of President Marcos has failed to generate a strong political movement with a coherent moderate leftist platform to tackle oligopoly, improve the tax system and raise investment in public goods, notably education and health. Meanwhile, the more extreme left has been stuck in a 1960s silo of Maoist doctrine and reliance on the specific grievances of minority indigenous groups to sustain its rural presence, and on protection money from mines and plantations.

The failure of the left, and also of a government unable to end insurgency, are the two sides of the same coin. It may also seem surprising given the left's past impact. The nationalism of the 1930s included Marxist as well as secular liberal ideas and saw the Communist Party take root. The Japanese occupation and its post-war aftermath saw the power of the insurgency at least in the core region of central Luzon. The Communist Party, particularly youth from the universities such as Rigoberto Tiglao and Cesar Melencio in the Manila-Rizal section, were active in opposing Marcos from the beginning of martial law and sustained their efforts despite many arrests, organizing strikes and forming links with grassroots and some church groups in Manila and rebuilding the NPA in rural Luzon. The strong revival of the NPA in the latter Marcos years which stretched the armed forces and worried the US was an important factor in the dictator's loss of support.

Its failure to capitalize on that role was primarily due to the ease with which traditional dynasties, headed by the Aquinos, regained their roles in the provinces as well as Manila. But the left had itself partly to blame for that. In 1978, the majority of the CPP leadership disagreed with the Manila-Rizal branch and opposed joining anti-Marcos allies, led from jail by Ninoy Aquino, in fighting an election which Marcos was forced to hold under pressure from the US. Though the result was rigged, it could have given the CPP an opportunity to show its importance. CPP candidates in Manila who had joined the coalition were ordered to withdraw at the last minute,[1] though they defied the order. The party was divided with the leadership believing in a Maoist revolution achieved by protracted guerrilla war. It eschewed cooperation with bourgeois parties and 'anti-Marcos reactionaries' – against to the advice of Lenin – and demoted Manila branch leaders.

This mindset repeated itself during the outpouring of anger at the assassination of Aquino where bourgeois parties with Church support seized the lead with the Justice for All, Justice for Aquino movement. Most fatally, the Maoist ideologues, buoyed by the growth of the revolutionary movement in Central Luzon, declined to join the Cory Aquino led-coalition in the 1986 election. Hence, the bourgeois groups were the sole beneficiaries of what followed – EDSA, the overthrow of Marcos and the return to power of pre-martial law elites. Worse still for the left, as President Aquino backtracked from early concessions on labour issues, and the release of JoMa Sison and an agreement to talks with the NDF. Assassinations of prominent leftists became frequent, setting a pattern almost as common under democracy as under the dictatorship. The movement in the countryside weakened after the overthrow of Marcos but an urban hit squad, the Alex Boncayao Brigade, was active in assassinating abusive policemen, though later turned to less violent actions to avoid alienating the middle class left.

Like all secretive revolutionary parties, the CPP was prone to paranoia. Faced with infiltration by government agents it could easily exaggerate their threat. Local units in Mindanao and Southern Tagalog had earlier large-scale assassinations of suspects but 1988 saw this purge reach core figures in Manila. Many were falsely accused, tortured for false confessions, and some killed. Other once-important figures left the party and drifted rightwards;

former Manila party secretary Tiglao, for example, after a career in mainstream journalism, became Arroyo's chief of staff, ambassador to Greece then a newspaper columnist supporting Duterte.

Already suffering from the weakening appeal of revolution after the fall of Marcos and some small steps on land reform, the CPP was devastated by the collapse of the Soviet Union and communism in Europe, though Sison, now in exile in Utrecht, blamed it all on the 'revisionism' of Brezhnev and Gorbachev. Although the left could claim some role through mass demonstration, in the 1992 rejection of renewal of the US bases agreement, ideological debates continued without conclusion. Rapid growth of the urban population might have been a basis for radicalization of workers but as most were self-employed in service jobs rather than in larger scale industry, organization was difficult. Also, a more appealing counter attraction for many was the 'opiate' offered by the populist religious preachers. A CPP consisting of a military wing, underground party organizers and above-ground union, peasant and student activists was fine in theory but needed a united policy and alliances with the non-CPP left. From a low point under Aquino, the NPA saw some revival in the 1990s but focused mostly on Mindanao and thus politically less significant to Manila than Central Luzon or Southern Tagalog.

The strategic confusion of the CPP, combining ideological rigidity with stabs at opportunism, was illustrated with the arrival of President Duterte at the national level. It supported him in 2016 on the basis of his anti-American sentiments, his de facto truce with the NPA in Davao and Sison's belief that Duterte, his former pupil, was genuinely set on ending the NPA insurgency. The CPP was thus able to put aside his proximity to the Marcos clan, Chinese business groups and local dynasts. In his campaign he had promised to release imprisoned CPP cadres and to allow Sison to return. In power, he initially ordered a ceasefire and appointed some leftists to his cabinet. Peace talks began in Norway. However, the ceasefire collapsed in early 2017. Likewise, many left-leaning professionals believed in Duterte's early claims to socialist sentiments and that his 'social technocrats' would prevail over the 'economic technocrats' of the Noynoy Aquino and Arroyo eras.[2] In practice, no such things happened.

The military had some success in anti-NPA operations but eliminating it proved elusive as it continued to draw recruits, particularly indigenous groups trying to protect their lands. Remote hill areas gave them ready refuge. The NPA was often accused of extortion of peasants as well as of businesses which paid protection money. However, it was also associated with efforts to promote health and education including in indigenous languages.

Far from further pursuing peace, Duterte opted for a policy, including assassinations, directed at visible urban-based figures within the NDF. In the second half of 2020, six NDF members formerly involved in the peace process and the daughter of one of the Bayan Muna representatives in

Congress were killed. The Duterte government also launched a broader attack on the left with the Anti-Terrorism Act which came into force in July 2020. Officially aimed at all those promoting political violence it had vague phrases such as to 'create an atmosphere to spread a message of fear', 'damage public property' and 'interfere with critical infrastructure'. It provided for the creation by the President of an Anti-Terrorism Council, which could designate suspects to be held without warrant for twenty-four days. Although strongly opposed by human rights groups and the Catholic Church, only two Senators opposed it. Duterte's National Task Force to End Local Communist Insurgency provided a platform for suppressing leftists generally, and indeed other critics such as of the drug war and failure to confront China. The Task Force was also a way to reward supporters via grants to local governments from the Barangay Development Fund for having been 'cleared of Communist influence'.

The anti-terrorism law was accompanied by a 'red tagging' campaign against institutions and individuals showing signs of NDF sympathy. This included leading universities such as Ateneo, Santo Tomas and Mindanao State University, described as 'recruitment havens' for the NPA. The campaign was particularly driven by some senior members of the armed forces involved in the National Task Force to End Local Communist Armed Conflict. It appeared designed to create a climate of fear among those tagged: 'red tagging' provided a way of linking the NPA to the CPP, the NDF and on to almost anyone engaged in land, labour or environmental issues. Extrajudicial killings were not reserved for drug suspects. The killings of activists had never stopped but were given new impetus. Senior military figures were prominent in naming alleged Communists. Locally anti-Communist vigilante squads backed by landowners and provincial politicians did the dirty work. Negros in particular saw killings including of lawyers and a prominent doctor. The killings aroused resentment in liberal and many Church circles but were, at least in the short term, a deterrent to leftist organizations however moderate.

Whilst the CPP, via the NPA, has sustained itself in some rural areas, the urban power of the left never recovered from the overthrow of Marcos. One reason was the division of organized labour between the CPP-aligned Kilusang Mayo Uno (KMU) and the umbrella movement of non-CPP unions, the Trade Union Congress of the Philippines. The total number of union members also fell after peaking in 2000. Unions increased in number but decreased in size, reducing their collective bargaining power. Employers – not least the government itself – also successfully avoided a prohibition on labour-only contracting via various non-permanent arrangements, taking more of the workforce into the informal sector not covered by wage agreements or even the minimum wage. Governments paid lip service to pushing labour rights and employers used the abundance of labour and the need to compete with mostly un-unionized workers in other Asian countries as reason to give them little scope. Contractualization then continued in barely disguised form. Thus, while labour-only contracting is banned and after six months all workers are supposed to become regular employees, in practice shorter terms periods are regularly renewed. In 2019, Duterte vetoed a bill to end contractual labour. 'The business community can now breathe a sigh of relief,' said Edgardo Lacson, chairman of the Employers Confederation of the Philippines. 'We thank President Duterte for looking beyond the interest of a few union leaders and vetoing the bill to protect the Philippine economy.'

Other obstacles to the labour movement included the fact that minimum wages were already more than most of the self-employed in the informal sector could earn. The slow growth of manufacturing industries and the influx of migrants meant that there was a declining share of workers in the more easily organized sectors. Those in the new services, such as BPO, employed the better educated who were less inclined towards unionism. The BPO industry was also fragmented. The same applied to service workers such as nurses due to the high proportion in the private sector.

The non-Communist left should, in theory, have been able to mobilize a broad spectrum of those, at least from the major cities, looking for deep but non-revolutionary change. However, while this is a huge constituency, it has proved incapable of organizing politically. The CPP and its allies within the NDF is unique in having an ideological basis but its extreme views and Leninist style organization limit its attraction. Otherwise, Philippine politics has been organized around personalities and provincial and city-level interest groups. The CPP's theories and language seems barely changed after the 1960s, perhaps not surprising given its leadership, from exile in the Netherlands, of one born in 1939, JoMa Sison. At the same time, it has remained such a potential threat to the establishment, and an actual one to the military, as to cause successive governments, notably those of Arroyo and Duterte, to use assassination as a weapon which both undermined the NDP and causes potential supporters of radical reform to shy away. The CPP meanwhile had made a fool of itself by supporting Duterte's election in the name of his anti-imperialism and anti-drugs postures.

Those seeking more modest but still substantial change had tended to see the Liberal Party as their best hope, bringing together reform-minded church groups, academia and progressive elements in the professional and business classes. Indeed, in the early post-Marcos years it had pushed through significant reforms and under Noynoy Aquino had made progress on increasing revenues and direct spending on the poor and pushing through the Reproductive Health Act. However, the party was built on dynastic foundations – Aquino, Roxas etc. – lacked cohesion and, as illustrated by its crushing defeat in 2019 elections had no answer to Duterte's crude populism.

Somewhere between the reformists in the Liberal Party and the NDF components lay the centre-left, Akbayan. It self-identified as socialist though it has been more active on social issues than economic ones, particularly since the resignation in 2016 of Walden Ballo, an academic long involved in the anti-globalization movement. Formed in 1998, it hoped to use the new Party List to gain a strong foothold in the system and at one point had three members in the House of Representatives, but it lost all in the 2019 Duterte landslide. It did have one Senator, Risa Hontiveros, elected in 2016.

Akbayan's loss in the House meant that the left was represented only by Bayan Muna with its three members and allies in the Makbayan bloc, which included the KMU, with eleven seats. Makbayan was headed by Satur Ocampo, former Bayan Muna representative and NDF negotiator. It was a varied group and had supported the Poe-Escudero slate in the 2019 elections but provided the main dissident voices in a Duterte and pork-dominated Congress. Progressive forces could find common ground on specific issues and legislation but such ideology as they still had was now often at odds with China's version of Communism, and its nationalist identity was aroused by China's actions in the South China Sea and the influx of the Chinese gambling industry.

Overall, however, there appeared no way that national, policy-based parties could make major electoral inroads against dynastic or celebrity-based politicians. At least while Congress failed to pass a law against dynasticism as required by the constitution. The left's best hope could be the emergence of a genuine populist leftist who acted to bring social and economic reform as ruthlessly as Duterte conducted his war on drugs. However, there is unlikely to be much gained in the longer run in partial replacement of a regressive economic and social structure with a Philippine version of Argentina's Juan Peron or Venezuela's Hugo Chavez, personality-based rule backed by a bodyguard of slogans which pleased lower income groups but damaged the real economy.

There is still the chance that Philippine democracy will mature as education and urbanization increase, that the far left and the NPA will abandon armed struggle which is destructive of those it is supposed to protect. More importantly, it requires that the forces of reaction and corruption cease their extra-judicial killings and 'red tagging' of those who seek social justice through peaceful organization. It also requires the reining in of dynastic and pork barrel politics.

The country may have many of the ingredients of a state ripe for revolution, but far from enough, given an economy so dependent on services and a population whose horizons are limited by low quality education and for whom the opportunity to work abroad acts as a safety valve. Meanwhile, the divisions and weakness of the left contribute to national foreign policy uncertainties. Suspicions of US imperialism linger even in the face of repeated Chinese incursions, and despite the role of ethnic Chinese capital in fostering relations with Beijing while suppressing labour movements at home. Nor does the left have significant ideological allies within the region with whom it can find common cause.

Notes

1   Cesar 'Sonny' Melencio, *Full Quarter Storms: Memoirs and Writings on the Philippine Left (1970–2010)*, Quezon City: Transform Asia, Inc., 2010.

2   Teresa S. Encarnacion Tadem, 'Technocracy and Class Politics in Policy-Making', in Mark R. Thompson and Eric Vincent C. Batalla (eds), *Routledge Handbook of the Contemporary Philippines*, Abingdon: Routledge, 2018.

21

Foreign policy: all at sea

Despite the presence of millions of Filipinos overseas, foreign policy has not been a topic much discussed other than in terms of the Philippines' relationships with the United States and more recently China. Those are now pivotal and will probably become more so as China shows no signs of letting up on its conquest and exploitation of a shared sea. However, rather than consistently making this its foreign policy priority, it has been all too easily distracted.

Every now and again in the Philippines the name Sabah intervenes, displaying, it may seem to outsiders, a weak state wanting to puff out its chest with a claim others mostly view with derision. It distracts from attention both to its relationship with big powers, and with its immediate neighbours. It also complicates its problems in the Bangsamoro region, and in Sulu in particular.

Thus in 2020, just as the Philippines and its maritime neighbours were facing growing pressure from an expanding China, President Duterte's Foreign Secretary Teodoro Locsin loudly repeated the claim to Sabah, to the great annoyance of Malaysia, a natural and ethnic ally in opposing Chinese moves, and irritation in Jakarta. It was also contrary to a cardinal principle of ASEAN – not to engage in disputes over colonial era boundaries and leave marginal issues to international courts. While other ASEAN states try to avoid raising potentially contentious border issues, Manila's politicians had found a cheap way to get some publicity at the cost of the nation's reputation.

To the outside world, the claim never had merit. The Philippines as a political entity was created by Spanish colonialism, passed to the US and hence to an independent nation. The Sultan of Sulu once controlled part of eastern Borneo which had been ceded to him by the Sultan of Brunei. This included what are now eastern Sabah and Indonesian North Kalimantan, but by the late nineteenth century the Sultan had no control over it and leased it to a British company overseen by the government in London. The same year, 1878, the Sultan relinquished all his claims to sovereignty to Spain. In 1885, Spain, Britain and Germany made an agreement recognizing Spain's claim on Sulu but not any Borneo territory. Likewise, the territory that Spain ceded to the US in 1898 excluded Borneo.

The post-independence claim dates to the presidency of Macapagal and the 1963 creation of Malaysia which joined the Malayan Federation to formerly British-ruled Borneo – Sabah and Sarawak. Macapagal was in principle a supporter of pan-Malay notions. The dreams of Rizal had been carried on in the twentieth century by radical anti-colonialists such as Tan Melaka from Indonesia, who proposed Davao as capital of a pan-Malay state, and Ibrahim Ya'acob from Malaya. In the Philippines its advocates included Wenceslao Vinzons congressman and author of the pan-Malay address *Malay Irredenta*. Another was leftist Pedro Abad Santos (see Chapter 4). Both were executed by the Japanese. However, after 1945 the realities of differing systems, differing religions, Cold War politics and new nationalism overtook dreams of Malay solidarity. Macapagal had promoted the idea of a Malay confederation, Maphilindo. Meeting in Tokyo he and President Sukarno and Malayan Prime Minister Tunku Abdul Rahman seemed to find common ground, but Sukarno decided the enlarged Malaya was a neo-colonialist creation and Macapagal could not tolerate Sabah joining Malaysia without a broader pan-Malay agreement. Both countries broke off relations with Kuala Lumpur and Indonesia began armed *konfrontasi* to undermine Malaysian rule. Indonesia under President Suharto was to recognize reality in 1967 and thereafter Indonesia did not challenge Malaysia. However, the Philippine claim continued to surface occasionally as an expression of nationalism by politicians.

Until the post-Marcos period, few saw an alternative to the US embrace. Anti-imperialist nationalism was a noisy but minority creed. The immediate post-war years were instinctively pro-American. Nationalism had some outlets in trade and investment rules but Sabah was an occasional diversion into territorial issues. So, in a minor but, as it proved, significant way was Kalayaan, the little islands, cays and reefs in the South China Sea west of Palawan.

The 'new southern islands' had been referred to by Vice-President Quirino in 1946 and the following year businessman Tomas Cloma[1] who ran a Visayan fishing company put in a claim for them but nothing happened until 1956 when Cloma with some unofficial backing from Vice-President Garcia landed with a group of men and declared them a territory called 'Freedomland' with himself as ruler under a Philippine protectorate. The Republic of China on Taiwan lodged a strong objection and the Philippines backed off. Nothing much further happened until President Marcos, noting the significance of the islands for oil search, arranged for the quiet occupation in 1970–1 of five of them and imprisoned Cloma until he agreed to renounce his claims. Three more features were occupied in 1977, 1978 and 1980 and one more by President Estrada in 1999. A sprinkling of soldiers stood guard. In 1978, the Municipality of Kalayaan was created as part of Palawan province. (Kalayaan means freedom).

What fifty years ago were obscure specks on the map are now part of a bigger battle for control of the sea as well as the islands. Kalayaan consists of four islands, four cays and three reefs. The largest island, Pag-asa in Filipino (known as Thitu in English), is thirty hectares and has an air strip. The Philippines' claims are based not simply on first occupation but the archipelagic principles enshrined in the UNCLOS[2] that they all fall within the Philippine 200 nautical mile EEZ. All the Spratly group, of which Kalayaan is a part, are claimed by China and Vietnam. Two reefs where Malaysia established a naval presence in 1986, Mariveles and Ardesier, fall within the Kalayaan claim as do several islands and reefs occupied by China and Vietnam.

The struggle for the Spratlys gathered momentum in the 1990s, which was unfortunate timing for the Philippines when domestic sentiments weakened its diplomatic and military capability. A generation which came of age during the Vietnam War and then lived through the years of the US-tolerated Marcos dictatorship saw the US bases as an affront to national sovereignty and as more a threat to drag the nation into war than to defend it when there seemed no serious external threats. The few who even thought about it considered Vietnam's encounters with China over the Paracels as a bilateral issue and took little notice of Chinese moves to occupy some Spratly reefs even though in 1988, sixty-four Vietnamese were killed by an invading Chinese force. Chinese media also began to make ominous references to a wealth of oil in the South China Sea and reminding the other states of the extent of China's claims which went as far as the James Shoal off the Borneo coast and twenty metres under water even at the lowest tides.

China had been late in its moves to exercise claims on the ground, with the only genuine islands already occupied, including Thitu, Northeast (Parola) and West York (Likas) and Nanshan (Lawak) while Taiwan remained on the largest, Itu Aba, and Vietnam three of the others. Reefs needed to be enlarged to be of any practical value and Malaysia started the process in the 1980s at Swallow Reef (Layang-Layang to Malaysians) which it eventually made into a little dive resort. The year 1992 was critical. In Manila, the Senate voted not to renew the US bases agreement, thereby also ending direct US support for the Philippine military. The same year the National People's Congress in Beijing approved a 'Law Concerning Territorial Waters and Adjacent Regions' formalizing a 1958 'Declaration on the Territorial Sea' and providing for the leasing of exploration blocks. It promptly leased a block of Vietnam to a freebooting American company, Crestone, overlapping with a block awarded to a PetroVietnam/Conoco Phillips consortium. The ensuing standoff has thwarted exploration ever since.

The year also saw Vietnam join ASEAN and the group begin a diplomatic dance with China over cooperation or confrontation in the South China Sea. Every now and then the music would stop as China made a step forward. After an interval the music would resume and talks about talks and codes of conduct would recommence. Thus in 1995, the Philippines was shocked to discover from one of its fishing boats which had been by detained by them that a Chinese fleet with a force of workmen had occupied Mischief (Panganiban) Reef, just 132 nautical miles southwest of Palawan. The unwelcome news was also a reminder of the Philippine navy's lack of surveillance capacity, let alone ability to resist. Although President Ramos was loud in his denunciation of China, he stopped short of calling it an invasion. An attempt in 1999 to establish a presence on Scarborough Shoal by grounding a ship there was met with Chinese protest. The ship was then towed away, a meek gesture of goodwill towards Prime Minister Zhu Rongji who was due to visit.

The neighbours, meanwhile, had taken note of Mischief Reef, notably Indonesia which was now aware that Chinese claims covered part of its gas field off its Natuna Islands. In 1996, Indonesia, Malaysia and Brunei conducted a joint naval exercise which was followed by a massive display of Indonesian force with twenty-seven ships and fifty-two aircraft exercising off the islands observed by Chinese vessels.[3] For the time being, China took the hint, but the Philippines lacked similar resources or resolve. Its weakness became more apparent with the advent of the administration of President Arroyo. Speaker of the House and former presidential candidate Jose de Venecia entered the picture. This wheeler-dealer businessman-politician had Chinese connections and links to the Department of Energy in Manila. Together, these proved weightier than the Department of Foreign Affairs (DFA) which was involved in the dance between ASEAN and China over maritime issues.

In a bid to try to avoid conflict by ending competitive prosecution of sea and island claims, ASEAN members and China had agreed in 2002 a Declaration on the Conduct of Parties in the South China Sea. Its clauses included accepting the UNCLOS, freedom of navigation, peaceful settlement of disputes, and self-restraint not to engage in actions which would aggravate disputes, including not inhabiting currently uninhabited islands, reefs and rocks. This led to years of on-off discussion on a formal code of conduct, meanwhile parties, most notably China, went ahead expanding its presence. The Philippines was an exception. It largely neglected to develop the ones where it had a toehold and failed to establish a permanent presence on Scarborough Shoal.

The lure of Chinese money was too much for a weak state and one with ministers eager for deals. In 2004, de Venecia and the Department of Energy put together a joint exploration venture with China National Offshore Oil Company (CNOOC). Arroyo signed off on this JMSU, covering some 140,000 square kilometres and played it up in a visit to Beijing. 'That is the institutional weakness in policy making' noted a later Energy Secretary, Rapael Lotilla, with individual interests and oil-men with no strategic or geopolitical experience capturing policy.[4]

Vietnam was furious and made its views very plain to Manila. The JMSU covered its claimed EEZ and was, contrary to the 2002 ASEAN agreement, not to aggravate disputes. However, as it could not stop the bilateral deal, it opted to join it as a third party. In practice it was heavily weighted towards China, which carried out the seismic work, with Vietnam processing it and the Philippines interpreting it. The work was complete by 2007 but trust in China's lead role was thin, Lotilla remarking that data for the crucial Reed (Recto) Bank was 'inconclusive and blurred'.[5]

The agreement was supposed to be renewed in 2008 but then the nationalist left took the issue to the Supreme Court on the grounds that it was unconstitutional. There it remained. Quite how much sovereignty the Philippines would have to surrender was revealed by a draft of a later proposal to revive the JMSU. It provided for CNOOC to do all the drilling and production work, the laws of the Professional Regulation Commission as well as the Philippines would apply and each party would pay tax to their respective governments.

Whilst the Aquino government did not pursue the JMSU it still harboured illusions about China's 'peaceful rise', but under Xi Jinping, who became its leader in 2012, China showed scant desire to put neighbourly relations ahead of pushing ahead with creating new facts in the South China Sea. In 2012, the Philippines navy tried to stop Chinese fisherman poaching in the Scarborough Shoal only to be confronted by Chinese Maritime Surveillance vessels. The struggle over Scarborough brought into sharp focus the role of the US and its Mutual Defence Treaty with the Philippines. It had long been understood in Manila that this did not extend to the Kalayaan Islands However, the US was obliged to defend the Philippines against aggression in Pacific area waters. Relations with the US military had remained strong despite the of the bases and were strengthened by the Visiting Forces Agreement in 1999 and by the common interest of fighting radical Muslims, notably after the 9/11 attacks in the US and the appearance of al-Qaeda in Mindanao and Sulu.

The Scarborough (Panatag) Shoal was an anomaly. It lay just outside the sea boundary delineated on the map of the 1898 Treaty of Paris by which Spain ceded the territory, but it had appeared on earlier maps, including the famously precise Murillo Velarde map of 1734. The US had even long paid the Philippines for its use as a bombing range.[6]

Yet in the face of China's claims to the whole South China Sea, its islands and resources, the US had no policy, just diplomats urging negotiation. The Commander of US forces in the Pacific was to remark in 2016: 'The primary weakness of American strategy is that it takes no position on the conflicting claims . . . the US needs to decide which claims it recognises . . . so that it can use its superior military force to set limits on Chinese aggression'.[7]

More cautious Americans believed US ambiguity over island claims would be a deterrent. In practice, China called its bluff. Accused of provocation at Scarborough Shoal, the Philippines meekly replaced its naval vessel with a coast guard ship. China then proceeded to send more vessels from its Fisheries Law Enforcement Command which blocked the sole Philippine ship from the shoal. At the height of the face off at Scarborough, US Undersecretary for East Asia, Kurt Campbell, was desperate to find a solution while some in Manila naively believed that once the transfer of power to Xi Jinping was complete China would be more accommodating. After a meeting with the Chinese ambassador in Washington, Campbell thought he had agreement for both sides to withdraw their ships. The Philippines vessels left, the Chinese craft may have done briefly but immediately returned and have never since left.

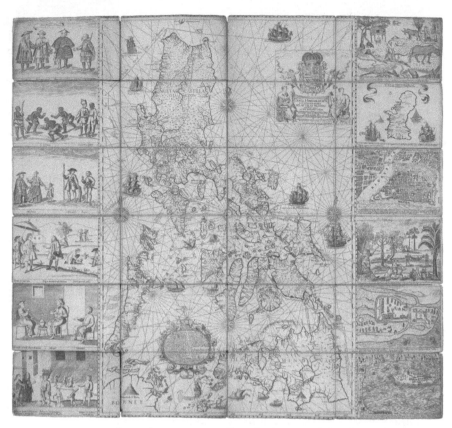

FIGURE 21.1 *Eighteenth century Murillo Velarde map of the Philippines showing the Panacot/Scarborough/Panatag Shoal. Cartographer: Murillo Velarde, Pedro, 1696–1753; engraver: Nicolás de la Cruz Bagay, 1701–71.*

The humiliation of Scarborough and the failure of ASEAN diplomacy to achieve the promised code of conduct demanded a new approach. It primarily took the work of Associate Justice Antonio Carpio who had been studying the issues since the 1990s helped by maritime law experts at the University of the Philippines. The country, they argued, must rely on UNCLOS and take its case to the international tribunal. Foreign Secretary del Rosario was keen and an exasperated Aquino agreed. The case was brought in 2013 and the judgement delivered in 2016 was a stunning victory for the Philippines (see Chapter 8).

The judgements were not just a victory for the Philippines but, in practice, also for Vietnam, Malaysia, Brunei and Indonesia, all of which had seas falling within the nine-dash line.

However, instead of following up on the stunning victory with a regional and international diplomatic offensive, the newly elected President Duterte, who had once promised to jet-ski to Panatag, turned his back on it. The sad state of Philippine politics was underlined by the eagerness with which Duterte and his followers looked to China for the boost to economic growth that they themselves could not provide because of corruption and bad management. It was a new form of an old curse, money politics. Six years on there was modest Chinese-financed infrastructure to show for Duterte's de facto attempt to sell national rights.

The DFA under Aquino had primed ASEAN members, and the littoral countries in particular, for a statement of support for international law and UNCLOS should the Philippines win its case. In the event, they were never asked. Foreign Secretary Perfecto Yasay, a college friend of Duterte, said it was a bilateral matter not for ASEAN. Any resolution would have been vetoed by Cambodia on China's behalf but Yasay's position astonished other ASEAN members.

From the day he entered office, Duterte was preparing to downplay any victory which came two weeks later. Nothing should stand in the way of Chinese money to build the Philippines. He was not the only Philippine politician to want to put Chinese money and friendship before national interest in the EEZ. Figures ranging from Arroyo and de Venecia preferred exploration deals. Estelito Mendoza, who had been Marcos' attorney-general, argued for negotiating with Beijing rather than annoying it – as though China had ever given any indication of willingness to compromise on its nine-dash line and associated claims. Money and domestic politics took precedence over using the judgement to assert national rights over some 375,000 square kilometres of sea, but Duterte's anti-American sentiments added to a reaction which left neighbours and allies, including Japan, stunned. Less than three months after the ruling, Duterte was in Beijing announcing his 'separation' from the US. 'I have realigned myself in your ideological flow', he proclaimed in the Great Hall of the People.

Duterte had previously blamed Aquino for the loss of Scarborough and suggested that they were an unreliable ally and no defence against China. It would thus be wiser for the Philippines to please Beijing, tread softly on Scarborough and reap economic rewards. Duterte, however, failed to develop an alternative foreign policy which would use the influence of regional middle powers to balance China. Japan took note of what was happening and quietly made efforts to develop its naval contacts with the Philippines and step up efforts to offer infrastructure finance. Between 2004 and 2016, the nation had only two foreign secretaries, both experienced in government. Alberto Romulo, 2004–11, had been among other posts, Secretary of Finance. Albert del Rosario, 2001–16, had been ambassador in Washington, but Duterte's and his successive secretaries were less attuned either to the language of international affairs, or to putting strategy above local politics.

Duterte's first pick, Perfecto Yasay, was not confirmed because he had been an American citizen. Next came Alan Peter Cayetano, a traditional politician with numerous relatives in elected offices, who had been Duterte's failed running mate for vice-president. Not only did Cayetano follow Duterte and Yasay in setting the 2016 judgement aside in pursuit of China relations but he gave away an earlier Philippine sea rights victory. In 2008, the Philippines had submitted a claim to the Benham (Philippine) Rise, a vast volcanic seamount east of Luzon, because it lay on its continental shelf and within its archipelagic baselines. In 2012, the UN Commission on the Limits to the Continental Shelf accepted this against China's opposition. Yet in 2018, Cayetano, brushing aside a French offer, gave consent to the Chinese Institute of Oceanography to survey the area. It later transpired that the Chinese had being doing so already, without consent. China then lodged Chinese names for the Rise's underwater features to the International Hydrographic Organization. Cayetano also described the West Philippine Sea as 'disputed' though the 2016 judgement gave all its resources to the Philippines.

In 2018, Cayetano was replaced by Teodoro 'Teddy Boy' Locsin, a lawyer and journalist much given, like Duterte, to florid language. On a more fundamental level, Duterte claimed that distancing from the US was a badly needed assertion of foreign policy independence. For too long the country had mostly followed wherever the US led. However, when US-China rivalry was gathering momentum distancing could only help China's South China Sea ambitions unless balanced by stronger regional cooperation, notably with Japan, Vietnam, Malaysia and Indonesia. Duterte's approach was at least partly explicable with the election of President Trump with his cancelling of the Trans-Pacific Partnership which would have joined the US to east Asia, excluding China, and Australia. Trump also seemed equivocal on maintaining the level of US forces in Asia and his sudden changes of mind were no encouragement to allies.

Initially, Duterte's anti-American stance found favour with the left but in the House it was the moderate left Akbayan and more radical Bayan Muna Party List representatives who were to be prominent in criticizing China and Duterte's alleged weakness in defending national sovereignty. On the right, the military leaders, with years of close ties to the US, were also a reluctant follower of the president.

More than four years into his efforts to befriend China, Duterte seemed to reverse course with a 2020 speech to the UN General Assembly drawing attention to the 2016 Court of Arbitration judgement and calling for international support for its implementation. However, it was unclear whether this was more than a rhetorical shift in response to public opinion. China had had four years to reclaim land around the rocks it had occupied, making them into fortified islands, four more years of harassing Philippine fishermen. Philippine reluctance to build on its court victory also discouraged neighbours from following suit with their own cases against China. Repeated mass presences of Chinese vessels, fishing boats and otherwise, in the Philippine's EEZ, effectively blocking Philippine fishers, met with protests from the Foreign Ministry to Beijing but minimal reaction on the part of the president. While surveys showed people were generally suspicious of China, the sea was not high up on their list of concerns. So massive was the Chinese presence in the Philippine EEZ that pressure did build on Duterte to be responsive at least rhetorically. Duterte also backed away from ending the Visiting Forces Agreement, ostensibly in return for a supply of US vaccines and September 2021 saw Locsin and Defence Secretary Delfin Lorenzana in Washington, Lorenzana calling for more US help and to 'upgrade' and 'update' the Mutual Defense Agreement, and Locsin welcomed the Australia-UK-US nuclear submarine pact for the Pacific, much to the annoyance of Beijing.

The Philippines made little effort to strengthen cooperation with Vietnam and Malaysia, and there was a push in Congress to expand the West Philippine Sea claim which would have further antagonized their ASEAN neighbours. However, with the formation of the informal anti-China Quad alliance of the US, Japan, India and Australia, the 2021 US/Australia/UK submarine treaty (AUKUS) and growing links between the US and Vietnam and Indonesia, there was scant space for ideas of Philippine neutrality.

Popular suspicion of China – and of Chinese immigration – ran deep, while links to Western countries were underpinned by the large Filipino communities there. There was also recognition in Manila of the importance of Japan and Korea to both trade and aid, and hence those countries' interest in keeping the South China Sea an open waterway. Overall, the Philippines lacked a clear foreign policy and defence strategy which would survive changes in government. However, US policy under President Biden was more predictable and brought together Japan, Australia and India in countering China's pressure, and engaged more closely with Vietnam and Indonesia. It was possible that a post-Duterte administration would take a more coherent stance to protect national interests, focusing more on its own sea and air defence capabilities and engaging with its neighbours. But the influence of Chinese money and commerce on the political class was likely to remain a factor in foreign policy

Notes

1 Bill Hayton, *The South China Sea: The Struggle for Power in Asia*, New Haven, CT: Yale University Press, 2014, ch. 3.

2 John G. Butcher and R.J. Elson: *Sovereignty and the Sea: How Indonesia Became an Archipelagic State,* Singapore: University of Singapore Press, 2017.

3 Hayton, *The South China Sea,* ch. 3.

4 Quoted in Vitug, *Rock Solid,* pp. 60–4.

5 Ibid., pp. 104–6.

6 Ibid.

7 Ibid.

Conclusion

The future

The history of maritime southeast Asia is, in a long perspective, summed up by the comings and goings of the sea. Now even a short forward perspective reveals a challenge that the islands must face, a challenge more fundamental than the other threats of nature to which it is accustomed. Yet while it is necessary to make assumptions about the next fifty to one hundred years, the challenges of today are not only more urgent for those living today or over the next decade or two. They are also the ones which can be addressed now and if not addressed will make adjustment to climate change all the more difficult. Governance in the broadest sense, and educational levels, are the most critical, to enable the nation to take and execute decisions on development issues – the location of buildings, the protection of existing structures, land use and agricultural policies focused on the medium to long term. Advances on these fronts are sorely needed.

The rise of the sea after the last Ice Age began some 22,000 years ago, stopped around 7,000 years ago and started again about 100 years ago. While the next thousand years is beyond prediction it is reasonable to assume that the next fifty years will see a rise of thirty to forty centimetres and possibly more if the melting of Arctic ice speeds up. That may not seem a major threat but given how much of its population lives close to the current sea margin, notably in the National Capital Region, there is not just the threat of loss of land for farming and housing but the increased susceptibility to floods. The same applies to parts of Central Luzon and Calabarzon – the latter being the most populous of all regions with nearly 15 million people. Indeed, 40 million are crammed into the three mostly low-lying regions of the NCR, Central Luzon and Calabarzon. Sea level and climate issues alone emphasize the importance of the future development of inland cities such as Bukidnon in central Mindanao, Tuguegarao in the Cagayan Valley and those on the coast least vulnerable to sea level rise and storm surges. Historically, all the most significant cities have been port cities, but that may have to change as part of climate change, presenting demands for inland infrastructure and a shift of service industries which mainly need good IT connections to these areas. Fisheries will likely be affected by warmer oceans, though the impact is as yet hard to judge. As for agriculture, the direct impact of a warmer climate is yet to be measured but if it sees more droughts or other extreme events the impact will be significant on a country which is a large net importer of food.

The sea level rise inundating some coastal areas and rising salinity in others emphasizes the importance of raising crop yields significantly to offset losses of agricultural land as well as raise the incomes of its farmer population. Climate changes offer the prospect of more extreme weather generally – more or more violent typhoons, changes in seasonal rainfall patterns, droughts, etc. which require greater readiness to address emergencies, re-location of settlements to less vulnerable areas and the willingness to adapt cropping to changing conditions, and perhaps reduce monocrops cultivation while also focusing on value-added rather than the ever-illusory food security. As we have seen, the existing problems with agriculture are already bad enough, a major contributor to poverty, poor health and income maldistribution. The nation already badly needs more effort and investment in agriculture to raise productivity.

Whatever the level of the Philippines' own effort in alleviating global warming – and a start has been made with no more new coal-fired power stations – it remains a very small contributor to the global problem. So, its response has to be led by forward thinking about how and where to house a still fast-growing growing population, how to limit threats to infrastructure

FIGURE 22.1 *Tacloban, Leyte, after typhoon Haiyan, November 2013. © Getty Images.*

by building in the safest locations, not just the cheapest or most influential. With help from international organizations the nation has the ability to plan better, but the nature of the political institutions and weakness of the bureaucracy makes implementation difficult. There is an immediate cost in terms of new infrastructure, but the key is smart decisions by governments which will attract private investment to new, less crowded, safter locations.

Sea levels and climate change are relatively new issues, but old natural challenges still need to be addressed. Most regions are prone to earthquakes and a few localities to volcanoes. Historically, buildings were lightweight and flexible, made of wood, bamboo and thatch. Today high-rise structures are built to survive earthquakes, but many constructed of concrete, brick and tile are vulnerable. Underlining the point, in 2012 the World Bank made a loan of $340 million to enhance the safety of public buildings in Manila alone, focused mainly on earthquake threats. According to one calculation, a 7.2 level earthquake, as hit Bohol in 2013, in Manila would cause 50,000 deaths and untold damage to housing and infrastructure.

Yet for all its problems, despite its fractured geography, socio-economic divides, linguistic variations, regional sympathies, the nation is extremely unlikely to break up. The interlinkages between Luzon, the Visayas and Mindanao are far stronger than the identity of the island groups which are themselves divided by the localisms such as those of Ilocos and Bicol. Muslim Mindanao is barely viable as it is, let alone as an independent state. Years of on-off warfare for independence or autonomy have shown both internal division and the impossibility of creating a separate entity which can prosper without close links with the rest of Mindanao. The only possible exception could be that the Sulu Archipelago might one day prefer to be part of Sabah than of the BARMM of which it became a rather reluctant member.

The much bigger problem is of governance. This more than population lies at the heart of the nation's underperformance. There have been many new starts: EDSA and the return of democracy, the Ramos presidency, the reforms of Noynoy Aquino, but the system has remained run by and for an elite of families and interests, provincial and central, with provincial politicians beholden to whoever is on top at the time. Improvements can and do happen over time and the fairly steady economic growth shown from 2000 to 2019 demonstrated this. However, abysmal educational standards are no help towards policy rather than personality-based politics. Post Duterte and post the pandemic, much may return to the status quo ante but making up for lost education is harder than making up for lost output due to lockdowns.

Good governance means strengthening the role of permanent positions in the bureaucracy and limiting those political and personal appointees whose main talent is loyalty to the president. Duterte appointed competent people to most economy-related posts but many others were based on loyalties, particularly to his Davao associates and engendered corruption. The administrative structure would benefit much from a reduction in the number of provinces – populations vary from 4 million to 17,000 – and fewer types of city. Fragmentation is a bigger curse than 'imperial Manila'. Other reforms to de-politicize decision-making would address the Supreme Court, particularly the tenure of justices. Dynastic politics is another issue which could be addressed if the incumbents did not have a vested interest in not enacting the legislation demanded by the constitution. Likewise, the capture of most of the Party List seats in the House by elites, and the power of the executive over budget allocation, make the House a rubber stamp of the incumbent. Governance issues rather than the strength of Communist ideology explain the continuation for decades of NPA activity in some rural areas where poverty and wealth gaps are extreme or traditional land rights threatened. An army pre-occupied with internal problems is debilitating as well as weakening external defence.

These problems derive more from the structure of government than policies per se. Macro-economic and central banking policies have been remarkably stable, remaining little altered through political changes. Technocrats have pushed for reforms such as in the tax regime, but they often struggle against vested interests with the ear of politicians, local as well as central. Meanwhile, other ministries with appropriate policies run up against a weak administrative structure on the ground. Especially stark is the failure either to develop its own manufacturing behind a tariff wall or invite foreign investment on the scale seen in Thailand, Malaysia, Vietnam and elsewhere.

The need for change is self-evident but how to get there is not. There may be a taste for strongman rule as evidenced by the early years of Marcos' martial law and by the popularity of gun-slinging Duterte, but Duterte was interested in power for its own sake, not because he had a radical reform agenda to force through. The drug war and an entirely rhetorical attack on corruption were showmanship by an adept manipulator of public opinion. The reputation of the police, always low, sank lower while their power and lack of accountability rose. A nation with an historically high homicide rate had a president, schooled by his years as boss of Davao, who encouraged it in the name of law and order.

By some measures, the Philippines needs a revolution, to throw off the old elites, end monopolies, open up to foreign competition, prioritize education, eliminate large-scale smuggling and enforce taxes. The weakness of a divided left plus the economic growth, however unequal, in the pre-pandemic years kept popular discontent well-contained with some progress in poverty reduction and income transfers to the poor. Things for the masses were not getting worse and the urban middle classes who had driven EDSA in 1986 were doing fine. The future may well offer more of the same, with OFW, remittances and BPO all continuing to provide foreign exchange and jobs while progress in infrastructure remains underpinned by foreign support. However, the world is changing too so continued growth of those two earners is not assured as demand from traditional labour importers in the Middle East stagnates and lack of skills limits upgrading needed in the BPO world. The country's biggest challenge, though, is not to export more people but to make better use at home of the tens of millions in informal jobs in cities and low productivity agriculture. Meanwhile, rebellion simmers on the margin of society and could yet grow much bigger again as in the latter Marcos days.

Political and economic domination by a China seeking regional hegemony is clearly a longer-term threat to the legacies of former foreign rulers – Christianity from Spain and a political and legal system from the US. China's relative economic power is not likely to wane soon while that of others such as Japan, the US and Australia may do. Yet with a foreign policy driven by strategic thinking, not by petty and often ignorant local politicians, the Philippines can be part of a non-military pact with significant neighbours, notably Indonesia and Vietnam in limiting China's ambitions, making Beijing pay a high international price for seeking to dominate the seas and be the 'Godfather' to the region. Greater awareness of its cultural links to the wider Malay world would also help, reducing its sense of distance from predominantly Muslim neighbours while diluting its sense of attachment to an American and Hispanic past. Philippine historiography often has a distinctly nationalist tone but more as reaction to Western imperialism than to a pre-colonial identity when there was no such place as the Philippines but, like Indonesia and Malaysia, a collection of lands of various kings, sultans and chiefs speaking related languages and trading and sometimes warring with each other.

There remains a lot to do in improving relations with non-Chinese neighbours. Apart from occasional squabbles about Sabah, there were few specific aggravations, but little effort was made to cultivate them and they often seem baffled by a Philippines unsure of its position as a significant Asian country. Duterte's back-tracking from the stunning 2016 victory over China stunned fellow littoral states which could take advantage of the ruling themselves. Future presidents may well come back to the ruling as a cornerstone of policy but will need to see issues in regional terms not simply as a China-US struggle for hegemony. General lack of interest in foreign and neighbouring country affairs was reflected in media coverage as well as in the simplistic notions of provincial politicians. Manila would have done well to look to Hanoi for guidance in balancing defence of its territorial rights with economic ties with China.

Meanwhile, Japan received modest attention in spite of its far larger role than China in private investment and aid for infrastructure. While the importance of China trade was much touted, the reality was that the merchandise trade is massively in China's favour while Philippines' remittance and service earnings are almost entirely from elsewhere. In strategic terms, China may seem an ever-rising power which has made some progress if making the South China Sea into a Chinese lake. However, US power in the western Pacific will remain formidable for the foreseeable future and find plenty of formal and informal allies among medium-sized states wary of China. US failures in the Middle East, and the Trump era, dented America's regional standing but at the same time focused more US attention on China's east Asian ambitions and its anti-China Quad group (with India, Japan and Australia) finds many quiet sympathizers in Indonesia, Malaysia and Korea.

As for the Philippines' military, though a proud and relatively disciplined force, it has spent seventy years fighting its own people. Its background political influence increased under Duterte and was a factor in persuading a reluctant president to renew the Visiting Forces Agreement with the US. Although still a small force and one yet to attempt a coup, an unstable regional outlook could draw the Philippine military closer to politics at home as well as in facing a more nationalist China under President Xi Jinping. The raised level of unpredictability over Taiwan as well as the nine-dash line claim made it more important than ever for the Philippines to maximize its diplomatic efforts to protect common interests while continuing to cooperate with the US and others on military issues. The Philippines has few natural resources to attract the Chinese but it does have a crucial position on the Luzon Strait as well as the owning (in theory) more EEZ rights in the South China Sea than any other littoral state.

For the longer term, it is possible to see demographic issues coming to play a bigger role in China relations – a fast aging China looking for man and (especially) women power which would in time make it, not the Middle East or US, a golden opportunity for Philippine job seekers, and hence an income source for the nation. At the same time, millions of Chinese might like to follow the example of many South Koreans and seek homes and retirement in a warmer climate with lower living costs. Of course, China itself may prefer to avoid either importing labour or exporting retirees, Filipinos may resist an influx of Chinese, even old ones, but the issue of people movement could become a key influence on the direction of China relations.

The decline in the fertility rate has been quickening but there are still two decades ahead when pressure to create jobs for school leavers will remain severe. However, the working percentage of the population will rise, and an increased share of national income should be able to go to education and investment. Further increasing labour export generates short-term gains to income but takes pressure off the need for getting work at home for those who have become remittance reliant. Despite much rhetoric about the plight of the poor, politics is seldom about specific measures other than the targeted support under the Pantawid programme. A more radical approach involving higher taxes and more competition runs up against the realities of the social and political power structure. That might change under a leader with a radical agenda and backed by populist sentiment but none has yet to emerge. Nor as yet does the Philippines have, for good or ill, a movement similar to Peronism in Argentina or to countries in Latin America and the Middle East with histories of left-leaning generals with populist slogans backed by an army. Even the old left might abandon outdated slogans and find a leader who can galvanize the masses.

There is no doubt that Filipinos remain eager participants in elections at every level even though choices are mostly limited to dynasts and media celebrities. They are proof that for all its faults and divides, the Philippines mostly remains an open and freewheeling society despite the efforts of would-be autocrats for executive rule and a populist desire among many for a 'strong leader' in the Marcos/Duterte mould who promises (but does not deliver) more effective government. For what it is worth, for all its myriad problems of poverty and lawlessness, the nation regularly rates much higher in the Global Happiness Index than its socio-economic position would suggest. Foreign countries welcoming its workers and migrants seem to agree.

The nation, like its archipelago, is made up of many odd-shaped pieces which make a whole. Its 500-year history is a bond of identity but also a curse of continuity of a socio-political structure in need of a shake-up which would enable its people's talents be better reflected in the state of the nation. More than anything it needs stronger state institutions, particularly honest and independent courts and genuine separation of executive and legislative powers, not ones at the mercy of dynasts and populists. Fewer but stronger local government units would help as would stable parties and the supremacy of policy issues over patronage. The 2022 election was seen by many as a test of the nation's ability to modernize itself

Seventy-five years after independence, the Philippines is searching for a political answer to its relative failure to keep up with the economic and social progress of its once poorer neighbours. Its problem is the very continuity of the social history of 500 years, binding the nation together but impeding its ability to change, but it is also a young country with a median age of twenty-six and hence has a greater potential than its neighbours for positive change.

BIBLIOGRAPHY

Abinales, Patricio N., *Orthodoxy and History in the Muslim-Mindanao Narrative* (Quezon City: Ateneo de Manila Press, 2010).

Abinales, Patricio N. and Donna J. Amoroso, *State and Society in the Philippines*, revised edn (New York: Rowman and Littlefield, 2017).

Abueva, Jose V., *Towards a Federal Republic of the Philippines with a Parliamentary Government* (Marikina: Centre for Social Policy and Governance, Kalayaan College, 2005).

Abuza, Zachary and Luke Lischin, *US Institute of Peace, Special Report 468* (June 2020).

Aguilar, Filomeno V. Jr, and Nicholas Sy, *Horatio de la Costa, Foreign Missionaries and the Quest for Filipinization* (Quezon City: Ateneo de Manila Press, 2017).

Alcina, Francisco, *Historia de las Islas e Indios de Bisaya*, Vols 1 and 3, trans. Cantius Kobak and Lucio Gutierrez (Manila: University of Santo Tomas, 2002).

Anderson, Benedict, 'Cacique Democracy in the Philippines', in Benedict Anderson, *The Spectre of Comparison; Nationalism, Southeast Asia and the World* (London: Verso Books, 1998).

Anderson, Benedict, *Imagined Communities Reflections on the Origin and Spread of Nationalism* (London: Verso Books, 2006).

Balisacan, Arsenio M. and Hal Hill, eds, *The Philippine Economy, Development Policies and Challenges* (New York: Oxford University Press), 2003.

Barrows, David P., *A History of the Philippines* (First Rate Publishers: San Bernardino, CA, [1903] 2020).

Bellwood, Peter, *Man's Conquest of the Pacific: The Pre-history of Southeast Asia and Oceania* (New York: Oxford University Press, 1979).

Berlow, Alan, *Dead Season A Story of Murder and Revenge on the Island of Negros* (New York: Pantheon Books, 1996).

Bonner, Raymond, *Waltzing with a Dictator* (New York: Times Books, 1987).

Boot, Max, *The Road Not Taken Edward Lansdale and the American Tragedy in Vietnam* (New York: Liveright Books, 2018).

Borton, James, ed., *Islands and Rocks in the South China Sea Post-Hague Ruling* (X-Libris.com, 2017).

Bowring, John, *A Visit to the Philippine Islands* (Manila: Filipiniana Book Guild, [1859] 1963).

Boxer Codex, *16th Century Exploration Accounts of East and Southeast Asia and the Pacific,* ed. Isaac Donoso, trans. Ma Luisa Garcia, Carlos Quirino, Mauro Garcia (Quezon City: Vibal Foundation, 2018).

Bulosan, Carlos, *America is in the Heart* (Seattle: University of Washington Press, [1946] 1973).

Burton, Sandra, *Impossible Dream: The Marcoses, The Aquinos and the Unfinished Revolution* (New York: Warner Books, 1989).

Butcher, John G. and R.J. Elson, *Sovereignty and the Sea: How Indonesia Became an Archipelagic State* (Singapore: University of Singapore Press, 2017).

Buzeta, Manuel, *Diccionario Geografico-Estadistico-Historico de las islas Filipinas* (Madrid: 1850).

Connaughton, Richard, John Pimlott, Duncan Anderson, *The Battle for Manila* (Novato, CA: Presidio Press, 1995).

Constantino, Renato, *History of the Philippines from the Spanish Conquest to the Second World War* (New York: Monthly Review Press, 1975).

Constantino, Renato, *The Philippines: A Past Revisited*, Vol. 1, (Quezon City: Tala Publishing Services, 1975).

Cole, Mabel Cook, *Philippine Folk Tales* (republished by Forgotten Books [1916] 2007/2020).

Coraming, Rommel A., 'Filipinos as Malays', in Maznah Mohamad and Syed Muhd Khairudin Aljunied, *Melayu: The Politics, Parties and Paradoxes of Malayness* (Singapore: National University of Singapore Press, 2012).

Corpuz, O.D., *Roots of the Filipino Nation*, 2 vols (Quezon City: University of the Philippines Press, 2005).

Doranila, Amando, *Afro-Asia in Upheaval* (Manila: Anvil Publishing, 1983).

Enrile, Juan Ponce, *A Memoir* (Quezon City: ABS/CBN, 2012).

Francia, Luis H., *A History of the Philippines* (New York: Overlook Press, 2014).

Garcia, Myles A., *Thirty Years Late Catching Up with Marcos Era Crimes* (Manila: MAG Publishing, 2016).

Geldart, Peter, *Mapping the Philippine Seas* (Manila: Philippine Map Collectors Society, 2017).

George, T.J.S., *Revolt in Mindanao: The Rise of Islam in Philippine Politics* (Oxford: Oxford University Press, 1980).

Giraldez, Arturo, *The Age of Trade: The Manila Galleons and the Dawn of the Global Economy* (New York: Rowman and Littlefield, 2015).

Hayton, Bill, *The South China Sea: The Struggle for Power in Asia* (New Haven, CT: Yale University Press, 2014).

Hicken, Alle, Edward Aspinall and Meredith Weiss, *Electoral Dynamics in the Philippines,* (Singapore: National University of Singapore Press, 2019).

Hutchcroft, Paul D., *Booty Capitalism: The Politics of Banking in the Philippines* (Ithaca: Cornell University Press, 1998).

Hutchcroft, Paul D. ed., *Mindanao: The Long Journey to Peace and Prosperity* (Mandaluyong City: Anvil Publishing, 2016).

Hutchcroft, Paul D. ed., *Strong Patronage, Weak Parties: The Case for Electoral System Redesign in the Philippines* (Mandaluyong City: Anvil Publishing, 2019).

Ileto, Reynaldo, *Pasyon and Revolution: Popular Movements in the Philippines, 1840–1910* (Quezon City: Ateneo de Manila University Press, 1979).

Karnow, Stanley, *In Our Image: America's Empire in the Philippines* (New York: Random House, 1989).

Kerkvliet, Benedict J., *The Huk Rebellion: A Study of Peasant Revolt in the Philippines* (New York: Roman and Littlefield [1977] 2002).

Kirk, Donald, *Looted: The Philippines After the Bases* (New York: St Martin's Press, 1998).

Jones, Gregg R., *Red Revolution Inside the Philippines Guerrilla Movement* (New York: Routledge [1989] 2019).

Junker, Laura Lee, *Raiding, Trading and Feasting: The Political Economy of Philippine Chiefdoms* (Honolulu: University of Hawaii Press, 1998).

Lanzona, Uma A., *Amazons of the Huk Rebellion* (Madison, WI: University of Wisconsin Press, 2009).

Larkin, John A., *Sugar and the Origins of Modern Philippine Society* (Berkeley, CA: University of California Press, 1993).

Legarda Jr, Benito J., *After the Galleons* (Quezon City: Ateneo de Manila University Press, 2002).

May, Glenn Anthony, *Inventing a Hero: The Posthumous Re-Creation of Andres Bonifacio* (Quezon City: New Day Publishers, 1997).

Mears, Leon A., Meliza H. Agabin, Teresa A. Anden, Rosalinda C. Marquez, *The Rice Economy of the Philippines* (Quezon City: University of the Philippines Press, 1974).

Melencio, Cesar 'Sonny', *Full Quarter Storms: Memoirs and Writing on the Philippine Left* (Quezon City: Transform Asia, 2010).

Miller, Jonathan, *Rodrigo Duterte Fire and Fury in the Philippines* (Melbourne and London: Scribe, 2018).

Morga, Antonio de, *Sucesos de las Islas Filipinas*, trans Henry E.J. Stanley (London: The Hakluyt Society, 1868).

Nery, John, *Revolutionary Spirit Jose Rizal in Southeast Asia* (Singapore: Institute of Southeast Asian Studies, 2011).

Ocampo, Anthony Christian, *The Latinos of Asia: How Filipino Americans Break the Rules on Race* (Palo Alto, CA: Stanford University Press, 2016).

Oviedo, Gonzalo Fernandez, *Spanish and Portuguese Conflict in the Spice Islands*, from Book XX of *The General and Natural History of the Indies*, ed. Glen F. Dille (London: The Hakluyt Society, London 2021).

Perouse, Jean-François de la Galaup, *The Journal 1785–1788*, 2 vols, trans John Dunmore (London: The Hakluyt Society, 1995).

Pigafetta, Antonio, *Magellan's Voyage*, 2 vols, trans R.A. Skelton (New York: Dover Publishing, 1969).

Pires, Tome, *Suma Oriental*, Vol. 1, trans. and ed. Armando Cortesao (New Delhi Asian Educational Services [1948] 2015, pp. 132–3.

Quezon III, Manuel L., 'An Epidemic of Clans', *Philippine Inquirer*, 9 June 2021.

Rafael, Vicente. L., *Contracting Colonialism Translation and Christian Conversion in Tagalog Society* (Quezon City: Ateneo de Manila University Press, 1988).

Reyes, Vicente Chua Jr., *Mapping the Terrain of Education Reform: Global Trends and Local Responses in the Philippines* (New York: Routledge, 2016).

Rizal, Jose, *Filipinos dentro cien anos* (Barcelona: La Solidaridad, 1889).

Rood, Steven, *What Everyone Needs to Know About the Philippines* (New York: Oxford University Press, 2019).

Rufo, Aries C., *Altar of Secrets Sex: Politics and Money in the Philippine Catholic Church* (Pasig: Journalism for Nation Building Foundation, 2013).

Salazar, Zeus A., *The Malayan Connection: Ang Filipinas sa Dunya Melayu*, (Quezon City: Palimbagan ng Lahi, 1998).

Saleeby, Najib M., *The History of Sulu* (Manila: Filipiniana Book Guild [1908] 1963).

Scott, William Henry, *Looking for the Pre-Hispanic Filipino* (Quezon City: New Day Publisher, 1992).

Scott, William Henry, *Prehispanic Source Materials for the Study of Philippine History* (Manila: University of Santo Tomas Press, 1968).

Seagrave, Sterling, *The Marcos Dynasty*, (New York: Harper & Row, 1988).

Solheim II, William G., *Archaeology and Culture in Southeast Asia: Unraveling the Nusantao* (Quezon City: University of the Philippines Press, 2006).

Steinberg, David Joel, *Philippine Collaboration in World War II* (Ann Arbor: University of Michigan Press, 1967).

Steinberg, David Joel, *The Philippines: A Singular and Plural Place*, 4th ed. (New York: Routledge, 2000).

Tabuga, Aubrey D., *A Probe into Filipino Migration Culture* (Quezon City: Philippine Institute for Development Studies, 2018).

Tadem, Teresa S. Encarnacion, 'Technocracy and Class Politics in Policy-Making', in Mark R. Thompson and Eric Vincent C. Batalla, eds, *Routledge Handbook of the Contemporary Philippines* (Abingdon: Routledge, 2018).

Tan, Samuel K., *A History of the Philippines* (Quezon City: University of the Philippines Press, 2009).

Thompson, Mark R., *The Marcos Regime* in *Sultanistic Regimes*, eds. Houchang E. Chehabi and Juan J. Linz (Baltimore: Johns Hopkins University Press, 1998).

Thompson, Mark R. and Eric Vincent C. Batalla, eds, *Routledge Handbook of the Contemporary Philippines* (New York: Routledge, 2018).

Tiglao, Rigoberto D., *Debunked Uncovering Hard Truths about EDSA, Martial Law, Marcos, Aquino, with a Special Section on the Duterte Presidency* (Manila: Akropolis Publishing, 2018).

Vitug, Marites Danguilan, *Power from the Forest The Politics of Logging* (Manila: Philippine Center for Investigative Journalism, 1993).

Vitug, Marites Danguilan, *Endless Journey: A Memoir of Jose T. Almonte* (Manila: Cleverheads Publishing, 2015).

Vitug, Marites Danguilan, *Hour Before Dawn: The Fall and Uncertain Rise of the Philippine Supreme Court* (Manila: Cleverheads Publishing, 2012).

Vitug, Marites Danguilan, *Rock Solid: How the Philippines Won its Maritime Case Against China* (Quezon City: Ateneo de Manila University Press, 2019).

Vitug, Marites Danguilan and Gloria M. Glenda, *Under the Crescent Moon Rebellion in Mindanao* (Manila: Ateneo Center for Social Policy, 2000).

Asian Development Bank
Asiasentinel
Asiaweek
Bangko Sentral ng Pilipinas
Business World
Far Eastern Economic Review
Forbes Magazine
Human Development Index (annual)
International Crisis Group
Manila Bulletin
Media and general sources
Newsbreak

Permanent Court of Arbitration, Case No. 2013–19, South China Sea Arbitration, decision 2016

Philippine Centre for Investigative Journalism

Philippine Daily Inquirer

Philippine Department of Agriculture

Philippine Department of Energy

Philippine Department of Health

Philippine Statistics Authority

Rappler

UN Development Programme

UNICEF

United Nations Convention on Law of the Sea

World Bank

World Development Report (annual)

INDEX